THE CONTEST FOR KNOWLEDGE

THE
OTHER VOICE
IN
EARLY MODERN
EUROPE

A Series Edited by Margaret L. King and Albert Rabil Jr.

RECENT BOOKS IN THE SERIES

Maria Gaetana Agnesi,
Giuseppa Eleonora Barbapiccola,
Diamante Medaglia Faini,
Aretafila Savini de' Rossi, and
the Accademia de' Ricovrati

THE CONTEST FOR
KNOWLEDGE

*Debates over Women's Learning
in Eighteenth-Century Italy*

ᴣ

*Edited and Translated by Rebecca Messbarger
and Paula Findlen, with an Introduction by
Rebecca Messbarger*

THE UNIVERSITY OF CHICAGO PRESS
Chicago & London

Maria Gaetana Agnesi, 1718–99
Giuseppa Eleonora Barbapiccola, ca. 1700–ca. 1740
Diamante Medaglia Faini, 1724–70
Aretafila Savini de' Rossi, 1687–?

Paula Findlen is Ubaldo Pierotti Professor in Italian History, Stanford University, where she codirects the Science, Technology, and Society Program. She is the editor or coeditor of four books, most recently *Athanasius Kircher: The Last Man Who Knew Everything* and *Possessing Nature: Museums, Collecting, and Scientific Culture in Early Modern Italy*.
Rebecca Messbarger is associate professor of Italian at Washington University in Saint Louis. She is the author of *The Century of Women: Representations of Women in Eighteenth-Century Italian Public Discourse*.

The University of Chicago Press, Chicago 60637
The University of Chicago Press, Ltd., London
© 2005 by The University of Chicago
All rights reserved. Published 2005
Printed in the United States of America

14 13 12 11 10 09 08 07 06 05   1 2 3 4 5

ISBN: 0-226-01054-6 (cloth)
ISBN: 0-226-01055-4 (paper)

Library of Congress Cataloging-in Publicaltion Data

The contest for knowledge : debates over women's learning in eighteenth-century Italy / Maria Gaetana Agnesi . . . [et al.] and the Accademia de' ricovrati ; edited and translated by Rebecca Messbarger and Paula Findlen ; with an introduction by Rebecca Messbarger.
p. cm. — (The other voice in early modern Europe)
Includes bibliographical references and index.
ISBN 0-226-01054-6 (cloth : alk. paper)—ISBN 0-226-01055-4 (pkb. : alk. paper)
1. Women—Education—Italy—History—18th century—Sources.
2. Women—Italy—Intellectual life—18th century—Sources.
3. Women—Italy—Social conditions—History—18th century—Sources.
4. Education—Italy—History—18th century—Sources.   5. Italy—Intellectual life—18th century—Sources.   6. Italy—Social conditions—18th century—Sources.
I. Agnesi, Maria Gaetana, 1718–1799.   II. Messbarger, Rebecca Marie.
III. Findlen, Paula.   IV. Accademia di Padova.   V. Title.   VI. Series.
LC2122.C66 2005
370.82'0945'09033—dc22   2004015825

For our parents, who educated us

CONTENTS

ACKNOWLEDGMENTS

We wish to recognize Albert Rabil for his sage guidance through the course of writing and revisions. We are grateful to the anonymous reader of the initial manuscript whose suggestions were invaluable during final revisions. We thank Randolph Petilos and Maia Rigas for seeing it to press. Special thanks go to Rachel Trotter Chaney for her initial draft of the translation of Agnesi's Latin "Oration." We owe a debt of gratitude to Valentina Ricci, Ken Gouwens, Pam Long, George Pepe, Elissa Weaver, and Jill Levin for their expert recommendations for correcting translations and revising introductory remarks. We thank the Department of Romance Languages and Literatures at Washington University in Saint Louis and the Program in the History and Philosophy of Science at Stanford University for their generous assistance with the production of this book, and the Vice Provost of Undergraduate Education at Stanford for a VPUE grant supporting Rachel Trotter Chaney's involvement in the project. Finally, we wish to thank the growing community of Settecentisti in the United States and Canada, whose enthusiasm for this material was a principal reason this volume came into being.

Rebecca Messbarger
Paula Findlen

THE OTHER VOICE IN
EARLY MODERN EUROPE:
INTRODUCTION TO THE SERIES

Margaret L. King and Albert Rabil Jr.

THE OLD VOICE AND THE OTHER VOICE

In western Europe and the United States, women are nearing equality in the professions, in business, and in politics. Most enjoy access to education, reproductive rights, and autonomy in financial affairs. Issues vital to women are on the public agenda: equal pay, child care, domestic abuse, breast cancer research, and curricular revision with an eye to the inclusion of women.

These recent achievements have their origins in things women (and some male supporters) said for the first time about six hundred years ago. Theirs is the "other voice," in contradistinction to the "first voice," the voice of the educated men who created Western culture. Coincident with a general reshaping of European culture in the period 1300–1700 (called the Renaissance or early modern period), questions of female equality and opportunity were raised that still resound and are still unresolved.

The other voice emerged against the backdrop of a three-thousand-year history of the derogation of women rooted in the civilizations related to Western culture: Hebrew, Greek, Roman, and Christian. Negative attitudes toward women inherited from these traditions pervaded the intellectual, medical, legal, religious, and social systems that developed during the European Middle Ages.

The following pages describe the traditional, overwhelmingly male views of women's nature inherited by early modern Europeans and the new tradition that the "other voice" called into being to begin to challenge reigning assumptions. This review should serve as a framework for understanding the texts published in the series The Other Voice in Early Modern Europe. Introductions specific to each text and author follow this essay in all the volumes of the series.

TRADITIONAL VIEWS OF WOMEN, 500 BCE–1500 CE

Embedded in the philosophical and medical theories of the ancient Greeks were perceptions of the female as inferior to the male in both mind and body. Similarly, the structure of civil legislation inherited from the ancient Romans was biased against women, and the views on women developed by Christian thinkers out of the Hebrew Bible and the Christian New Testament were negative and disabling. Literary works composed in the vernacular of ordinary people, and widely recited or read, conveyed these negative assumptions. The social networks within which most women lived—those of the family and the institutions of the Roman Catholic Church—were shaped by this negative tradition and sharply limited the areas in which women might act in and upon the world.

GREEK PHILOSOPHY AND FEMALE NATURE. Greek biology assumed that women were inferior to men and defined them as merely childbearers and housekeepers. This view was authoritatively expressed in the works of the philosopher Aristotle.

Aristotle thought in dualities. He considered action superior to inaction, form (the inner design or structure of any object) superior to matter, completion to incompletion, possession to deprivation. In each of these dualities, he associated the male principle with the superior quality and the female with the inferior. "The male principle in nature," he argued, "is associated with active, formative and perfected characteristics, while the female is passive, material and deprived, desiring the male in order to become complete."[1] Men are always identified with virile qualities, such as judgment, courage, and stamina, and women with their opposites—irrationality, cowardice, and weakness.

The masculine principle was considered superior even in the womb. The man's semen, Aristotle believed, created the form of a new human creature, while the female body contributed only matter. (The existence of the ovum, and with it the other facts of human embryology, was not established until the seventeenth century.) Although the later Greek physician Galen believed there was a female component in generation, contributed by "female semen," the followers of both Aristotle and Galen saw the male role in human generation as more active and more important.

In the Aristotelian view, the male principle sought always to reproduce

---

1. Aristotle, *Physics* 1.9.192a20–24, in *The Complete Works of Aristotle*, ed. Jonathan Barnes, rev. Oxford trans., 2 vols. (Princeton: Princeton University Press, 1984), 1:328.

itself. The creation of a female was always a mistake, therefore, resulting from an imperfect act of generation. Every female born was considered a "defective" or "mutilated" male (as Aristotle's terminology has variously been translated), a "monstrosity" of nature.[2]

For Greek theorists, the biology of males and females was the key to their psychology. The female was softer and more docile, more apt to be despondent, querulous, and deceitful. Being incomplete, moreover, she craved sexual fulfillment in intercourse with a male. The male was intellectual, active, and in control of his passions.

These psychological polarities derived from the theory that the universe consisted of four elements (earth, fire, air, and water), expressed in human bodies as four "humors" (black bile, yellow bile, blood, and phlegm) considered, respectively, dry, hot, damp, and cold and corresponding to mental states (melancholic, choleric, sanguine, and phlegmatic). In this scheme the male, sharing the principles of earth and fire, was dry and hot; the female, sharing the principles of air and water, was cold and damp.

Female psychology was further affected by her dominant organ, the uterus (womb), *hystera* in Greek. The passions generated by the womb made women lustful, deceitful, talkative, irrational, indeed—when these effects were in excess—"hysterical."

Aristotle's biology also had social and political consequences. If the male principle was superior and the female inferior, then in the household, as in the state, men should rule and women must be subordinate. That hierarchy did not rule out the companionship of husband and wife, whose cooperation was necessary for the welfare of children and the preservation of property. Such mutuality supported male preeminence.

Aristotle's teacher, Plato, suggested a different possibility: that men and women might possess the same virtues. The setting for this proposal is the imaginary and ideal Republic that Plato sketches in a dialogue of that name. Here, for a privileged elite capable of leading wisely, all distinctions of class and wealth dissolve, as, consequently, do those of gender. Without households or property, as Plato constructs his ideal society, there is no need for the subordination of women. Women may therefore be educated to the same level as men to assume leadership. Plato's Republic remained imaginary, however. In real societies, the subordination of women remained the norm and the prescription.

The views of women inherited from the Greek philosophical tradition became the basis for medieval thought. In the thirteenth century,

2. Aristotle, *Generation of Animals* 2.3.737a27–28, in *Complete Works*, 1:1144.

the supreme Scholastic philosopher Thomas Aquinas, among others, still echoed Aristotle's views of human reproduction, of male and female personalities, and of the preeminent male role in the social hierarchy.

ROMAN LAW AND THE FEMALE CONDITION. Roman law, like Greek philosophy, underlay medieval thought and shaped medieval society. The ancient belief that adult property-owning men should administer households and make decisions affecting the community at large is the very fulcrum of Roman law.

About 450 BCE, during Rome's republican era, the community's customary law was recorded (legendarily) on twelve tablets erected in the city's central forum. It was later elaborated by professional jurists whose activity increased in the imperial era, when much new legislation was passed, especially on issues affecting family and inheritance. This growing, changing body of laws was eventually codified in the *Corpus of Civil Law* under the direction of the emperor Justinian, generations after the empire ceased to be ruled from Rome. That *Corpus*, read and commented on by medieval scholars from the eleventh century on, inspired the legal systems of most of the cities and kingdoms of Europe.

Laws regarding dowries, divorce, and inheritance pertain primarily to women. Since those laws aimed to maintain and preserve property, the women concerned were those from the property-owning minority. Their subordination to male family members points to the even greater subordination of lower-class and slave women, about whom the laws speak little.

In the early republic, the *paterfamilias*, or "father of the family," possessed *patria potestas*, "paternal power." The term *pater*, "father," in both these cases does not necessarily mean biological father but denotes the head of a household. The father was the person who owned the household's property and, indeed, its human members. The *paterfamilias* had absolute power—including the power, rarely exercised, of life or death—over his wife, his children, and his slaves, as much as his cattle.

Male children could be "emancipated," an act that granted legal autonomy and the right to own property. Those over fourteen could be emancipated by a special grant from the father or automatically by their father's death. But females could never be emancipated; instead, they passed from the authority of their father to that of a husband or, if widowed or orphaned while still unmarried, to a guardian or tutor.

Marriage in its traditional form placed the woman under her husband's authority, or *manus*. He could divorce her on grounds of adultery, drinking wine, or stealing from the household, but she could not divorce him. She could neither possess property in her own right nor bequeath any to her children upon her death. When her husband died, the household property passed not to her but to his male heirs. And when her father died, she had no claim to any family inheritance, which was directed to her brothers or more remote male relatives. The effect of these laws was to exclude women from civil society, itself based on property ownership.

In the later republican and imperial periods, these rules were significantly modified. Women rarely married according to the traditional form. The practice of "free" marriage allowed a woman to remain under her father's authority, to possess property given her by her father (most frequently the "dowry," recoverable from the husband's household on his death), and to inherit from her father. She could also bequeath property to her own children and divorce her husband, just as he could divorce her.

Despite this greater freedom, women still suffered enormous disability under Roman law. Heirs could belong only to the father's side, never the mother's. Moreover, although she could bequeath her property to her children, she could not establish a line of succession in doing so. A woman was "the beginning and end of her own family," said the jurist Ulpian. Moreover, women could play no public role. They could not hold public office, represent anyone in a legal case, or even witness a will. Women had only a private existence and no public personality.

The dowry system, the guardian, women's limited ability to transmit wealth, and total political disability are all features of Roman law adopted by the medieval communities of western Europe, although modified according to local customary laws.

CHRISTIAN DOCTRINE AND WOMEN'S PLACE. The Hebrew Bible and the Christian New Testament authorized later writers to limit women to the realm of the family and to burden them with the guilt of original sin. The passages most fruitful for this purpose were the creation narratives in Genesis and sentences from the Epistles defining women's role within the Christian family and community.

Each of the first two chapters of Genesis contains a creation narrative. In the first "God created man in his own image, in the image of God he created him; male and female he created them" (Gn 1:27). In the second, God created Eve from Adam's rib (2:21–23). Christian theologians relied principally on Genesis 2 for their understanding of the relation between man and woman, interpreting the creation of Eve from Adam as proof of her subordination to him.

The creation story in Genesis 2 leads to that of the temptations in Genesis 3: of Eve by the wily serpent and of Adam by Eve. As read by Christian theologians from Tertullian to Thomas Aquinas, the narrative made Eve responsible for the Fall and its consequences. She instigated the act; she deceived her husband; she suffered the greater punishment. Her disobedience made it necessary for Jesus to be incarnated and to die on the cross. From the pulpit, moralists and preachers for centuries conveyed to women the guilt that they bore for original sin.

The Epistles offered advice to early Christians on building communities of the faithful. Among the matters to be regulated was the place of women. Paul offered views favorable to women in Galatians 3:28: "There is neither Jew nor Greek, there is neither slave nor free, there is neither male nor female; for you are all one in Christ Jesus." Paul also referred to women as his coworkers and placed them on a par with himself and his male coworkers (Phlm 4:2–3; Rom 16:1–3; 1 Cor 16:19). Elsewhere, Paul limited women's possibilities: "But I want you to understand that the head of every man is Christ, the head of a woman is her husband, and the head of Christ is God" (1 Cor 11:3).

Biblical passages by later writers (although attributed to Paul) enjoined women to forgo jewels, expensive clothes, and elaborate coiffures; and they forbade women to "teach or have authority over men," telling them to "learn in silence with all submissiveness" as is proper for one responsible for sin, consoling them, however, with the thought that they will be saved through childbearing (1 Tm 2:9–15). Other texts among the later Epistles defined women as the weaker sex and emphasized their subordination to their husbands (1 Pt 3:7; Col 3:18; Eph 5:22–23).

These passages from the New Testament became the arsenal employed by theologians of the early church to transmit negative attitudes toward women to medieval Christian culture—above all, Tertullian (*On the Apparel of Women*), Jerome (*Against Jovinian*), and Augustine (*The Literal Meaning of Genesis*).

THE IMAGE OF WOMEN IN MEDIEVAL LITERATURE. The philosophical, legal, and religious traditions born in antiquity formed the basis of the medieval intellectual synthesis wrought by trained thinkers, mostly clerics, writing in Latin and based largely in universities. The vernacular literary tradition that developed alongside the learned tradition also spoke about female nature and women's roles. Medieval stories, poems, and epics also portrayed women negatively—as lustful and deceitful—while praising good housekeepers and loyal wives as replicas of the Virgin Mary or the female saints and martyrs.

There is an exception in the movement of "courtly love" that evolved in southern France from the twelfth century. Courtly love was the erotic love between a nobleman and noblewoman, the latter usually superior in social rank. It was always adulterous. From the conventions of courtly love derive modern Western notions of romantic love. The tradition has had an impact disproportionate to its size, for it affected only a tiny elite, and very few women. The exaltation of the female lover probably does not reflect a higher evaluation of women or a step toward their sexual liberation. More likely it gives expression to the social and sexual tensions besetting the knightly class at a specific historical juncture.

The literary fashion of courtly love was on the wane by the thirteenth century, when the widely read *Romance of the Rose* was composed in French by two authors of significantly different dispositions. Guillaume de Lorris composed the initial four thousand verses about 1235, and Jean de Meun added about seventeen thousand verses—more than four times the original—about 1265.

The fragment composed by Guillaume de Lorris stands squarely in the tradition of courtly love. Here the poet, in a dream, is admitted into a walled garden where he finds a magic fountain in which a rosebush is reflected. He longs to pick one rose, but the thorns prevent his doing so, even as he is wounded by arrows from the god of love, whose commands he agrees to obey. The rest of this part of the poem recounts the poet's unsuccessful efforts to pluck the rose.

The longer part of the *Romance* by Jean de Meun also describes a dream. But here allegorical characters give long didactic speeches, providing a social satire on a variety of themes, some pertaining to women. Love is an anxious and tormented state, the poem explains: women are greedy and manipulative, marriage is miserable, beautiful women are lustful, ugly ones cease to please, and a chaste woman is as rare as a black swan.

Shortly after Jean de Meun completed *The Romance of the Rose*, Mathéolus penned his *Lamentations*, a long Latin diatribe against marriage translated into French about a century later. The *Lamentations* sum up medieval attitudes toward women and provoked the important response by Christine de Pizan in her *Book of the City of Ladies*.

In 1355 Giovanni Boccaccio wrote *Il Corbaccio*, another antifeminist manifesto, although ironically by an author whose other works pioneered new directions in Renaissance thought. The former husband of his lover appears to Boccaccio, condemning his unmoderated lust and detailing the defects of women. Boccaccio concedes at the end "how much men naturally surpass women in nobility" and is cured of his desires.[3]

---

3. Giovanni Boccaccio, *The Corbaccio, or The Labyrinth of Love*, trans. and ed. Anthony K. Cassell, rev. ed. (Binghamton, NY: Medieval and Renaissance Texts and Studies 1993), 71.

WOMEN'S ROLES: THE FAMILY. The negative perceptions of women expressed in the intellectual tradition are also implicit in the actual roles that women played in European society. Assigned to subordinate positions in the household and the church, they were barred from significant participation in public life.

Medieval European households, like those in antiquity and in non-Western civilizations, were headed by males. It was the male serf (or peasant), feudal lord, town merchant, or citizen who was polled or taxed or succeeded to an inheritance or had any acknowledged public role, although his wife or widow could stand as a temporary surrogate. From about 1100, the position of property-holding males was further enhanced: inheritance was confined to the male, or agnate, line—with depressing consequences for women.

A wife never fully belonged to her husband's family, nor was she a daughter to her father's family. She left her father's house young to marry whomever her parents chose. Her dowry was managed by her husband, and at her death it normally passed to her children by him.

A married woman's life was occupied nearly constantly with cycles of pregnancy, childbearing, and lactation. Women bore children through all the years of their fertility, and many died in childbirth. They were also responsible for raising young children up to six or seven. In the propertied classes, that responsibility was shared, since it was common for a wet nurse to take over breast-feeding and for servants to perform other chores.

Women trained their daughters in the household duties appropriate to their status, nearly always tasks associated with textiles: spinning, weaving, sewing, embroidering. Their sons were sent out of the house as apprentices or students, or their training was assumed by fathers in later childhood and adolescence. On the death of her husband, a woman's children became the responsibility of his family. She generally did not take "his" children with her to a new marriage or back to her father's house, except sometimes in the artisan classes.

Women also worked. Rural peasants performed farm chores, merchant wives often practiced their husbands' trades, the unmarried daughters of the urban poor worked as servants or prostitutes. All wives produced or embellished textiles and did the housekeeping, while wealthy ones managed servants. These labors were unpaid or poorly paid but often contributed substantially to family wealth.

WOMEN'S ROLES: THE CHURCH. Membership in a household, whether a father's or a husband's, meant for women a lifelong subordination to others.

In western Europe, the Roman Catholic Church offered an alternative to the career of wife and mother. A woman could enter a convent, parallel in function to the monasteries for men that evolved in the early Christian centuries.

In the convent, a woman pledged herself to a celibate life, lived according to strict community rules, and worshiped daily. Often the convent offered training in Latin, allowing some women to become considerable scholars and authors as well as scribes, artists, and musicians. For women who chose the conventual life, the benefits could be enormous, but for numerous others placed in convents by paternal choice, the life could be restrictive and burdensome.

The conventual life declined as an alternative for women as the modern age approached. Reformed monastic institutions resisted responsibility for related female orders. The church increasingly restricted female institutional life by insisting on closer male supervision.

Women often sought other options. Some joined the communities of laywomen that sprang up spontaneously in the thirteenth century in the urban zones of western Europe, especially in Flanders and Italy. Some joined the heretical movements that flourished in late medieval Christendom, whose anticlerical and often antifamily positions particularly appealed to women. In these communities, some women were acclaimed as "holy women" or "saints," whereas others often were condemned as frauds or heretics.

In all, although the options offered to women by the church were sometimes less than satisfactory, they were sometimes richly rewarding. After 1520, the convent remained an option only in Roman Catholic territories. Protestantism engendered an ideal of marriage as a heroic endeavor and appeared to place husband and wife on a more equal footing. Sermons and treatises, however, still called for female subordination and obedience.

THE OTHER VOICE, 1300–1700

When the modern era opened, European culture was so firmly structured by a framework of negative attitudes toward women that to dismantle it was a monumental labor. The process began as part of a larger cultural movement that entailed the critical reexamination of ideas inherited from the ancient and medieval past. The humanists launched that critical reexamination.

THE HUMANIST FOUNDATION. Originating in Italy in the fourteenth century, humanism quickly became the dominant intellectual movement in

Europe. Spreading in the sixteenth century from Italy to the rest of Europe, it fueled the literary, scientific, and philosophical movements of the era and laid the basis for the eighteenth-century Enlightenment.

Humanists regarded the Scholastic philosophy of medieval universities as out of touch with the realities of urban life. They found in the rhetorical discourse of classical Rome a language adapted to civic life and public speech. They learned to read, speak, and write classical Latin and, eventually, classical Greek. They founded schools to teach others to do so, establishing the pattern for elementary and secondary education for the next three hundred years.

In the service of complex government bureaucracies, humanists employed their skills to write eloquent letters, deliver public orations, and formulate public policy. They developed new scripts for copying manuscripts and used the new printing press to disseminate texts, for which they created methods of critical editing.

Humanism was a movement led by males who accepted the evaluation of women in ancient texts and generally shared the misogynist perceptions of their culture. (Female humanists, as we will see, did not.) Yet humanism also opened the door to a reevaluation of the nature and capacity of women. By calling authors, texts, and ideas into question, it made possible the fundamental rereading of the whole intellectual tradition that was required in order to free women from cultural prejudice and social subordination.

A DIFFERENT CITY. The other voice first appeared when, after so many centuries, the accumulation of misogynist concepts evoked a response from a capable female defender: Christine de Pizan (1365–1431). Introducing her *Book of the City of Ladies* (1405), she described how she was affected by reading Mathéolus's *Lamentations*: "Just the sight of this book . . . made me wonder how it happened that so many different men . . . are so inclined to express both in speaking and in their treatises and writings so many wicked insults about women and their behavior."[4] These statements impelled her to detest herself "and the entire feminine sex, as though we were monstrosities in nature."[5]

The rest of *The Book of the City of Ladies* presents a justification of the female sex and a vision of an ideal community of women. A pioneer, she has received the message of female inferiority and rejected it. From the fourteenth to the

---

4. Christine de Pizan, *The Book of the City of Ladies*, trans. Earl Jeffrey Richards, foreword by Marina Warner (New York: Persea Books, 1982), 1.1.1, pp. 3–4.

5. Ibid., 1.1.1–2, p. 5.

seventeenth century, a huge body of literature accumulated that responded to the dominant tradition.

The result was a literary explosion consisting of works by both men and women, in Latin and in the vernaculars: works enumerating the achievements of notable women; works rebutting the main accusations made against women; works arguing for the equal education of men and women; works defining and redefining women's proper role in the family, at court, in public; works describing women's lives and experiences. Recent monographs and articles have begun to hint at the great range of this movement, involving probably several thousand titles. The protofeminism of these "other voices" constitutes a significant fraction of the literary product of the early modern era.

THE CATALOGS. About 1365, the same Boccaccio whose *Corbaccio* rehearses the usual charges against female nature wrote another work, *Concerning Famous Women*. A humanist treatise drawing on classical texts, it praised 106 notable women: 98 of them from pagan Greek and Roman antiquity, 1 (Eve) from the Bible, and 7 from the medieval religious and cultural tradition; his book helped make all readers aware of a sex normally condemned or forgotten. Boccaccio's outlook nevertheless was unfriendly to women, for it singled out for praise those women who possessed the traditional virtues of chastity, silence, and obedience. Women who were active in the public realm—for example, rulers and warriors—were depicted as usually being lascivious and as suffering terrible punishments for entering the masculine sphere. Women were his subject, but Boccaccio's standard remained male.

Christine de Pizan's *Book of the City of Ladies* contains a second catalog, one responding specifically to Boccaccio's. Whereas Boccaccio portrays female virtue as exceptional, she depicts it as universal. Many women in history were leaders, or remained chaste despite the lascivious approaches of men, or were visionaries and brave martyrs.

The work of Boccaccio inspired a series of catalogs of illustrious women of the biblical, classical, Christian, and local pasts, among them Filippo da Bergamo's *Of Illustrious Women*, Pierre de Brantôme's *Lives of Illustrious Women*, Pierre Le Moyne's *Gallerie of Heroic Women*, and Pietro Paolo de Ribera's *Immortal Triumphs and Heroic Enterprises of 845 Women*. Whatever their embedded prejudices, these works drove home to the public the possibility of female excellence.

THE DEBATE. At the same time, many questions remained: Could a woman be virtuous? Could she perform noteworthy deeds? Was she even, strictly speaking, of the same human species as men? These questions were debated over four centuries, in French, German, Italian, Spanish, and English, by authors male and female, among Catholics, Protestants, and Jews, in ponderous volumes and breezy pamphlets. The whole literary genre has been called the *querelle des femmes*, the "woman question."

The opening volley of this battle occurred in the first years of the fifteenth century, in a literary debate sparked by Christine de Pizan. She exchanged letters critical of Jean de Meun's contribution to *The Romance of the Rose* with two French royal secretaries, Jean de Montreuil and Gontier Col. When the matter became public, Jean Gerson, one of Europe's leading theologians, supported de Pizan's arguments against de Meun, for the moment silencing the opposition.

The debate resurfaced repeatedly over the next two hundred years. *The Triumph of Women* (1438) by Juan Rodríguez de la Camara (or Juan Rodríguez del Padron) struck a new note by presenting arguments for the superiority of women to men. *The Champion of Women* (1440–42) by Martin Le Franc addresses once again the negative views of women presented in *The Romance of the Rose* and offers counterevidence of female virtue and achievement.

A cameo of the debate on women is included in *The Courtier*, one of the most widely read books of the era, published by the Italian Baldassare Castiglione in 1528 and immediately translated into other European vernaculars. *The Courtier* depicts a series of evenings at the court of the duke of Urbino in which many men and some women of the highest social stratum amuse themselves by discussing a range of literary and social issues. The "woman question" is a pervasive theme throughout, and the third of its four books is devoted entirely to that issue.

In a verbal duel, Gasparo Pallavicino and Giuliano de' Medici present the main claims of the two traditions. Gasparo argues the innate inferiority of women and their inclination to vice. Only in bearing children do they profit the world. Giuliano counters that women share the same spiritual and mental capacities as men and may excel in wisdom and action. Men and women are of the same essence: just as no stone can be more perfectly a stone than another, so no human being can be more perfectly human than others, whether male or female. It was an astonishing assertion, boldly made to an audience as large as all Europe.

THE TREATISES. Humanism provided the materials for a positive counterconcept to the misogyny embedded in Scholastic philosophy and law and inherited from the Greek, Roman, and Christian pasts. A series of humanist treatises on marriage and family, on education and deportment, and on the nature of women helped construct these new perspectives.

The works by Francesco Barbaro and Leon Battista Alberti—*On Marriage* (1415) and *On the Family* (1434–37)—far from defending female equality, reasserted women's responsibility for rearing children and managing the housekeeping while being obedient, chaste, and silent. Nevertheless, they served the cause of reexamining the issue of women's nature by placing domestic issues at the center of scholarly concern and reopening the pertinent classical texts. In addition, Barbaro emphasized the companionate nature of marriage and the importance of a wife's spiritual and mental qualities for the well-being of the family.

These themes reappear in later humanist works on marriage and the education of women by Juan Luis Vives and Erasmus. Both were moderately sympathetic to the condition of women without reaching beyond the usual masculine prescriptions for female behavior.

An outlook more favorable to women characterizes the nearly unknown work *In Praise of Women* (ca. 1487) by the Italian humanist Bartolommeo Goggio. In addition to providing a catalog of illustrious women, Goggio argued that male and female are the same in essence, but that women (reworking the Adam and Eve narrative from quite a new angle) are actually superior. In the same vein, the Italian humanist Maria Equicola asserted the spiritual equality of men and women in *On Women* (1501). In 1525 Galeazzo Flavio Capra (or Capella) published his work *On the Excellence and Dignity of Women*. This humanist tradition of treatises defending the worthiness of women culminates in the work of Henricus Cornelius Agrippa *On the Nobility and Preeminence of the Female Sex*. No work by a male humanist more succinctly or explicitly presents the case for female dignity.

THE WITCH BOOKS. While humanists grappled with the issues pertaining to women and family, other learned men turned their attention to what they perceived as a very great problem: witches. Witch-hunting manuals, explorations of the witch phenomenon, and even defenses of witches are not at first glance pertinent to the tradition of the other voice. But they do relate in this way: most accused witches were women. The hostility aroused by supposed witch activity is comparable to the hostility aroused by women. The evil deeds the victims of the hunt were charged with were exaggerations of the vices to which, many believed, all women were prone.

The connection between the witch accusation and the hatred of women is explicit in the notorious witch-hunting manual *The Hammer of Witches* (1486) by two Dominican inquisitors, Heinrich Krämer and Jacob Sprenger. Here the inconstancy, deceitfulness, and lustfulness traditionally associated with women are depicted in exaggerated form as the core features of witch behavior. These traits inclined women to make a bargain with the devil—sealed by sexual intercourse—by which they acquired unholy powers. Such bizarre claims, far from being rejected by rational men, were broadcast by intellectuals. The German Ulrich Molitur, the Frenchman Nicolas Rémy, and the Italian Stefano Guazzo all coolly informed the public of sinister orgies and midnight pacts with the devil. The celebrated French jurist, historian, and political philosopher Jean Bodin argued that because women were especially prone to diabolism, regular legal procedures could properly be suspended in order to try those accused of this "exceptional crime."

A few experts, such as the physician Johann Weyer, a student of Agrippa's, raised their voices in protest. In 1563 he explained the witch phenomenon thus, without discarding belief in diabolism: the devil deluded foolish old women afflicted by melancholia, causing them to believe they had magical powers. Weyer's rational skepticism, which had good credibility in the community of the learned, worked to revise the conventional views of women and witchcraft.

WOMEN'S WORKS. To the many categories of works produced on the question of women's worth must be added nearly all works written by women. A woman writing was in herself a statement of women's claim to dignity.

Only a few women wrote anything before the dawn of the modern era, for three reasons. First, they rarely received the education that would enable them to write. Second, they were not admitted to the public roles—as administrator, bureaucrat, lawyer or notary, or university professor—in which they might gain knowledge of the kinds of things the literate public thought worth writing about. Third, the culture imposed silence on women, considering speaking out a form of unchastity. Given these conditions, it is remarkable that any women wrote. Those who did before the fourteenth century were almost always nuns or religious women whose isolation made their pronouncements more acceptable.

From the fourteenth century on, the volume of women's writings rose. Women continued to write devotional literature, although not always as cloistered nuns. They also wrote diaries, often intended as keepsakes for their children; books of advice to their sons and daughters; letters to family members and friends; and family memoirs, in a few cases elaborate enough to be considered histories.

A few women wrote works directly concerning the "woman question," and some of these, such as the humanists Isotta Nogarola, Cassandra Fedele, Laura Cereta, and Olympia Morata, were highly trained. A few were professional writers, living by the income of their pens; the very first among them was Christine de Pizan, noteworthy in this context as in so many others. In addition to *The Book of the City of Ladies* and her critiques of *The Romance of the Rose*, she wrote *The Treasure of the City of Ladies* (a guide to social decorum for women), an advice book for her son, much courtly verse, and a full-scale history of the reign of King Charles V of France.

WOMEN PATRONS. Women who did not themselves write but encouraged others to do so boosted the development of an alternative tradition. Highly placed women patrons supported authors, artists, musicians, poets, and learned men. Such patrons, drawn mostly from the Italian elites and the courts of northern Europe, figure disproportionately as the dedicatees of the important works of early feminism.

For a start, it might be noted that the catalogs of Boccaccio and Alvaro de Luna were dedicated to the Florentine noblewoman Andrea Acciaiuoli and to Doña María, first wife of King Juan II of Castile, while the French translation of Boccaccio's work was commissioned by Anne of Brittany, wife of King Charles VIII of France. The humanist treatises of Goggio, Equicola, Vives, and Agrippa were dedicated, respectively, to Eleanora of Aragon, wife of Ercole I d'Este, Duke of Ferrara; to Margherita Cantelma of Mantua; to Catherine of Aragon, wife of King Henry VIII of England; and to Margaret, Duchess of Austria and regent of the Netherlands. As late as 1696, Mary Astell's *Serious Proposal to the Ladies, for the Advancement of Their True and Greatest Interest* was dedicated to Princess Anne of Denmark.

These authors presumed that their efforts would be welcome to female patrons, or they may have written at the bidding of those patrons. Silent themselves, perhaps even unresponsive, these loftily placed women helped shape the tradition of the other voice.

THE ISSUES. The literary forms and patterns in which the tradition of the other voice presented itself have now been sketched. It remains to highlight the major issues around which this tradition crystallizes. In brief, there are four problems to which our authors return again and again, in plays and catalogs, in verse and letters, in treatises and dialogues, in every language: the problem of chastity, the problem of power, the problem of speech, and the problem of knowledge. Of these, the greatest, preconditioning the others, is the problem of chastity.

THE PROBLEM OF CHASTITY. In traditional European culture, as in those of antiquity and others around the globe, chastity was perceived as woman's quintessential virtue—in contrast to courage, or generosity, or leadership, or rationality, seen as virtues characteristic of men. Opponents of women charged them with insatiable lust. Women themselves and their defenders— without disputing the validity of the standard—responded that women were capable of chastity.

The requirement of chastity kept women at home, silenced them, isolated them, left them in ignorance. It was the source of all other impediments. Why was it so important to the society of men, of whom chastity was not required, and who more often than not considered it their right to violate the chastity of any woman they encountered?

Female chastity ensured the continuity of the male-headed household. If a man's wife was not chaste, he could not be sure of the legitimacy of his offspring. If they were not his and they acquired his property, it was not his household, but some other man's, that had endured. If his daughter was not chaste, she could not be transferred to another man's household as his wife, and he was dishonored.

The whole system of the integrity of the household and the transmission of property was bound up in female chastity. Such a requirement pertained only to property-owning classes, of course. Poor women could not expect to maintain their chastity, least of all if they were in contact with high-status men to whom all women but those of their own household were prey.

In Catholic Europe, the requirement of chastity was further buttressed by moral and religious imperatives. Original sin was inextricably linked with the sexual act. Virginity was seen as heroic virtue, far more impressive than, say, the avoidance of idleness or greed. Monasticism, the cultural institution that dominated medieval Europe for centuries, was grounded in the renunciation of the flesh. The Catholic reform of the eleventh century imposed a similar standard on all the clergy and a heightened awareness of sexual requirements on all the laity. Although men were asked to be chaste, female unchastity was much worse: it led to the devil, as Eve had led mankind to sin.

To such requirements, women and their defenders protested their innocence. Furthermore, following the example of holy women who had escaped the requirements of family and sought the religious life, some women began to conceive of female communities as alternatives both to family and to the cloister. Christine de Pizan's city of ladies was such a community. Moderata Fonte and Mary Astell envisioned others. The luxurious salons of the French *précieuses* of the seventeenth century, or the comfortable English drawing rooms of the next, may have been born of the same impulse. Here women not only might escape, if briefly, the subordinate position that life in the family entailed but might also make claims to power, exercise their capacity for speech, and display their knowledge.

THE PROBLEM OF POWER. Women were excluded from power: the whole cultural tradition insisted on it. Only men were citizens, only men bore arms, only men could be chiefs or lords or kings. There were exceptions that did not disprove the rule, when wives or widows or mothers took the place of men, awaiting their return or the maturation of a male heir. A woman who attempted to rule in her own right was perceived as an anomaly, a monster, at once a deformed woman and an insufficient male, sexually confused and consequently unsafe.

The association of such images with women who held or sought power explains some otherwise odd features of early modern culture. Queen Elizabeth I of England, one of the few women to hold full regal authority in European history, played with such male/female images—positive ones, of course—in representing herself to her subjects. She was a prince, and manly, even though she was female. She was also (she claimed) virginal, a condition absolutely essential if she was to avoid the attacks of her opponents. Catherine de' Medici, who ruled France as widow and regent for her sons, also adopted such imagery in defining her position. She chose as one symbol the figure of Artemisia, an androgynous ancient warrior-heroine who combined a female persona with masculine powers.

Power in a woman, without such sexual imagery, seems to have been indigestible by the culture. A rare note was struck by the Englishman Sir Thomas Elyot in his *Defence of Good Women* (1540), justifying both women's participation in civic life and their prowess in arms. The old tune was sung by the Scots reformer John Knox in his *First Blast of the Trumpet against the Monstrous Regiment of Women* (1558); for him, rule by women, defects in nature, was a hideous contradiction in terms.

The confused sexuality of the imagery of female potency was not reserved for rulers. Any woman who excelled was likely to be called an Amazon, recalling the self-mutilated warrior women of antiquity who repudiated all men, gave up their sons, and raised only their daughters. She was often said to have "exceeded her sex" or to have possessed "masculine virtue"—as the very fact of conspicuous excellence conferred masculinity even on the female subject. The catalogs of notable women often showed those female heroes dressed in armor, armed to the teeth, like men. Amazonian heroines romp through the epics of the age—Ariosto's *Orlando Furioso* (1532) and Spenser's *Faerie Queene* (1590–1609). Excellence in a woman was perceived as a claim for power, and power was reserved for the masculine realm. A woman who possessed either one was masculinized and lost title to her own female identity.

THE PROBLEM OF SPEECH. Just as power had a sexual dimension when it was claimed by women, so did speech. A good woman spoke little. Excessive speech was an indication of unchastity. By speech, women seduced men. Eve had lured Adam into sin by her speech. Accused witches were commonly accused of having spoken abusively, or irrationally, or simply too much. As enlightened a figure as Francesco Barbaro insisted on silence in a woman, which he linked to her perfect unanimity with her husband's will and her unblemished virtue (her chastity). Another Italian humanist, Leonardo Bruni, in advising a noblewoman on her studies, barred her not from speech but from public speaking. That was reserved for men.

Related to the problem of speech was that of costume—another, if silent, form of self-expression. Assigned the task of pleasing men as their primary occupation, elite women often tended toward elaborate costume, hairdressing, and the use of cosmetics. Clergy and secular moralists alike condemned these practices. The appropriate function of costume and adornment was to announce the status of a woman's husband or father. Any further indulgence in adornment was akin to unchastity.

THE PROBLEM OF KNOWLEDGE. When the Italian noblewoman Isotta Nogarola had begun to attain a reputation as a humanist, she was accused of incest—a telling instance of the association of learning in women with unchastity. That chilling association inclined any woman who was educated to deny that she was or to make exaggerated claims of heroic chastity.

If educated women were pursued with suspicions of sexual misconduct, women seeking an education faced an even more daunting obstacle: the assumption that women were by nature incapable of learning, that reasoning was a particularly masculine ability. Just as they proclaimed their chastity, women and their defenders insisted on their capacity for learning. The major work by a male writer on female education—that by Juan Luis Vives, *On the Education of a Christian Woman* (1523)—granted female capacity for intellection but still argued that a woman's whole education was to be shaped around the requirement of chastity and a future within the household. Female writers of the following generations—Marie de Gournay in France, Anna Maria van Schurman in Holland, and Mary Astell in England—began to envision other possibilities.

The pioneers of female education were the Italian women humanists who managed to attain a literacy in Latin and a knowledge of classical and Christian literature equivalent to that of prominent men. Their works implicitly and explicitly raise questions about women's social roles, defining problems that beset women attempting to break out of the cultural limits that had bound them. Like Christine de Pizan, who achieved an advanced education through her father's tutoring and her own devices, their bold questioning makes clear the importance of training. Only when women were educated to the same standard as male leaders would they be able to raise that other voice and insist on their dignity as human beings morally, intellectually, and legally equal to men.

THE OTHER VOICE. The other voice, a voice of protest, was mostly female, but it was also male. It spoke in the vernaculars and in Latin, in treatises and dialogues, in plays and poetry, in letters and diaries, and in pamphlets. It battered at the wall of prejudice that encircled women and raised a banner announcing its claims. The female was equal (or even superior) to the male in essential nature—moral, spiritual, and intellectual. Women were capable of higher education, of holding positions of power and influence in the public realm, and of speaking and writing persuasively. The last bastion of masculine supremacy, centered on the notions of a woman's primary domestic responsibility and the requirement of female chastity, was not as yet assaulted—although visions of productive female communities as alternatives to the family indicated an awareness of the problem.

During the period 1300–1700, the other voice remained only a voice, and one only dimly heard. It did not result—yet—in an alteration of social patterns. Indeed, to this day they have not entirely been altered. Yet the call for justice issued as long as six centuries ago by those writing in the tradition of the other voice must be recognized as the source and origin of the mature feminist tradition and of the realignment of social institutions accomplished in the modern age.

We thank the volume editors in this series, who responded with many suggestions to an earlier draft of this introduction, making it a collaborative enterprise. Many of their suggestions and criticisms have resulted in revisions of this introduction, although we remain responsible for the final product.

PROJECTED TITLES IN THE SERIES

Isabella Andreini, *Mirtilla*, edited and translated by Laura Stortoni

Tullia d'Aragona, *Complete Poems and Letters*, edited and translated by Julia Hairston

Tullia d'Aragona, *The Wretch, Otherwise Known as Guerrino*, edited and translated by Julia Hairston and John McLucas

Francesco Barbaro et al., *On Marriage and the Family*, edited and translated by Margaret L. King

Laura Battiferra, *Selected Poetry, Prose, and Letters*, edited and translated by Victoria Kirkham

Francesco Buoninsegni and Arcangela Tarabotti, *Menippean Satire: "Against Feminine Extravagance" and "Antisatire,"* edited and translated by Elissa Weaver

Rosalba Carriera, *Letters, Diaries, and Art*, edited and translated by Shearer West

Madame du Chatelet, *Selected Works*, edited by Judith Zinsser

Vittoria Colonna, Chiara Matraini, and Lucrezia Marinella, *Marian Writings*, edited and translated by Susan Haskins

Princess Elizabeth of Bohemia, *Correspondence with Descartes*, edited and translated by Lisa Shapiro

Isabella d'Este, *Selected Letters*, edited and translated by Deanna Shemek

Fairy Tales by Seventeenth-Century French Women Writers, edited and translated by Lewis Seifert and Domna C. Stanton

Moderata Fonte, *Floridoro*, edited by Valeria Finucci and translated by Julia Kisacki

Moderata Fonte and Lucrezia Marinella, *Religious Narratives*, edited and translated by Virginia Cox

Catharina Regina von Greiffenberg, *Meditations on the Life of Christ*, edited and translated by Lynne Tatlock

In Praise of Women: Italian Fifteenth-Century Defenses of Women, edited and translated by Daniel Bornstein

Louise Labé, *Complete Works*, edited and translated by Annie Finch and Deborah Baker

Lucrezia Marinella, *L'Enrico, or Byzantium Conquered*, edited and translated by Virginia Cox

Lucrezia Marinella, *Happy Arcadia*, edited and translated by Susan Haskins and Letizia Panizza

Chiara Matraini, *Selected Poetry and Prose*, edited and translated by Elaine MacLachlan

Alessandro Piccolomini, *Rethinking Marriage in Sixteenth-Century Italy*, edited and translated by Letizia Panizza

Christine de Pizan, *Life of Charles V*, edited and translated by Nadia Margolis

Christine de Pizan, *The Long Road of Learning*, edited and translated by Andrea Tarnowski

Madeleine and Catherine des Roches, *Selected Letters, Dialogues, and Poems*, edited and translated by Anne Larsen

Oliva Sabuco, *The New Philosophy: True Medicine*, edited and translated by Gianna Pomata

Margherita Sarrocchi, *La Scanderbeide*, edited and translated by Rinaldina Russell

Justine Siegemund, *The Court Midwife*, edited and translated by Lynne Tatlock

Gabrielle Suchon, *"On Philosophy" and "On Morality,"* edited and translated by Domna Stanton with Rebecca Wilkin

Sara Copio Sullam, *Sara Copio Sullam: Jewish Poet and Intellectual in Early Seventeenth-Century Venice*, edited and translated by Don Harrán

Arcangela Tarrabotti, *Convent Life as Inferno: A Report*, introduction and notes by Francesca Medioli, translated by Letizia Panizza

Laura Terracina, *Works*, edited and translated by Michael Sherberg

Katharina Schütz Zell, *Selected Writings*, edited and translated by Elsie McKee

Signed miniature (1732) by Leonardo Sconzani showing Laura Bassi lecturing in the Sala del Consiglio of the Palazzo Pubblico. Courtesy of the Bologna State Archive (Anziani consoli, Insignia, vol. XIII, c. 94). Photograph courtesy of Rebecca Messbarger.

THE ITALIAN ENLIGHTENMENT REFORM
OF THE QUERELLE DES FEMMES

Woman has an extra-fine intellect,
But the shrewd man will not let her study.
If woman were educated, sorry man
Would be seen to spin at the distaff.
And if a woman uses her intellect,
Man will be on the bottom and woman on top.

—Carlo Goldoni

THE OTHER VOICE

During the course of the Italian Enlightenment (1700–1789),[1] four women, Giuseppa Eleonora Barbapiccola, Aretafila Savini de' Rossi, Maria Gaetana Agnesi, and Diamante Medaglia Faini, joined the vigorous and prolific debate over the education of women waged by learned men across the peninsula. These enlightened *letterate* epitomize the unprecedented authority attained by women during the Settecento within the academic establishment and their increasing ability to influence the public discourse. In sharp contrast to the restricted presence of women in centers for intellectual exchange in the past and in other contemporary European countries, they asserted arguments in favor of the education of their sex within the leading institutions that constituted the Enlightenment Republic of Letters[2]—in the

This introduction summarizes arguments and literary and historical analysis in my book *The Century of Women: Representations of Women in Eighteenth-Century Italian Public Discourse* (Toronto: University of Toronto Press, 2002).

1. This periodization of the Italian Enlightenment reflects the substantive changes in political discourse generally and in the controversy about women specifically that came about in response to the French Revolution.

2. Dena Goodman, in her interpretation and extension of the theories of Jürgen Habermas, has perhaps best defined the eighteenth-century Republic of Letters in her book of the same name.

pages of respected scholarly publications and from the lecterns of scientific and literary academies to which they belonged. This shift in the locus of women's defenses of women from the perimeters to the hubs of intellectual exchange is paralleled by their rhetoric and arguments, which, with rare exceptions, scrupulously adhere to the ruling discursive conventions in their moderation of tone and their commitment to rational critical analysis founded on *esperienze* and aimed, ultimately, at practical social reform. Individually and as a whole, these four arguments in defense of women's learning elucidate women's evolving agency and discursive strategies in the pivotal contest for knowledge during the Italian Enlightenment.

THE QUERELLE DES FEMMES IN
SEVENTEENTH-CENTURY ITALY

The same cannot be said for the earlier *querelle des femmes* instituted by men and typified by such misogynist harangues as Giuseppe Passi's *On Feminine Defects* (1599).[3] In *The Nobility and Excellence of Women and the Defects and Vices of Men* (1600),[4] the Venetian writer and scholar Lucrezia Marinella (1571–1653) countered Passi's thirty-five chapters point by point, opposing his descriptions of such wicked women as the jealous, the ambitious, the lustful, the inconstant, the hateful, the thieving, the tyrannical, and the hypocritical with thirty-five chapters of her own defending women's virtue and castigating male villainy and abuse. From her convent cell, Marinella's Venetian contemporary, Arcangela Tarabotti (1604–52) similarly rebutted Valens Acidalius's exasperated misogynist tract *A New Disputation against Women Which Proves That They Are Not Human.*[5] Tarabotti's vigorous and systematic counter-

---

She describes it as a lettered community, influenced to an unprecedented degree by women, ideally engaged "at the very center of the public sphere" in the egalitarian exchange of ideas and the circulation of socially relevant knowledge and information. In contrast to the situation in France, however, the eighteenth-century Italian Republic of Letters was not defined strictly outside of the academic establishment by the woman-governed salon, but also comprised scientific and literary academies to which women in Italy could very often also belong. Dena Goodman, *The Republic of Letters: A Cultural History of the French Enlightenment* (Ithaca, NY: Cornell University Press, 1994).

3. Giuseppe Passi, *I donneschi diffetti nuovamente formati e posti in luce* (Venice: Iacobo Antonio Somascho, 1599).

4. Lucrezia Marinella, *The Nobility and Excellence of Women and the Defects and Vices of Men* (*Nobilità et l'eccellenza delle donne, co' difetti et mancamenti degli uomini*, 1600), ed. and trans. Anne Dunhill (Chicago: University of Chicago Press, 1999).

5. Valens Acidalius, *Disputatio nova contra mulieres, qua probatur eas homines non esse* (n.p.: H. Osthausen, 1595), translated into Italian by Orazio Plata in 1637.

argument, *That Women Are of the Same Species as Men*,[6] refuted "word by word, argument by argument, and concept by concept" each of her opponent's "deceptions" with "counterproofs" derived from scripture and common truth.[7] In 1600, the year in which Marinella published *The Nobility and Excellence of Women*, Moderata Fonte, another celebrated Venetian, constructed a literary refuge from the plague of male abuse in her fictional dialogue *The Worth of Women*.[8] However, the target of Fonte's fictional conversation among seven women secluded in a palace garden was not a single male adversary but the entrenched misogynist tradition, both literary and actual.

As the titles of these arguments for and against women make plain, the worth, the integrity, and, indeed, the very humanity of the female sex were at issue in the seventeenth-century Italian *querelle des femmes*. Constance Jordan has demonstrated that both sides of the quarrel invoked the authority of natural and divine law, and mined both scripture and the classical master narratives, especially the work of Plato and Aristotle, for proofs of women's inherent virtue or corruption and their inferiority, equality, or even superiority to men.[9] Writers in the genre commonly compiled catalogs of illustrious and infamous women from miscellaneous sources—historical, religious, and mythological—to establish women's intrinsic nature and appropriate roles. Indeed, as Jordan, Ruth Kelso, Marc Angenot, Linda Woodbridge, Virginia Cox, and others have shown, before the Enlightenment, the dispute about women constituted a genre with set themes, tropes, and authorities that academicians often exploited to display their rhetorical skill and ingenuity, at times even arguing both sides of the debate.[10]

6. Arcangela Tarabotti, *Che le donne siano della spetie degli Huomini* (Norimbergh: Cherchenbergher, 1651).

7. Ibid., 5: "parole a parole, ragione a ragione, concetti a concetti."

8. Moderata Fonte, *The Worth of Women: Wherein Is Clearly Revealed Their Nobility and Their Superiority to Men*, ed. and trans. Virginia Cox (Chicago: University of Chicago Press, 1997).

9. Constance Jordan, *Renaissance Feminism: Literary Texts and Political Models* (Ithaca, NY: Cornell University Press, 1990).

10. Ruth Kelso, *Doctrine for the Lady of the Renaissance* (Urbana: University of Illinois Press, 1956); Marc Angenot, *Les champions des femmes: examen du discours sur la supériorité des femmes, 1400–1800* (Montreal: Presses de l'Université de Québec, 1977); Joan Kelly, "Did Women Have a Renaissance," in *Women, History and Theory: The Essays of Joan Kelly*, ed. Catherine Stimpson (Chicago: University of Chicago Press, 1984), 19–50; Linda Woodbridge, *Women and the English Renaissance: Literature and the Nature of Womankind, 1540–1620* (Urbana: University of Illinois Press, 1984); Virginia Cox, "Moderata Fonte and *The Worth of Women*," in *The Worth of Women*, by Fonte, 1–23.

EIGHTEENTH-CENTURY EXTENSIONS AND TRANSFORMATIONS OF THE CONTROVERSY ABOUT WOMEN

The potent reprisals of Marinella, Tarabotti, and Fonte and the misogynist literary discourse that prompted them serve as a critical point of comparison for the public discourse about women that characterized the eighteenth century in Italy. As the historian Ginevra Conti Odorisio has observed, the misogynist literature of the seventeenth century was "particularly violent and dense with religious references which continued to fade during the eighteenth century."[11] With the rise of Enlightenment ideals of rational civil law, secular moral philosophy, and utilitarian social ethics, the authority of natural and divine law that had been so integral to the earlier *querelle* was increasingly displaced, thus radically altering the criteria for defining and assessing feminine virtue and women's proper roles. A self-conscious drive to scientifically define and classify fields of knowledge, social and political institutions, the parts and functions of the human body, the operations of the mind, and the formation and range of human behaviors gave rise to such influential texts as Gaetano Filangieri's *The Science of Legislation*, Giambattista Vico's *The New Science* of the origins and evolution of human society, Cesare Beccaria's systematic and disinterested examination of *Crimes and Punishments*. Less noted but influential studies included Trojano Spinelli's *The Science of Currency*, Giuseppe Pizzati's *Science of Sounds and Harmony*, and Giovanni Maria Torre's *Science of Nature*.[12] This same drive also compelled Enlightenment thinkers to reconceive the formal controversy about women. The *illuministi* undertook a modernization of the terms and methods of the *querelle*, effectively developing a new "science of woman," an offshoot of the flourishing "science of man." They applied the principles of modern medicine, physiology and anatomy, natural philosophy, economics, and political and social ethics in an effort to determine women's practical value and her appropriate roles

11. Ginevra Conti Odorisio, *Donna e società nel Seicento: Lucrezia Marinelli e Arcangela Tarabotti* (Rome: Bulzoni, 1979), 36.

12. Gaetano Filangieri, *La Scienza della Legislazione* [1780], ed. Vittorio Frosini (Rome: Istituto Poligrafico e Zecca dello Stato, 1984); Giambattista Vico, *Principj di scienza nuova di Giambattista Vico d'intorno alla comune natura delle nazioni* (Naples: Stamperia Muziana, 1744); Cesare Beccaria, *Dei delitti e delle pene* (Livorno, 1764); Trojano Spinelli, *Riflessioni politiche sopra alcuni punti della scienza della moneta* (Naples, 1750); Giuseppe Pizzati, *La scienza de' suoni e dell'armonia, diretta specialmente a render ragione de' fenomeni, ed a conoscer la natura e le leggi della medesima, ed agiovare alla pratica del contrappunto* (Venezia: Giovanni Gatti, 1782); Giovanni Maria Torre, *Scienza della Natura* (Naples: Serafino Regio Stampatore, 1748–49).

in modern society and the state.[13] The empirical method served the pursuit of the "facts" of feminine difference, difference translated in the terms of the Enlightenment project itself.

For the authoritative intellectual class of the *illuministi*, the crux of the "woman question" shifted in the eighteenth century from women's inherent "worth" to their practical functions and their potential influence over the collective welfare—the "public good" or "bene pubblico." Noted male intellectuals across the peninsula discussed women's proper role in contemporary society, both as a crucial subject in its own right and in relation to such pressing contemporary issues as public health, education, child rearing, birth rates, the private and the public economies, social morality, bourgeois consumerism, and the nature and duties of citizenship. Luciano Guerci rightly states that "those who wrote about marriage, breast-feeding, conversations, the education of women, etc., did so well aware that they were confronting issues fundamental to the organization of society."[14] Indeed, of all the "old questions" revised and revisited during the Italian Enlightenment, the "woman question" stood at the center of public debate.

The currency and ubiquity of these issues are evident in the number and prominence of the *letterati* who formally addressed them. Participants in the controversy included the Venetian poet, prose writer, gazetteer, and critic Gasparo Gozzi; the Paduan scientist and philosopher Antonio Conti; the Milanese political economist, journalist, and government official Pietro Verri; the Venetian playwrights Carlo Goldoni and Pietro Chiari; the Neapolitan political theorist Gaetano Filangieri; the Venetian writer and adventurer Giovanni Casanova; the Milanese economist Carlo Sebastiano Franci; and the Venetian intellectual and cosmopolitan Francesco Algarotti.

This is not to say, however, that the vehement misogyny expressed a century earlier by Passi and Acidalius vanished during the Italian Enlightenment. Echoes of the seventeenth-century misogynists' discourse clearly survive in numerous popular texts of the Settecento. Foremost among these

13. On the development of a "science of women," see Ludmilla Jordanova, "Sex and Gender," in *Inventing Human Science*, ed. Christopher Fox, Roy Porter, and Robert Wokler (Berkeley: University of California Press, 1995), 152–83; Londa Schiebinger, *The Mind Has No Sex? Women in the Origins of Modern Science* (Cambridge, MA: Harvard University Press, 1989); Thomas Laqueur, *Making Sex: Body and Gender from the Greeks to Freud* (Cambridge, MA: Harvard University Press, 1990); and Jonathan Sawday, *The Body Emblazoned: Dissection and the Human Body in Renaissance Culture* (New York: Routledge, 1995).

14. Luciano Guerci, *La discussione sulla donna nell'Italia del Settecento* (Turin: Tirrenia Stampatori, 1987), 17: "Color che scrissero del matrimonio, dell'allattamento, delle conversazioni, dell'istruzione femminile ecc. lo fecero essendo ben consapevoli di occuparsi di temi fondamentali per l'organizzazione della società."

are Ferdinando Galiani's semiserious tract *Croquis d'un dialogue sur les femmes* with its description of women as sick, weak and, indeed, deranged animals; the *soi-disant* anti-*philosophe* Giuseppe Antonio Constantini's *Lettere critiche* commanding men to subjugate those "haughty, deceitful female beasts"; and Diunilgo Valdecio's nearly seven thousand rhyming verses vilifying women as the *Ruin of Humanity* (*Lo scoglio dell'umanità*).[15] But the *illuministi* generally viewed these texts as frivolous and outmoded and consigned them to the margins of contemporary intellectual debate.

In contrast with the rhetorical formality and practical inconsequence of the *querelle des femmes*, the eighteenth century witnessed relatively little controversy about women's educability and ample debate over what and how much they should be taught. The *illuministi* increasingly viewed educating women as a reasonable and practical way to improve both the private and the public welfare. In the words of *illuminista* Pier Domenico Soresi, women were the "linchpin of public happiness" through their roles as guardians of the hearth, a site deemed by another Enlightenment thinker, Melchiorre Delfico, the new "cradle of [modern] deportment and reason."[16] Limited academic preparation for women thus gained broad acceptance as necessary to help them educate the nation's young and manage their household economies. However, some *illuministi* went further and considered the education of women crucial to the refinement of social life and to cultural progress generally. In the Age of Sociability, as it was known,[17] the influence of women, especially those from the upper classes, extended beyond the home to shape social life in limited but pivotal ways. Women often joined men in the elite art of the "conversazione"; they consumed material and cultural commodities—from fashionable goods to fashion magazines; and they entered the Enlightenment Republic of Letters with new authority and in unprecedented numbers.

15. Ferdinando Galiani, *Croquis d'un dialogue sur les femmes* [1772], in *Opere di Ferdinando Galiani*, ed. Furio Diaz and Luciano Guerci, vol. 6 of *Illuministi Italiani* (Milan: Riccardo Ricciardi, 1975), 613–42; Giuseppe Antonio Constantini, *Lettere critiche, giocose, morali, scientifiche, ed erudite, alla moda, ed al gusto del secolo presente*, 7 vols. (Venice: Pietro Bassaglia, 1751); and Diunilgo Valdecio [Carlo Maria Chiaraviglio], *Lo scoglio dell'umanità, ossia Avvertimento salutare alla gioventù per cautelarsi contro le male qualità delle donne cattive. Operetta lepido-critica-poetica-morale di Diunilgo Valdecio, pastor arcade* (Venice: Zatta, 1779).

16. Pier Domenico Soresi, *Saggio sopra la necessità e la facilità di ammaestrare le fanciulle* (Milan: Federico Agnelli, 1774), 38; Melchiorre Delfico, *Saggio filosofico sul matrimonio* (Teremo, 1774), 128.

17. Among others, the Venetian playwright Pietro Chiari applied this epithet to the Settecento. See his popular *Lettere d'un solitario a sua figlia per formarle il cuore, e lo spirito nella scuola del mondo*, part 1 (Venice: Battifoco, 1777), 171–72. See also Guerci's discussion of this text and its celebration of contemporary sociability in *La discussione sulla donna*, 80–81.

WOMEN'S PARTICIPATION IN EIGHTEENTH-CENTURY
ITALIAN ENLIGHTENMENT CULTURE

When Marinella, Tarabotti, and Fonte put their quills to paper to castigate men's abuse of women, they wrote from the cultural borderline, as isolated and remote voices. Tarabotti was physically sequestered in her convent cell, but all three could be said to have occupied the private and obscure terrain that Margaret King so eloquently describes as the "book-lined cell."[18] By contrast, the eighteenth century in Italy witnessed a marked relaxation of the borders that separated female from male writers and intellectuals. In other parts of Europe, notably France and England, women intellectuals exerted their influence in the shadow academic world of the salon because they were forbidden entry into academies and universities. In Italy, though, a number of learned Italian women achieved true institutional authority, beginning perhaps in 1678, when the thirty-two-year-old Paduan aristocrat Elena Cornaro Piscopia (1646–84) became the first woman to receive a university degree. More than twenty thousand spectators, including native and foreign political and ecclesiastical leaders, heard her defend her thesis in philosophy and saw her admitted into the rarefied, hitherto wholly masculine, domain of the Paduan *studiosi*.[19] To acknowledge her unique achievement, several scientific and literary academies made her a member, including the Academy of the Ricovrati of Padua, among whose founders had been the patriarch of the "new science," Galileo Galilei.[20] Although the University of Padua closed its doors to women less than a year later, Cornaro Piscopia's admission into the academic establishment signaled an opening, narrow as it may have been, of an institutional acceptance of learned women that continued throughout the century.[21]

When Laura Bassi Veratti (1711–78) became the second woman to receive a university degree in 1732, women had become increasingly present

18. Margaret King, "Book-Lined Cells: Women and Humanism in the Early Italian Renaissance," in *Beyond Their Sex: Learned Women of the European Past*, ed. Patricia H. Labalme (New York: New York University Press, 1980), 66–90.

19. On Cornaro Piscopia, see Marta Cavazza, "Dottrici e lettrici dell'Università di Bologna nel Settecento," *Annali di storia delle università italiane* 1 (1997): 109–26; and Patricia H. Labalme, "Women's Roles in Early Modern Venice: An Exceptional Case," in *Beyond Their Sex*, ed. Labalme, 129–52.

20. On the origins of the academy and Cornaro Piscopia's induction, see Diego Valeri, *L'Accademia dei Ricovrati Alias Accademia Patavina di Scienze Lettere ed Arti* (Padua: Sede dell'Accademia, 1987).

21. Labalme, "Women's Roles"; Paula Findlen, "Science as a Career in Enlightenment Italy: The Strategies of Laura Bassi," *Isis* 84 (1993): 441–69.

within the centers of intellectual exchange. Bassi defended her degree in philosophy at the University of Bologna before an elite crowd that included the Bolognese Senate and civic, cultural, and church leaders. Subsequently, the Senate appointed her lecturer of universal philosophy and designated her an honorary member of the Bolognese Academy of Sciences. In 1745 Pope Benedict XIV appointed her as a regular member of the *Benedettini* of the Academy of Sciences, a separate society he had established that year to distinguish the leaders of the Bolognese scientific community. As part of her civic duties as *Bologna Minerva*, Bassi presented Latin treatises at the Institute of Sciences and lectures at public anatomies, frequently on Newtonian optics and physics, on which she was a recognized expert. In 1776 she was named professor of experimental physics in the Institute of Sciences.[22] After Bassi, the legal scholar Maria Pellegrina Amoretti (1756–87), the Newtonian philosopher Cristina Roccati (1734–1814), and the classics scholar Clotilde Tambroni (1758–1817) also received university professorships,[23] and several other learned women were appointed to posts at the University of Bologna. Pope Benedict XIV, the former Archbishop of Bologna and a zealous advocate of modern scientific study, had been instrumental in bringing about Bassi's appointment to the university. Later, he sought to install the Milanese mathematician Maria Gaetana Agnesi (1718–99) as honorary chair of mathematics, but Agnesi declined the offer.[24] He also sanctioned

---

22. My thanks to Marta Cavazza for clarifying the details of Bassi's academic and professional trajectory. On Bassi, see Findlen, "Science as a Career"; Marta Cavazza, "Laura Bassi e il suo gabinetto di fisica sperimentale: realtà e mito," *Nuncius: Annali di storia della scienza* 10.2 (1995): 715–53; Cavazza, "Laura Bassi 'Maestra' di Spallanzani," in *Il cerchio della vita: Materiali del Centro Studi Lazzaro Spallanzani di Scandiano sulla storia della scienza del Settecento*, ed. Walter Bernardi and Paola Manzini (Florence: Olschki, 1999), 185–202; Cavazza, "Riflessi letterari dell'opera di Newton: Algarotti, Manfredi e Laura Bassi," in *Radici, significato, retaggio dell'opera newtoniana*, ed. G. Tarozzi and M. Van Vloten (Bologna: Società italiana di Fisica, 1989), 352–66; Cavazza, "Dottrici e lettrici dell'Università di Bologna nel Settecento," *Annali di storia delle università italiane* 1 (1997): 109–26; Alberto Elena, "In lode della filosofessa di Bologna: An Introduction to Laura Bassi," *Isis* 82 (1991): 510–18; Elio Meli, "Laura Bassi Verati: Ridiscussioni e nuovi spunti," in *Alma Mater Studiorum: La Presenza Femminile* (Bologna: CLUEB, 1988), 71–79; and Beate Ceranski, *"Und sie fürchtet sich vor niemandem": Die Physikerin Laura Bassi (1711–1778)* (Frankfurt: Campus Verlag, 1996).

23. On Roccati, see Paula Findlen, "A Forgotten Newtonian: Women and Science in the Italian Provinces," in *The Sciences in Enlightened Europe*, ed. William Clark and Jan Golinski (Chicago: University of Chicago Press, 1999), 313–49. On Amoretti and other female intellectuals of the eighteenth century, see Maria Bandini Buti, *Poetesse e scrittrici: Enciclopedia biografica e bibliografica italiana*, vol. 6 (Rome: E.B.B.I., 1942); Ginevra Canonici Fachini, *Prospetto biografico delle donne italiane rinomate in letteratura dal secolo decimoquarto fino a' giorni nostri* (Venice: Tipografia di Alvisopoli, 1824); and Jolanda de Blasi, *Antologia delle scrittrici italiane* (Florence: Nemi, 1931).

24. On Agnesi, see Paula Findlen's introduction to her 1727 oration in this volume and Giovanna Tilche, *Maria Gaetana Agnesi* (Milan: Rizzoli, 1984).

the appointment of Anna Morandi Manzolini (1714–74), the internationally known anatomist and anatomical wax modeler, as lecturer of anatomical design at the University of Bologna.[25]

As the century advanced, so did women's presence in elite academic institutions, a development unquestionably linked to the growing influence of Enlightenment ideals and their social and political practice. Growing numbers of women, Italian and foreign alike, were inducted into the most prestigious Italian scientific and literary academies. Even more impressively, Bianca Laura Saibante Vannetti (1723–99) and Clelia del Grillo Borromeo (1684–1777) founded, respectively, the Academy of the Agiati of Rovereto and the Academy of the Vigilanti.[26] By the middle of the eighteenth century, the Arcadia Academy, which was founded in 1690 at the inspiration of Queen Christina of Sweden but whose colonies eventually spanned the peninsula, had become a center of literary production and exchange shaped by the presence of women. As Elisabetta Graziosi has observed, this discursive site, where the poetic voices of the shepherdesses vied equally with those of shepherds, "relegated to the past the misogynistic closure of the seventeenth-century Italian intellectual class."[27] The crowning in 1776 as poet laureate of the Arcadian improviser Corilla Olimpica (Maria Maddelena Morelli Fernandez, 1727–1800), the only woman in Italy ever to achieve this distinction, shows the real and symbolic institutional gains women had made by the last quarter of the century.[28]

Beyond the worlds of the academy and the university, a small but influential group of women purveyed contemporary texts and ideas as editors, publishers, and journalists. Foremost among these was the Venetian *bourgeoise* Elisabetta Caminer Turra (1751–96), who collaborated with her father, Domenico Caminer, in the publication of the literary journal *Europa letteraria* and who directed on her own the *Giornale enciclopedico* (1774–82), the *Nuovo giornale enciclopedico* (1782–89), and the *Nuovo giornale enciclopedico d'Italia* (1790–97). Caminer Turra contributed to the development of the method

---

25. On Morandi Manzolini, see Rebecca Messbarger, "Waxing Poetic: The Anatomical Wax Sculptures of Anna Morandi Manzolini," *Configurations* 9 (2001): 65–97; and Messbarger, "Remembering a Body of Work: Re-Constructing the Lifework of Anatomist Anna Morandi Manzolini," *Studies in Eighteenth-Century Culture* 32 (2003): 123–54.

26. On Saibante Vannetti and del Grillo Borromeo, see Buti, *Poetesse e scrittrici*.

27. Elisabetta Graziosi, "Arcadia Femminile: Presenze e Modelli," in *Filologia e critica* 17 (1992): 321–58.

28. On Corilla Olimpica, see Paola Giuli, "Traces of a Sisterhood: Corilla Olimpica as Corinne's Unacknowledged Alter Ego," in *The Novel's Seductions: Stael's Corinne in Critical Inquiry*, ed. Karyne Samurlo (Lewisburg, PA: Bucknell University Press, 1999), 165–84.

and terms of modern literary critique in her journals, which reviewed major contemporary literary, scientific, and philosophical works published in and outside of Italy. Remarkably, for fifteen years she also oversaw her own publishing house, the Stamperia Turra.[29] Other contemporary women journalists of note include Caterina Cracas (1691–1771), the director of the Roman periodical *Il Caracas*, and Eleanora de Fonseca Pimentel Chavez (1752–99), the director of the Jacobin periodical *Monitore partenopeo*.[30]

Translation was perhaps the most common way for women to exercise authority within the contemporary Italian Republic of Letters. Caminer Turra promoted the dissemination of European Enlightenment thought in Italy not only by her work as an editor and journalist, but also by her translations of the bourgeois dramas of Gotthold Ephraim Lessing, Henry Fielding, Francois-Marie Arouet Voltaire, Louis-Sébastien Mercier, and others. Her Venetian compatriots Luisa Bergalli Gozzi (1703–99) and Giustina Renier Michiel (1755–1832) translated Jean Racine and William Shakespeare, respectively. Women also translated the texts of the "new science and philosophy." Giuseppa Eleonora Barbapiccola (n.d.), a Cartesian philosopher and a member of Vico's intellectual circle, sought to redress women's intellectual servitude by translating René Descartes's *Principles of Philosophy* expressly for them.[31] Another Neapolitan philosopher, Maria Angela Ardinghelli (1728–1825), produced the first translations into Italian of the works of the English botanist and physiologist Stephen Hales.[32]

Eighteenth-century Italian women were thus present, not merely symbolically but actually, at primary sites of intellectual exchange from which they had been excluded in the past. Women, albeit a select few, now occu-

---

29. On Caminer Turra, see Catherine Sama's introduction and bibliography in Elisabetta Caminer Turra, *Selected Writings of an Eighteenth-Century Venetian Woman of Letters*, ed. and trans. Catherine Sama (Chicago: University of Chicago Press, 2003), 1–95; Sama, "Becoming Visible: A Biography of Elisabetta Caminer Turra (1751–1796) during Her Formative Years," *Studi Veneziani* (fall 2002): 349–88; Sama, "Liberty, Equality, Frivolity! An Eighteenth-Century Critique of Fashion Periodicals in Italy," *Eighteenth-Century Studies* 37, no. 3 (2004): 389–414; and Rita Unfer Lukoschik, ed., *Elisabetta Caminer Turra (1751–1796): Una letterata veneta verso l'Europa* (Verona: Essedue, 1998).

30. For a useful summary of women's cultural influence during the period, see Paola Giuli, "Enlightenment," in *The Feminist Encyclopedia of Italian Literature*, ed. Rinaldina Russell (Westport, CT: Greenwood Press, 1997), 79–82.

31. On Barbapiccola, see Paula Findlen's introduction to her in this volume, pp. 37–46; see also Rebecca Messbarger, "Barbapiccola, Giuseppa Eleonora (Eighteenth Century)," in *Feminist Encyclopedia of Italian Literature*, ed. Russell, 27–29.

32. Paula Findlen, "Translating the New Science: Women and the Circulation of Knowledge in Enlightenment Italy," *Configurations* 3 (1995): 193; on Ardinghelli generally, 193–205.

pied the halls and chairs of universities and the seats, the podiums, and the scientific laboratories of academies. They spoke from the pages of influential academic and popular journals, some of which they also edited, and they published notable works both of fiction and nonfiction. This is not to say, though, that the Italian Enlightenment Republic of Letters replaced the entrenched tradition of academic misogyny with egalitarian, gender-indifferent intellectual exchange. The learned women recognized by the intellectual establishment were most often honorary or otherwise exceptional members. Their academic brethren typically called them *illustri*, an epithet that in fact relegated them to positions apart from their fellows in the academy and far from the common mass of women, to whom institutional access was unfailingly denied.[33] Yet while the learned woman's authority within the contemporary Republic of Letters was indisputabley limited, she was present and exerted unprecedented authority within established centers of intellectual exchange. This new and increasing presence helped transform the age-old controversy about women's education.

MALE RESPONSES TO FEMALE CULTURAL PRESENCE IN EIGHTEENTH-CENTURY ITALY

In his grand two-volume *Treatise on the Education of Women* (*Trattato degli studi delle donne*, 1740), Giovanni Bandiera built his argument for women's ability to master such sublime disciplines as metaphysics and mathematics on Poullain de la Barre's famous claim that "the mind has no sex"[34] and cited as evidence such contemporary learned women as Luisa Bergalli Gozzi, Giuseppa Eleonora Barbapiccola, and Laura Bassi.[35] The Bolognese *filosofessa* Bassi, renowned for her public lectures on Newtonian physics, inspired, in part, the fictional dialogue between the Marchioness of E—— and her philosopher companion in Francesco Algarotti's celebrated *Newtonianism for Ladies* (*Il Newtonianismo per le dame*, 1737),[36] a popular explication of Newtonian optics. Similarly, in the *Defense of Women* (*Difesa delle donne*) that he

33. Mary Sheriff provides an excellent theoretical analysis of the designation "exceptional woman" and of the (masculinist) politics that often underpin it, in *The Exceptional Woman: Elisabeth Vigée-Lebrun and the Cultural Politics of Art* (Chicago: University of Chicago Press, 1996), esp. 1–10.

34. François Poullain de la Barre, *Three Cartesian Feminist Treatises*, ed. and trans. Marcelle Maistre Welch and Vivien Bosley (Chicago: University of Chicago Press, 2002), 82.

35. Giovanni Bandiera, *Trattato degli studi delle donne in due parti divise* (Venice: Francesco Pitteri, 1740).

36. Francesco Algarotti, *Il Newtonianismo per le dame ovvero Dialoghi sopra la luce, i colori, e l'attrazione* (Naples: Giambatista Pasquali, 1739). See especially the reference to Bassi on pages 6 and 7.

published in the premier Italian Enlightenment journal *Il Caffè* (1764–66),[37] the Milanese *illuminista* Carlo Sebastiano Franci repeatedly extolled Empress Maria Theresa's sound judgment and exemplary moral fortitude to illustrate the characteristics of the ideal female education. For his part, when the *illuminista* and pedagogical theorist Pier Domenico Soresi cited examples of learned women throughout history in his *Essay on the Necessity and the Facility of Educating Girls* (1774),[38] his female contemporaries Maria Gaetana Agnesi, Elisabetta Caminer Turra, Luisa Bergalli Gozzi, Laura Bassi, and Aretafila Savini de' Rossi were prominent among them. At the same time, however, all these authors advocated rigorous limitations on women's presence in the academy and on their education generally. Ambivalence about the place and purpose of women in contemporary society and, by extension, about the purpose of their education lies at the core of the defenses of women's education written by even the most progressive *illuministi*.

Luciano Guerci summed up this ambivalence: women "are able, but they shouldn't."[39] In other words, although women may possess the same intellectual capability as men, they should not receive the same education. Bandiera's invocation of his learned female contemporaries, for example, and his defense of women's ability to grasp even the most esoteric sciences (claims that nearly put his tract on the *Index*) do not preclude his recommending that women be schooled only in subjects directly relevant to their domestic lives and their maternal duties. Carlo Sebastiano Franci, the author of *Il Caffè*'s "Defense of Women," likewise calls upon his fellow *illuministi* to recognize the practical benefits to the modern state, no less than to modern family life, of formally educating women. But his instruction is intended primarily to encourage women's domesticity and their renunciation of such worldly diversions as masquerades, the theater, and card games. In effect, he preaches women's compliant return to their traditional responsibilities to hearth and husband. Franci's repeated invocation of Maria Theresa, that most public of contemporary women, as the model for this ideal devotion to an enlightened domesticity reveals the ideological ambivalence at the heart of his argument. Even Pier Domenico Soresi, who censures those "irrational men" who would subjugate women by denying their "equal right" to an education,[40] nonetheless bans metaphysics, calculus, and other "sublime

---

37. Carlo Sebastiano Franci, "La difesa delle donne," in *Il Caffè, 1764–1766*, ed. Gianni Francioni and Sergio Romagnoli (Turin: Bollati Boringhieri, 1993), 245–56.

38. Soresi, *Saggio.*

39. Guerci, *Discussione sulla donna*, 133: "son capaci, ma non devono."

40. Soresi, *Saggio*, 23–24: "Io non oserei imaginarmi, che fosse effetto d'invidia il non partecipare alle femmine un tanto bene, il ritenere questo sesso amabile tra gli odiosi ceppi d'un

studies" from his ideal feminine curriculum,[41] and describes the perfectly educated women in traditional, masculinist terms. Soresi's educated woman will
dutifully withdraw from *il mondo* into her home to attend to the well-being of
her family, and especially to the primary education of the nation's young.[42]
Like Bandiera, Franci, and other Enlightenment defenders of women's education, Soresi maintains that "to liberate the fair sex from ignorance" is no
longer a merely rhetorical imperative but "a matter of public utility,"[43] and
yet he, too, conflates women's "public utility" with their domesticity.

Even those *illuministi* who praised women's expanding "sociability" as a
sign of contemporary progress rejected an equal education for women. In his
popular *Venetian Gazette* (1760–62), the journalist and critic Gasparo Gozzi
repeatedly defends the current practice of social conversation between men
and women. He insists that the sexes possess the same intellectual capacities
and contends that any difference in their mastery of certain subjects stems
from the different education they have traditionally received.[44] Yet Gozzi
still describes an education for women that accords with the needs and desires of men:

> Today, custom requires that women often find themselves in the com-
> pany of men and that they converse about things other than laun-
> dry, fabrics, or similar domestic affairs. It is therefore necessary that
> women acquire *some useful glimmer of learning*, such that, when they find
> themselves at a social gathering in which intellectual subjects are being
> discussed, they will not seem surprised; they will not yawn; they will
> not act as if they are dying of boredom; or, with their mouths sealed
> shut, as though they are silently begging the heavens for the discussion
> to end, of which they do not comprehend the first syllable.[45] (emphasis
> added)

The Venetian playwright Pietro Chiari even goes so far in his adamant defense of the "sociable woman" living in the current "Sociable Century" as to

---

ozio illiberale, al quale non è nato; il porre come un muro divisorio tra i nobili studj e lui; il
nascondergli sempre mai la bella faccia della verità, alla quale ciascun ha uguale diritto."

41. Soresi, *Saggio*, 106: "Nè vogliamo già immergere il bel sesso nella Metafisica, o nel Calcolo,
ne seppellirlo in altri Studj sublimi e profondi."

42. Soresi, *Saggio*, 90–108.

43. Soresi, *Saggio*, 108: "Nel proporre di liberare dall'ignoranza il bel sesso io non ho pensato
di adularlo: ho avuto unicamente in mira l'utilità pubblica, che è il fine delle mie, qualunque
siano, letterarie occupazioni."

44. Gasparo Gozzi, *Gazzetta veneta*, ed. Antonio Zardo (Florence: G. C. Sansoni, 1957), 160. On
Gozzi's constructions of femininity in the *Gazette*, see Rebecca Messbarger, "Double-Crossing:
Female Impersonation in Gasparo Gozzi's *Gazzetta veneta*," *M/MLA Journal* 35.1 (2002): 1–13.

45. Gozzi, *Gazzetta veneta*, 361.

approve the custom among aristocratic and upper bourgeois ladies of taking a *cicisbeo*, or gallant.[46] Yet, while he finds nothing indecorous in a woman's socializing with a man other than her husband, he warns his fair readers against the unseemliness of too much learning.[47]

Pietro Verri, editor of *Il Caffè* and a leading architect of the Italian Enlightenment, was perhaps most candid in his ambivalence about the proper role and intellectual preparation of the enlightened *cittadina* (female citizen). In the informal conduct manual he composed for his newborn daughter, Verri realistically outlined what she must do to live happily and garner respect in the world as an "honest" woman. He opened his *Advice for My Daughter* (*Ricordi a mia figlia*, 1777) by bluntly contrasting the broad scope of men's opportunities to shape their reputations in the world with women's domestic isolation and virtual powerlessness to affect their social standing, or indeed the very course of their lives:

> A man, either through a career in the military, in the Church, in academia, or the government has the means to shape and to silence rumors about him, and goes forth as a warrior conquering public opinion. But a woman lacks these resources. Weak, graceful, and timid by nature, she has no means but sweetness, placid goodness, and the virtues of the heart. These are the attributes that procure her a husband, that endear her to others, and that elevate her to that level of happiness to which you may aspire.[48]

In modern society, according to Verri, "l'opinione pubblica" determines a woman's public and private fortune, her reputation in the world and, most important, her marriageability and the ongoing respect of her spouse. For this reason, although he sanctions a liberal education for his daughter that comprises music, painting, an introduction to the natural sciences, classic and contemporary literature including novels, and the pedagogical works of John Locke and Jean-Jacques Rousseau,[49] he cautions his daughter that "the woman of *esprit* keeps her knowledge to herself."[50] Verri takes a generally positive view of the increasing social interaction between the sexes of the period and encourages his daughter to learn the newest card games, to

---

46. Chiari uses the terms "sociable woman" (*donna socievole*) and "Sociable Century" (*Secolo Socievole*) in *Lettere d'un solitario a sua figlia per formarle il cuore*, 174–76.

47. On Chiari's treatment of the "woman question," see Guerci, *Discussione sulla donna*, 117–19.

48. Pietro Verri, *Ricordi a mia figlia* in *Opere varie*, vol. 1, ed. Nino Valeri (Florence: Felice Le Monnier, 1947), 297.

49. Verri, *Ricordi*, 331–32; 347–48.

50. Verri, *Ricordi*, 306.

practice dancing and singing, to be a refined hostess, and to keep abreast of changing fashions. At the same time, however, he insists that she veil her intellectual strengths, warning that "a lady, or indeed any woman, who exceeds the limits of a basic education will have difficulty finding a mate."[51]

Ultimately, even the most enlightened advocates for the education of women prescribed a curriculum restricted to the subjects considered most germane to domestic life, including morally sound literature, sacred history, moral philosophy, rudimentary arithmetic and, in rare instances, contemporary novels and an introduction to the natural sciences. The education of women and the belief in women's educability gained new acceptance during the Italian Enlightenment, but the object and nature of women's formal instruction continued to reflect traditional notions of women as the keepers of the domestic space. Despite explicit claims made by the *illuministi* about treating the woman question "without prejudice and without passion,"[52] in order to arrive at the "useful truth" (*utile verità*) purified of "all that is personal" or "self-serving,"[53] the "truth" they discovered was generally less useful to women than it was to men. An education, they thought, would make women better administrators of the home, better primary educators of the young, and less insipid conversationalists—in brief, more capable mothers, wives, and companions for men.

EIGHTEENTH-CENTURY ITALIAN WOMEN'S VIEWS ABOUT THE QUERELLE DES FEMMES

What did women themselves have to say on the issue, and to what extent did they exploit the themes and methods of the dominant contemporary discourse to defend their claims? This volume gathers together the most important arguments women made in defense of the education of their sex during the Italian Settecento. The book begins with Giuseppa Eleonora Barbapiccola's preface to her 1722 translation of Descartes's *Principles of Philosophy*, in which she contests the conventional belief that women "are not capable of learning because their minds are of a distinctly different and lesser quality than those of men"[54] by directing her translation especially at women, "who,

51. Verri, *Ricordi*, 332.

52. Soresi, *Saggio*, 3: "cerchiamo su questo punto la verità senza pregiudizio e senza passione."

53. Delfico, *Saggio filosofico*, 4: "non essendo entrato nelle mie idee nulla di personale, nè alcun riguardo particolare . . . io spero che in favore dell'utile verità, che è stata la mia sola ed unica mira, il Lettore non mi giudicherà su le sue antecedenti idee."

54. Giuseppa Eleonora Barbapiccola, "La traduttrice a' lettori," in *I principi della filosofia di Renato Des-Cartes tradotto da Giuseppa Eleonora Barbapiccola* (Turin: Francesco Mairesse, 1722), sig. +3r–

in the words of that same René, . . . are more suited for philosophy than men."[55] Barbapiccola cites Descartes to argue that elite women will be taught more than "catechism, sewing, and other small tasks, singing, dancing, doing one's hair up, curtsying finely, and conversing politely."[56] The foundation of their education should instead be rational philosophy, for which, she averred, they possessed a natural talent. Her translation would ideally serve to expand the ranks of "Cartesian women" like herself.[57] Barbapiccola is indeed a transitional figure in the shift away from the tradition of the *querelle* and toward the Enlightenment revaluation of the "woman question." The preface to her translation of Descartes constitutes a forceful apology for her own contributions to philosophical discourse as well as a key by which all literate Italian women can unlock philosophy, that ultimate sanctuary of male privilege and authority. But Barbapiccola's vigorous case for women's right to and facility for learning rests on a traditional convention of the *querelle*—the catalog of illustrious women, ancient and modern. As the century wore on, the catalog was increasingly displaced from women's defenses of their sex by practical arguments that focused on the public good and the concerns of everyday life. Yet, even as she adheres to this convention of the genre, Barbapiccola establishes a distinct female genealogy that privileges those learned precursors most like herself, women who disseminated knowledge by teaching and translating great texts and ideas.

One year after Barbapiccola published her translation, the prestigious Ricovrati Academy in Padua held a formal debate on women's education. The debate sparked a fierce reaction from women both in and outside the Veneto, who objected to its misogynist arguments and its conservative outcome, which advocated preserving elite women's intellectual privilege, while denying education to the rest. To assuage its female public and to strengthen its reputation as a center for modern, rational intellectual exchange, the Ricovrati published an amended version of the 1723 debate that included defenses of an education for women written by the Sienese noble-

---

+3v: "non sian capaci de' Studj per essere gli animi loro da quei degli Uomini di qualità affatto diversa e da meno."

55. Barbapiccola, "La traduttrice a' lettori," sig. +6v: "Io m'invogliai di tradurla in Italiano per farla ad altri molti partecipe, in particolare alle Donne, le quali, al dire dello stesso *Renato* . . . , meglio che gli Uomini alla Filosofia atte sono."

56. Barbapiccola, "La traduttrice a' lettori," sig. +3r: "il Catechismo, la cucitura, e diversi piccioli lavori, catare, ballare, acconciarsi alla moda, far bene la riverenza, e parlar civilmente." I have here cited Findlen's translation of Barbapiccola in this volume, p. 47.

57. Erica Harth uses this eptithet in her exceptional study of early French women followers of Descartes, *Cartesian Women: Versions and Subversions of Rational Discourse in the Old Regime* (Ithaca: Cornell University Press, 1992).

woman Aretafila Savini de' Rossi and the nine-year-old Milanese prodigy Maria Gaetana Agnesi. This transformation of the Ricovrati debate from the traditional all-male intellectual sporting event of 1723 into the published polemic of 1729 that incorporated the dissenting voices of women demonstrates, as no other event during the century, women's increasing presence and influence in the contemporary intellectual world. Aretafila Savini de' Rossi cast her unprecedented two-part rebuttal to Giovanni Antonio Volpi's original argument in the debate against women's education as both a traditional scholarly rejoinder and as a series of derisive footnotes appended to Volpi's argument, an intervention unique within the genre. In her formal response, Savini de' Rossi met the demands of modern empirical analysis by systematically rebutting her opponent's faulty generalizations about women's weakness and inferiority with specific proofs of women's penchant and need for learning that she drew from the lives of her famous contemporaries and from women's everyday experience. In addition, the 1729 volume included a Latin oration defending the education of women that the nine-year-old Maria Gaetana Agnesi had given to members of the Milanese nobility in 1727. Although biographers have questioned Agnesi's role in composing the oration, her defense offered a spectacular contrast to the Ricovrati's original dispute, not just because a female child delivered the erudite argument in Latin, but also because Agnesi's eloquence and rhetorical finesse, which included the use of irony, proved to be equal, if not superior to that of her opponent, Giovanni Antonio Volpi. Systematically challenging Volpi's citation of social custom, female incapacity, and the fear of social disorder as reasons to proscribe women's learning, Agnesi used Cartesian rationalism, the writings of the ancients and the Church fathers, and a catalog of learned women, ancient and modern, to defend women's education as a universal public good. Throughout her oration, unsurprisingly, she insisted determinedly on women's need and right to speak eloquently, whether in public or at home.

The Ricovrati debate and its subsequent publication reverberated for decades. In 1763, forty years after the event in Padua, the poet and mathematician Diamante Medaglia Faini returned to the conservative conclusion of the original debate as the point of departure for her extraordinary oration, "Which Studies Are Fitting for Women," addressed to the Unanimi Academy in Salò, of which she was both a member and the reigning Princess.[58] Medaglia Faini's oration elucidates the gains made by women

---

58. On Medaglia Faini's membership in the academy, see Paula Findlen, "Becoming a Scientist: Gender and Knowledge in Eighteenth-Century Italy," *Science and Context* 16 (2003): 59–87.

within the Republic of Letters at the height of the Enlightenment, but also accepts masculinist assumptions about women's moral and intellectual deficiency to justify their rigorous instruction in the natural sciences, mathematics, and philosophy at the expense of a more traditional literary training, particularly in the reading and writing of poetry.

Medaglia Faini's argument epitomizes the strategic use of the "double-voiced" discourse that simultaneously defied and affirmed misogynist constructions of femininity and that female authors and orators often exploited to defend the education of women.[59] Directed as they were at an authoritative male public, women's apologies for their sex frequently embedded their demands for women's education within a broader discourse about the moral deficiencies of contemporary women and their need to acquire at least basic literacy to fulfill more competently their primary roles as wives and mothers. This strategy, coupled with an appropriation of the themes of Enlightenment discourse and the reasoned method derived from the "new science and philosophy," allowed women to turn the vocabulary and rhetoric of the contemporary Republic of Letters to their advantage. Contemporary women's vanity and profligacy were frequently cited in women's writing on female education as proof of the risks an unschooled female populace posed to the realization of a truly modern and enlightened state and society.

Prior to the French Revolution, eighteenth-century Italy produced no unambiguously militant prowoman arguments to rival Marinella's, Tarabotti's, and Fonte's earlier tracts. But the relative restraint of women's defenses of their sex during the Italian Settecento resulted largely from the paradoxical, if limited, increase in intellectual authority that women had acquired in the Enlightenment Republic of Letters. Speaking from recognized centers of intellectual exchange—the academy, the university, and publications both scholarly and popular—women who defended their sex necessarily followed the conventions of contemporary intellectual exchange and adopted the demeanor and modes of argument expected by their academic fellows: a dispassionate scholarly tone, "reasonable" arguments based on *esperienza*, and the advocacy of moderate reforms of women's education rather than of their civil rights and status.

As will be seen in the texts that follow, these defenses defy easy categorization. Remarkable proposals like Savini de' Rossi's that women themselves educate other members of their sex regardless of class, or calls like Medaglia

---

59. On the subject of "double-voiced discourse," see Elaine Showalter, "Feminist Criticism in the Wilderness," in *The New Feminist Criticism: Essays on Women, Literature and Theory*, ed. Elaine Showalter (New York: Pantheon Books, 1985), 243–70.

Faini's that women be thoroughly instructed in mathematics and physics, nonetheless endorse the orthodox view of women as naturally subordinate and domestic and are directed explicitly at an authoritative male public. Women's newly acquired membership in elite institutions of intellectual exchange unmistakably demanded an attitude of deference to the customs and discursive practices of those institutions as well as to the male authorities who invited women to join them in the first place. But the temperate mode and demands of eighteenth-century Italian women's defenses of their sex should not obscure the political and discursive shifts their arguments manifest. For in these shifts may be discerned the practical and theoretical foundations of the organized feminist activism of the nineteenth century.

FORTUNES AND INFLUENCE OF ITALIAN ENLIGHTENMENT DISCOURSE ABOUT WOMEN

Since Enlightenment writers themselves lauded the progress exemplified by women's new presence as the subjects and objects of intellectual exchange, scholarship focused on this critical aspect of the age has been meager. Not only did historians consistently ignore the subject until recently, but the many texts about women from the Italian Settecento have remained largely in manuscript form and have undergone a virtual erasure as a result. Indeed, none of the texts translated in this volume has ever been reissued since its original publication in the eighteenth century.

Giulio Natali's expansive scholarly study *Il Settecento*, published in 1929, was the first to treat eighteenth-century Italian women's roles and influence and the question of their education as an important subject for historical analysis. In a lengthy chapter titled "The Education of Women," Natali comprehensively cataloged illustrious eighteenth-century women poets, writers, scientists, academicians, journalists, artists, musicians, and *salonnières* and compiled a vast bibliography of primary works by and about them. At the heart of this chapter, he surveyed the leading arguments that learned men and women of the age had made about women's education.[60] The "storehouse of people, facts, and book titles"[61] Natali included in his discussion of the eighteenth-century Italian "woman question" was unprecedented and began an essential revision of the period, albeit one that lacked analytical depth. After Natali, the major historians of the Italian eighteenth century remained silent on the subject until 1987–88, when Luciano Guerci published his path-

---

60. Giulio Natali, *Il Settecento* (Milan: F. Vallardi, 1929).
61. Carpanetto and Ricuperati, *Italy in the Age of Reason, 1685–1789*, 322.

breaking studies *The Discourse about Women in Eighteenth-Century Italy* and *The Obedient Wife: Woman and Marriage in Eighteenth-Century Italian Discourse.*[62]

In these books, Guerci sought to answer critical questions about the rise and dominant features of what he accurately deemed "the gigantic and proliferating eighteenth-century discourse about women."[63] He analyzed the origins, themes, and contemporary reception of an extensive range of texts, academic and popular, religious and libertine, literary and philosophical. Guerci included discussion of the "specific contribution of Italian Enlightenment thinkers to the discourse about women,"[64] but he was more interested in the arguments about women made by the influential but often neglected "other Settecento" in its non-Enlightenment and reactionary anti-Enlightenment discourse. Guerci's critical survey of the discourse about women, and particularly of the debate about women's education, elucidated the themes and rhetoric dominant in the writings of male authors; however, he excluded analysis of women's own writings about women.

More recent scholarship has begun to fill this void and to enhance our understanding of women's explicit roles in the Italian Enlightenment Republic of Letters. Indeed, since Guerci's books, and undoubtedly in part in response to them, a number of biographical and cultural studies, published and forthcoming, have illuminated the lives and the potent cultural influence of learned women of the Italian Settecento. Paula Findlen[65] and Marta Cavazza[66] have effected a reconception of the eighteenth-century cultural landscape through their studies of the marked presence and influence of scientific women during the age. Other significant contributions to the understanding of women's roles and representation within the Italian scientific culture of the eighteenth century include studies by Beate Ceranski, Gabriella Berti Logan, Massimo Mazzotti, Paola Govoni, Gianna Pomata, Claudia Pancino, and Londa Schiebinger. My investigation of the life and work of the Bolognese anatomist and anatomical wax modeler Anna Morandi Manzolini (1714–1774) has also sought to increase knowledge of women's impact and struggles working on the periphery of the scientific

---

62. Guerci, *Discussione sulla donna* and *La sposa obbediente: Donna e matrimonio nella discussione dell'Italia del Settecento* (Turin: Tirrenia Stampatori, 1988).

63. Guerci, *Discussione sulla donna*, 17.

64. Ibid.

65. By Findlen, see especially "Becoming a Scientist"; "A Forgotten Newtonian"; "Science as a Career"; "The Scientist's Body: The Nature of a Woman Philosopher in Enlightenment Italy," in *The Faces of Nature in Enlightenment Europe*, ed. Gianna Pomata and Lorraine Daston (Berlin: Berliner Wissenschafs-Verlag, 2003), 211–36; and "Translating the New Science," 184–91.

66. By Cavazza, see especially those works cited in n. 22 above.

establishment.[67] Numerous recent essays, books, and anthologies have also served to extend understanding of the presence and sway of women within eighteenth-century Italian literary culture, including the work of Luisa Ricaldone, Adriana Chemello, Gabriella Zarri, Letizia Panizza, Sharon Wood, Pamela Stewart, Franco Fido, and Maria Ines Bonatti.[68] Catherine Sama and Rita Unfer Lukoschik have made visible the hitherto neglected life and literary work of the powerful editor, journalist, translator, and playwright Elisabetta Caminer Turra.[69] Elisabetta Graziosi has our enhanced understanding of women's roles in eighteenth-century Italian academic culture through her intricate studies of the Arcadia.[70] In her account and interpretation of the life of improvisational poet Corilla Olimpica, Paola Giuli has shed light on

67. Among works by these authors, see Ceranski, *"Und sie fürchtet sich vor niemandem"*; Gabriella Berti Logan, "The Desire to Contribute: An Eighteenth-Century Italian Woman of Science," *American Historical Review* 99 (June 1994): 785–812; Berti Logan, "Women and the Practice and Teaching of Medicine in Bologna in the Eighteenth and Early Nineteenth Centuries," *Bulletin of the History of Medicine* 77.3 (Fall 2003): 506–35; Massimo Mazzotti, "Maria Gaetana Agnesi: The Unusual Life and Mathematical Work of an Eighteenth-Century Woman," *Isis* 92 (2001): 657–83; Paola Govoni, *Un pubblico per la scienza. La divulgazione scientifica nell'Italia in formazione* (Roma: Carrocci, 2002), esp. pp. 56–72; Gianna Pomata, "Donne e Rivoluzione Scientifica: verso un nuovo bilancio," in *Corpi e storia: Donne e uomini dal mondo antico all'età contemporanea,* ed. Nadia Filippini et al. (Rome: Viella, 2002), 165–192; Pomata, "Risposta a Pigmalione: Le origini della storia delle donne alla London School of Economics," *Quaderni Storici* 110.2 (2002): 505–44; Pomata, "Gender and the Family," in *Short Oxford History of Italy: Early Modern Italy, 1550–1796,* ed. John Marino (Oxford: Oxford University Press, 2002), 69–86; Claudia Pancino, "L'ostetricia del Settecento e la scuola Bolognese di Giovanni Antonio Galli," *Ars obstetricia bononiensis* (Bologna: CLUEB, 1988), 24–31; Pancino, "Donne e scienza," in *La memoria di lei: Storia delle donne, storia di genere,* ed. Gabriella Zarri (Turin: Società Editrice Internazionale, 1996), 89–94; Londa Schiebinger, *The Mind Has No Sex?*; Rebecca Messbarger, "Waxing Poetic"; Messbarger, "Remembering a Body of Work."

68. Luisa Ricaldone, "Il dibattito sulla donna nella letteratura del Triennio (1796–1799)," *Italienische Studien* Heft 7 (1984): 23–46; Ricaldone, "Diodata Saluzzo e la sua attività nell'Accademia delle Scienze," *Atti del Convegno. I primi due secoli dell'Accademia delle Scienze di Torino,* Novembre 1983, 10–12; Ricaldone, "Letterate e immagini di letterate nel Settecento italiano: proposte per una ricerca," *Literatur ohne Grenzen, Festschrift für Erika Kanduth* (Wein: Peter Lang, 1993), 339–50; Ricaldone, "Immagini di donne di lettere nel teatro goldoniano," *Italienische Studien* (1993): 75–82; Ricaldone, *La scrittura nascosta: Donne di lettere e loro immagini tra Arcadia e Restaurazione* (Paris-Fiesole: Champion-Cadmo, 1996); Ricaldone, ed., *Le avventure del poeta,* by Luisa Bergalli (Rome: Vecchiarelli, 1997); Ricaldone, "Aurelio de' Giorgi Bertola e la gentildonna," in *Un europeo del Settecento: Aurelio De' Giorgi Bertola riminese,* ed. A. Battistini (Ravenna: Longo, 2000), 119–50; Ricaldone and Adriana Chemello, eds., *Geografie e genealogie letterarie: Erudite, biografe, croniste, narratrici, "épistolières", utopiste tra Settecento e Ottocento* (Padua: Il Poligrafo, 2000); Letizia Panizza and Sharon Wood, eds., *History of Women's Writing in Italy* (Cambridge: Cambridge University Press, 2000); Gabriella Zarri, ed., *La memoria di lei: Storia delle donne e storia di genere* (Turin: Società Editrice Internazionale, 1996); Pamela Stewart, "Rosaura, the Blue-Stocking Heroine of Goldoni's *Donna di Garbo,"* in *Women's Voices in Italian Literature,* special issue, *Annali d'Italianistica* 7 (1989): 242–52; Franco Fido, "Italian Contributions to the Eighteenth-Century Debate on Women," *Annali*

the precarious role and public reception of literary women.[71] Susan Dalton's work shows how elite women appropriated and adapted behavioral norms and commonly held ideas about femininity to participate in political and intellectual life in the eighteenth-century Republic of Venice.[72] My own study *The Century of Women: Representations of Women in Eighteenth-Century Italian Public Discourse* focuses on the characteristics of the dominant discourse about women among male Italian Enlightenment thinkers and the counter-discourse that women authors produced to assert their distinct authority over constructions of femininity and the public sphere.[73]

The current swell of scholarly publication on women's distinctive influence over eighteenth-century Italian literary and cultural production promises to promote further inquiry and debate. Ideally, this volume will serve as yet another catalyst for new research and analysis.

Rebecca Messbarger

d'Italianistica 7 (1989): 216–25; Maria Ines Bonatti, "L'educazione femminile nel pensiero degli Illuministi e nei romanzi di Chiari," *Annali d'Italianistica* 7 (1989): 226–41.

69. For works on Caminer Turra, see note 29 above.

70. See especially, Graziosi, "Arcadia Femminile."

71. See the following works by Giuli, "Women Poets and Improvisers: Cultural Assumptions and Literary Values in Arcadia," *Studies in Eighteenth-Century Culture* 32 (2003): 69–92; "Corilla Olimpica *improvisatrice*: Toward a Reappraisal of Her Life and Work," in *Corilla Olimpica e la poesia del Settecento. Atti del Convegno Internazionale*, ed. Moreno Fabbri (Pistoia: Maschietto e Musolino, 2002), 155–72; "Traces of a Sisterhood"; "Enlightenment" and "*Querelle des femmes*," in *Feminist Encyclopedia of Italian Literature*, 77–82 and 273–75.

72. See Susan Dalton, *Engendering the Republic of Letters: Reconnecting Public and Private Spheres in Eighteenth-Century Europe* (Montreal: McGill-Queen's University Press, 2004).

73. Messbarger, *The Century of Women*. In contrast to previous scholarship that has broadly surveyed eighteenth-century Italian writing on the topic, my analysis centers instead on five paradigmatic and ideologically divergent eighteenth-century Italian texts about women written by male and female authors, including three of the texts translated here. I analyze each of the contributions to the Ricovrati debate, Aretafila Savini de' Rossi's response, and Diamante Medaglia Faini's oration.

VOLUME EDITORS'
BIBLIOGRAPHY

PRIMARY SOURCES

Agnesi, Maria Gaetana. *Istituzioni analitiche ad uso della gioventù italiana.* 2 vols. Milan: Richini, 1748.

———. *Oratio, quâ ostenditur: artium liberalium studia à femineo sexu neutiquam abhorrere. Habita a Maria de Agnesis rethoricae operam dante anno aetatis suae nono nondum exacto, die 18 Augusto 1727.* Milan: J. R. Malatestam, 1727.

———. *Propositiones philosophicae.* Milan, 1738.

Agrippa, Henricus Cornelius. *Declamation on the Nobility and Preeminence of the Female Sex.* Edited and translated by Albert Rabil Jr. Chicago: University of Chicago Press, 1996.

Aletino, Benedetto [Giovanni Battista Benedetti]. *Lettere apologetiche in difesa della teologia scolastica e della filosofia peripatetica.* Naples, 1694.

Alfani, Tommaso Maria. *Istoria degli anni santi, dal di loro solenne cominciamento per insino a quello del regnante Sommo Pontefice Benedetto XIII.* Naples, 1725.

Algarotti, Francesco. *Il Newtonianismo per le dame ovvero Dialoghi sopra la luce, i colori, e l'attrazione.* Naples: Giambatista Pasquali, 1739.

Alighieri, Dante. *Purgatorio.* Translated by Allen Mandelbaum. New York: Bantam Books, 1982.

Alla nobile fanciulla D. Maria Gaetana Agnesi, Milanese, che nell'età di anni cinque parla mirabilmente il francese. Milan, 1723.

Anianus. *Codicis Theodosiani lib. xvi. Quam emendatissimis adiectis quas certis locis fecerat Aniani interpretationibus* (Lyon, 1566).

Ariosto, Ludovico. *Orlando Furioso.* Translated by Barbara Reynolds. New York: Penguin Books, 1975.

———. *Orlando Furioso.* Translated by Guido Waldman. Oxford: Oxford University Press, 1983.

Aristotle. *Minor Works.* Translated by W. S. Hett. London: William Heinemann, 1936.

———. *Oeconomica.* Translated by E. S. Forster. Oxford: Clarendon Press, 1920.

Augustine. "The Advantage of Believing." Translated by Luanne Meagner. In *Writings of Saint Augustine,* vol. 4 of *The Fathers of the Church,* edited by Ludwig Schopp, 2:381–442. New York: Cima Publishing, 1947.

Bacon, Francis. *The Essays or Counsels, Civill and Morall.* 2nd ed. Edited by Michael Kiernan. Oxford: Clarendon, 2000.

Baillet, Adrien. *Ristretto della vita di Renato Descartes: altramente detto Cartesio, ò Sig. delle Carte: in cui si descrive la storia della sua filosofia, e dell'altre sue opere.* Basilea, 1713.

Bandiera, Giovanni. *Trattato degli studj delle Donne in due parti diviso. Opera d'un Accademico Intronato.* 2 vols. Venice: Francesco Pitteri, 1740.

Barbapiccola, Giuseppa Eleonora. "La traduttrice a' lettori." In *I Principi della filosofia di Renato Des-cartes tradotti dal francese col confronto del latino in cui l'autore gli scrisse.* Turin: Mariesse, 1722.

Bartoli, Danielo. *Dell'huomo di lettere difeso et emendato.* Venice, 1655.

Baruffaldi, Girolamo. "Il Grillo." Venice: Houdon Bettanino, 1738.

————. "Il Poeta, commedia d'Enante Vignajuolo [pseud.]." Bologna: Stamperia di L. Dalla Volpe, 1734.

————. "La Tabaccheide." Ferrara: Per gli eredi di B. Pomatelli, 1714.

Basil, Bishop of Caesarea. "Address to Young Men on Reading Greek Literature." In *Saint Basil, the Letters,* translated by Roy J. Defarrari, 4:363–435. London: W. Heinemann, 1926.

Beccaria, Cesare. *Dei delitti e delle pene.* Livorno, 1764.

Becelli, Guido Cesare. *Trattato della divisione degli ingegni.* Verona: 1738.

Bergalli Gozzi, Luisa. *Componimenti poetici delle più illustri rimatrici d'ogni secolo.* 2 vols. Venice: Antonio Mora, 1726.

Boccaccio, Giovanni. *The Decameron.* Translated by G. H. McWilliam. New York: Penguin Books, 1972.

————. *Famous Women.* Edited and translated by Virginia Brown. Cambridge, MA: Harvard University Press, 2001.

Brognoli, Antonio. *Elogi di Bresciani per dottrina eccellenti del secolo XVIII.* Bologna: Forni Editore, 1972.

Caminer Turra, Elisabetta. *Selected Writings of an Eighteenth-Century Venetian Woman of Letters.* Edited and translated by Catherine Sama. Chicago: University of Chicago Press, 2003.

Cano, Melchior. *Locorum theologicum libri 12.* Cologne, 1585.

Cereta, Laura. *Collected Letters of a Renaissance Feminist.* Translated and edited by Diana Robin. Chicago: University of Chicago Press, 1977.

Chastagnol, André, ed. *Histoire auguste.* Paris: Éditions Robert Laffont, 1994.

Chiari, Pietro. *Lettere d'un solitario a sua figlia per formarle il cuore, e lo spirito nella scuola del mondo.* Venice: Battifoco, 1777.

Cicero, Marcus Tullius. *De Oratore.* Translated by Edward William Sutton. Cambridge, MA: Harvard University Press, 1942.

Clement of Alexandria. *Il pedagogo.* Translated by Boatti Abele. Turin: Società Editrice Internazionale, 1953.

————. *Selections from the Protreptikos.* Translated by Thomas Merton. New York: New Directions, 1962.

————. *Stromateis: Books One to Three.* Translated by John Ferguson. Washington, DC: Catholic University of America Press, 1991.

Corsignani, Pietro Antonio. *Reggia Marsicana, ovvero Memorie topografico-storiche di varie colonie e città antiche e moderne della provincia de i Mari e di Valeria.* Edited by Tommaso Maria Alfani. N.p., 1738.

Crescimbeni, Giovanni, et al. *Le Vite degli Arcadi illustri,* vol. 6. Rome: Antonio de' Rossi, 1751.

Dacier, André, and Anne Lefèvre Dacier. *Reflexions morales de l'empereur Marc Antonin avec des remarques de Mr. & de Mad. Dacier.* 2 vols. Paris, 1690–91.

Dacier, Anne Lefèvre. *Des causes de la corruption du goût.* Paris, 1714.

————. *L'Iliade d'Homère traduite en français avec des remarques de Madame Dacier.* 3 vols. Paris, 1711.

————. *L'Iliade d'Homere, traduite en françois, avec des remarques par Madame Dacier.* 4th ed. 3 vols. Amsterdam, 1731.

Delfico, Melchiorre. *Saggio filosofico sul matrimonio.* Teremo, 1774.

Descartes, René. *Correspondance avec Elisabeth et autres lettres.* Edited by Jean-Marie Beyssade and Michelle Beyssade. Paris: Flammarion, 1989.

————. *The Philosophical Writings of Descartes.* Translated by John Cottingham, Robert Stoothoff, and Dugal Murdoch. 3 vols. Cambridge: Cambridge University Press, 1985–91.

Diogenes Laertius. *Lives of Eminent Philosophers.* Translated by R. D. Hicks. 1925. Reprint, Cambridge, MA: Harvard University Press, 1979–80.

Discorsi accademici di vari autori viventi intorno agli studi delle donne. Padua: Giovanni Manfrè, 1729.

Di Porcia, G. A. *Notizie della vita e degli studi del Kavalier Antonio Vallisneri.* Edited by Dario Generali. Bologna: Patron, 1986.

Doria, Paolo Mattia. *Ragionamenti di Paolo Mattia D'Oria indirizzati alla Signora D'Aurelia D'Este Duchessa di Limatola: ne' quali si dimostra la donna, in quasi che tutte le virtù più grandi, non essere all'uomo inferiore.* Frankfurt, 1716.

————. *Dissertazione di Paolo Mattia Doria intorno alla nuova geometria di Cartesio.* Venice, 1721.

————. *Discorsi critici filosofici intorno alla filosofia degli antichi e dei moderni ed in particolare intorno alla filosofia di Renato Des Cartes.* Venice [Naples], 1724.

Eunapius. "Lives of the Philosophers." In *Philostratus and Eunapius: The Lives of the Sophists,* edited and translated by Wilmer Cave Wright. Cambridge, MA: Harvard University Press, 1952.

Filangieri, Gaetano. *La Scienza della Legislazione.* Edited by Vittorio Frosini. Rome: Istituo Poligrafico e Zecca della Stato, 1984.

Fleury, Claude. *Traité du choix et de la methode des etudes.* Paris, 1687.

Fontanini, Giusto. *De antiquitatibus Hortae coloniae Etruscorum.* Rome, 1708.

Fonte, Moderata. *Tredici canti del Floridoro di Mad. Moderata Fonte alli Serenissimi Gran Duca et gran Duchessa di Thoscana.* Venice: Stamperia de' Rampazetti, 1581.

————. *The Worth of Women: Wherein Is Clearly Revealed Their Nobility and Their Superiority to Men.* Edited and translated by Virginia Cox. Chicago: University of Chicago Press, 1997.

Forteguerri, Nicolo. *Ricciardetto di Niccolo Carteromaco* [pseud.]. 2 vols. Paris [Venice]: Francesco Pitteri, 1738.

Franci, Carlo Sebastiano. "La difesa delle donne." In *Il Caffè, 1764–1766,* edited by Gianni Francioni and Sergio Romagnoli, 245–56. Turin: Bollati Boringhieri, 1993.

Giornale delle adunanze. Accademia Patavina, Padua, MS B.

Giornale de' letterati d'Italia 32 (1719): 506–13.

Gozzi, Gasparo. *Gazzetta veneta.* Edited by Antonio Zardo. Florence: G. C. Sansoni, 1957.

Green, Monica, ed. and trans. *The Trotula: An English Translation of the Medieval Compendium of Women's Medicine*. Philadelphia: University of Pennsylvania Press, 2001.

Gregory of Nazianzus. *Opera . . . quo Poemata omne Graece et Latine*. Cologne, 1690.

Grimaldi, Costantino. *Risposta alla terza lettera apologetica contra il Cartesio creduto da piu d'Aristotele di Benedetto Aletino [pseud.] Opera, in cui dimostrasi quanto falda, e pia sia la filosofia di Renato delle Carte*. Cologne [Naples], 1703.

Guarini, Giovan Battista. *Il Pastor Fido*. London: A. Dulau, 1800.

Herodotus. *Histories*. Translated by J. Enoch Powell. Oxford: Clarendon Press, 1949.

Homer. *Iliad*. Translated by Stanley Lombardo. Indianapolis: Hackett, 1997.

————. *Odyssey*. Translated by Martin Hammond. London: Duckworth, 2000.

Horace. *The Art of Poetry*. Translated by James Hynd. Albany: State University of New York Press, 1974.

————. *Satires, Epistles and Ars Poetica*. Translated by H. Rushton Fairclough. 1926. Reprint, Cambridge, MA: Harvard University Press, 1999.

Jerome. *Selected Letters*. Edited and translated by F. A. Wright. London: William Heinemann, 1933.

Juvenal. *The Sixteen Satires*. Translated by Peter Green. New York: Penguin Books, 1967.

King, Margaret L., and Albert Rabil Jr., eds. and trans. *Her Immaculate Hand: Selected Works by and about the Women Humanists of Quattrocento Italy*. Rev. ed. Binghamton, NY: Medieval and Renaissance Texts and Studies, 1992.

Lattanzi, Carolina. *Schiavitù delle donne* [1792]. Edited by Gilberto Zacchè. Mantua: Edizioni Lombarde, 1976.

Launoy, Jean de. *Theologia de varia Aristotelis in Academia Parisiensi fortuna, extraneis hinc inde adornata praesidiis liber*. Paris, 1662.

Mabillon, Jean. *Traité des études monastiques*. Paris, 1691–92.

Marinella, Lucrezia. *The Nobility and Excellence of Women and the Defects and Vices of Men*. Edited and translated by Anne Dunhill. Chicago: University of Chicago Press, 1999.

Martello, Pier Jacopo. *Teatro*. Edited by Hannibal S. Noce. Rome: Laterza, 1980.

Mazza, Antonio. *Historiarum Epitome de rebus salernitanis*. Naples, 1681.

Medaglia Faini, Diamante. *Versi e prose di Diamante Medaglia Faini con alti componimenti di diversi autori e colla vita dell'autrice*. Salò: Bartolomeo Righetti, 1774.

Ménage, Giles. *The History of Women Philosophers*. Translated and edited by Beatrice H. Zedler. Lanham, MD: University Press of America, 1984.

Muratori, Ludovico Antonio. *Della perfetta poesia italiana spiegata e dimostrata con varie osservazioni*. Venice: Sebastiano Coleti, 1724.

————. *Riflessioni sopra il buon gusto nelle scienze e nelle arti*. Venice, 1708.

Nogarola, Isotta. *Letterbook, Dialogue on Adam & Eve, Orations*. Edited and translated by Margaret L. King and Diana Robin. Chicago: University of Chicago Press, 2003.

Ovid. *Tristia. Ex Ponto*. Translated by Arthur Leslie Wheeler and revised by G. P. Goold. 2nd ed., 1988. Reprinted with corrections, Cambridge, MA: Harvard University Press, 1996.

Pardies, Ignace Gaston. *Dell'anima delle bestie, e sue funzioni. Nel quale si disputa la celebre questione de' moderni se gli animali bruti sian mere machine automate senza cognizione, ne senso come gli orologi*. Translated by Andrea Poletti. Venice, 1696.

Passi, Giuseppe. *I donneschi difetti nuovamente formati e posti in luci.* Venice: Iacobo Antonio Somasco, 1599.

Paterculus, Velleius. *Compendium of Roman History.* Translated by Frederick W. Shipley. New York: G. P. Putnam's Sons, 1924.

Petrarca, Francesco. *The Canzoniere or Rerum vulgarium fragmenta.* Edited and translated by Mark Musa. Bloomington: University of Indiana Press, 1994–2000.

————. *Opere.* Edited by Emilio Bigi. Milan: Mursia, 1963–79.

Pizzati, Giuseppe. *La scienza de' suoni e dell'armonia, diretta specialmente a render ragione de' fenomeni, ed a conoscer la natura e le leggi della medesima, ed agiovare alla pratica del contrappunto.* Venice: Giovanni Gatti, 1782.

Plato. *Alcibiades.* Edited by Nicholas Denyer. Cambridge: Cambridge University Press, 2001.

Poullain de la Barre, François. *Three Cartesian Feminist Treatises.* Edited and translated by Marcelle Maistre Welch and Vivien Bosley. Chicago: University of Chicago Press, 2002.

Propertius, Sextus. *The Poems.* Translated by Guy Lee. Oxford: Clarendon Press, 1994.

Rahner, H., S.J. *St. Ignatius Loyola: Letters to Women.* New York: Herder & Herder, 1960.

Recanati, Giovanni Batista. *Poesie italiane di rimatrici viventi raccolte da Teleste Ciparissia Pastore Arcade.* Venice: Sebastiano Coleti, 1716.

Registri de' Ragionamenti recitati nell'Accademia detta de' Discordi di Salò, ed ora de' Pescatori Benacensi. Biblioteca dell'Atneo, Salò, MS 101 (c. 23), n. 4.

Revese, Antonio. *L'impossibile ovvero la riforma delle donne nella loro educazione.* Vicenza: Stamperia Turra, 1787.

Rohault, Jacques. *Entretiens sur la philosophie.* Paris, 1672.

Rollin, Charles. *De la manière d'enseigner et d'étudier les belles-lettres par raport a l'esprit & au coeur, ou Traité des études.* Paris: Chez la veuve Etienne & Fils, 1748.

Rondel, Jacques du. *De vita et moribus Epicuri autori Iacobo Rondello.* Amsterdam, 1693.

Salvini, Anton Maria. *Discorsi accademici di Anton Maria Salvini, gentiluomo fiorentino, lettore di Lettere greche nello Studio di Firenze e accademico della Crusca, sopra alcuni dubbj proposti nell'Accademia degli Apatisti.* 3 vols. Venice: Pasinelli, 1735.

Savini de' Rossi, Aretafila. "Apologia in favore degli Studi delle Donne, contra il precedente Discorso del signor Gio. Antonio Volpi." In *Discorsi Accademici di vari autori viventi intorno agli Studi Delle Donne,* edited by Giovanni Antonio Volpi, 50–65. Padua: Giovanni Manfrè, 1729.

Schurman, Anna Maria van. *Whether a Christian Woman Should Be Educated and Other Writings from Her Intellectual Circle.* Edited and translated by Joyce L. Irwin. Chicago: University of Chicago Press, 1998.

Serry, Jacques Hyacinthe. *Praelectiones theologicae: theologicae, dogmaticae, polemicae, scholasticae habitae in celeberrima Patavina Academia.* Venice, 1742.

Soresi, Pier Domenico. *Saggio sopra la necessità e la facilità di ammaestrare le fanciulle.* Milan: Federico Agnelli, 1774.

Spinelli, Francesco. *Riflessioni . . . su le principali materia della prima filosofia fatte ad occasione di esaminare la prima parte d'un libro intitolato Discorsi critici filosofici intorno alla filosofia degli antichi e de' moderni & di Paolo Mattia Doria.* Naples, 1733.

Spinelli, Trojano. *Riflessioni politiche sopra alcuni punti della scienza della moneta.* Naples, 1750.

Tarabotti, Arcangela. *Che le donne sian della spetie degli Huomini.* Norimbergh: Cherchenbergher, 1651.

Valletta, Giuseppe. *Opere filosofiche.* Edited by Michele Rak. Florence: Olschki, 1974.

Vallisneri, Antonio. "Introduzione." In *Discorsi Accademici di vari autori viventi intorno agli Studi Delle Donne,* edited by Giovanni Antonio Volpi, 1–5. Padua: Giovanni Manfrè, 1729.

———. *Epistolario.* Edited by Dario Generali. Milan: Franco Angeli, 1991.

Velleius Paterculus. *Compendium of Roman History.* Translated by Frederick W. Shipley. New York: G. P. Putnam's Sons, 1924.

Verri, Pietro. *Ricordi a mia figlia.* In *Opere Varie,* edited by Nino Valeri, 295–351. Florence: Felice Le Monnier, 1947.

Vico, Giambattista. *De antiquissima Italorum sapientia.* Naples, 1710.

———. *The Autobiography of Giambattista Vico.* Translated by Max Harold Fisch and Thomas Goddard Bergin. Ithaca, NY: Cornell University Press, 1944.

———. *On the Most Ancient Wisdom of the Italians.* Translated by Lucia M. Palmer. Ithaca, NY: Cornell University Press, 1988.

———. *Principj di scienza nuova di Giambattista Vico d'intorno alla comune natura delle nazioni.* Naples: Stamperia Muziana, 1744.

———. *Scritti vari e pagine sparse.* Edited by Fausto Nicolini. Bari: Laterza, 1940.

Virgil. *The Aeneid of Virgil, Books VII–XII.* Edited by T. E. Page. London: Macmillan, 1964.

———. *The Aeneid.* Translated by Edward McCrorie. Ann Arbor: University of Michigan Press, 1995.

Volpi, Giovanni Antonio, ed. *Discorsi accademici di vari autori viventi intorno agli studi delle donne.* Padua: Giovanni Manfrè, 1729.

———. "Dedicatoria." In *Discorsi Accademici di vari autori viventi intorno agli Studi Delle Donne,* edited by Giovanni Antonio Volpi, sig. a3r–sig. a7v. Padua: Giovanni Manfrè, 1729.

———. "Discorso Accademico, Che non debbono ammettersi le Donne allo Studio delle Scienze, e delle Belle Arti; da lui recitato in Padova nell'Accademia de' Ricovrati il dì 16 giugno 1723 sopra il Problema proposto dall'Ill. Sign. Antonio Vallisneri, Pubblico Primario Professore di Medicina Teorica nello Studio di Padova, e Principe di essa Accademia." In *Discorsi Accademici di vari autori viventi intorno agli Studi Delle Donne,* edited by Giovanni Antonio Volpi, 27–45. Padua: Giovanni Manfrè, 1729.

———. "Prefazione." In *Discorsi Accademici di vari autori viventi intorno agli Studi Delle Donne,* edited by Giovanni Antonio Volpi, sig. a8r–sig. a10v. Padua: Giovanni Manfrè, 1729.

SECONDARY SOURCES

Ajello, Raffaele. "Cartesianismo e la cultura oltremontana al tempo dell' 'Istoria civile.'" In *Pietro Giannone e il suo tempo,* edited by Raffael Ajello, 1:1–181. Naples: Jovene, 1980.

Åkerman, Susanna. *Queen Christina of Sweden and Her Circle: The Transformation of a Seventeenth-Century Philosophical Libertine.* Leiden: Brill, 1991.

Angenot, Marc. *Les champions des femmes*. Montreal: Les Presses de l'Université de Québec, 1977.

Anzoletti, Luisa. *Maria Gaetana Agnesi*. Milan: L. F. Cogliati, 1900.

Badaloni, Nicola. *Antonio Conti: Un abate libero pensatore tra Newton e Voltaire*. Milan: Feltrinelli, 1968.

Bandini Buti, Maria. *Poetesse e scrittrici*. *Enciclopedia biografica e bibliografica italiana*, vol. 6. Rome: E.B.B.I., 1942.

Bellù, Adele, Giulio Giacometti, Anna Serralunga Bardazza, and Piero Sessa. *Maria Gaetana Agnesi ricercatrice di Gesù Cristo*. 2 vols. Milan: NED, 1999.

Benson, Pamela Joseph. *The Invention of the Renaissance Woman: The Challenge of Female Independence in the Literature and Thought of Italy and England*. University Park: Pennsylvania State University Press, 1992.

Berti Logan, Gabriella. "The Desire to Contribute: An Eighteenth-Century Italian Woman of Science." *American Historical Review* 99 (1994): 785–812.

———. "Women and the Practice and Teaching of Medicine in Bologna in the Eighteenth and Early Nineteenth Centuries." *Bulletin of the History of Medicine* 77.3 (Fall 2003): 506–35.

Bonatti, Maria Ines. "L'educazione femminile nel pensiero degli Illuministi e nei romanzi di Chiari." *Annali d'Italianistica* 7 (1989): 226–41.

Brigidi, Sebastiano. *Vita di Lodovico-Antonio Muratori: La sua mente e il suo cuore*. Florence: Galileiana, 1871.

Busolini, D. "Giusto Fontanini." In *Dizionario biografico degli italiani*, 48:747–52. Rome: Enciclopedia Italiana, 1964– .

Bustico, Guido. "Diamante Medaglia Faini." In *Pagine Benacensi*. Salò: Pietro Veludari, 1909.

———. "Diamante Medaglia Faini." *Rassegna Nazionale* (Rome), 1941, 3–5.

Callegari, Marco. "La tipografia Volpi-Cominiana (1717–1756): Gestione dell'azienda ed attività commerciale." *Bollettino del Museo Civico di Padova* 80 (1991): 279–301.

———. " 'Tipografi umanisti' a Padova nel '700: I fratelli Volpi e la Stamperia Cominiana." *Archivio Veneto* 145 (1995): 31–63.

Candler Hayes, Julie. "Of Meaning and Modernity: Anne Dacier and the Homer Debate." *EMF: Studies in Early Modern France* 8, edited by David Lee Rubin (2002): 173–95.

Canepa, Nancy. "The Writing Behind the Wall: Arcangela Tarabotti's *Inferno monacale* and Cloistral Autobiography in the Seventeenth Century." *Forum Italicum* 30 (Spring 1996): 1–23.

Canonici Fachini, Ginevra. *Prospetto biografico delle donne italiane rinomate in letteratura dal secolo decimoquarto fino a' giorni nostri*. Venice: Tipografia di Alvisopoli, 1824.

Carpanetto, Dino, and Giuseppe Ricuperati, eds. *Italy in the Age of Reason, 1685–1789*. New York: Longman, 1987.

Cavazza, Marta. " 'Dottrici' e lettrici dell'Università di Bologna nel Settecento." *Annali di storia delle università italiane* 1 (1997): 109–26.

———. "Laura Bassi e il suo gabinetto di fisica sperimentale: Realtà e mito." *Nuncius: Annali di storia della scienza* 10, no. 2 (1995): 715–53.

———. "Laura Bassi 'Maestra' di Spallanzani." In *Il cerchio della vita. Materiali del Centro Studi Lazzaro Spallanzani di Scandiano sulla storia della scienza del Settecento*, edited by Walter Bernardi and Paolo Manzini, 185–202. Florence: Olschki, 1999.

————. "Riflessi letterari dell'opera di Newton: Algarotti, Manfredi e Laura Bassi." In *Radici, significato, retaggio dell'opera newtoniana*, edited by G. Tarozzi and M. Van Vloten, 352–66. Bologna: Società italiana di Fisica, 1989.

Ceranski, Beate. *"Und sie fürchtet sich vor niemandem": Die Physikerin Laura Bassi (1711–1778)*. Frankfurt: Campus Verlag, 1996.

Cirillo, Antonio. *Napoli ai tempi di Giambattista Vico*. Naples: Edizioni Tempo Lungo, 2000.

Clark, Gillian. *Women in Late Antiquity: Pagan and Christian Lifestyles*. Oxford: Clarendon, 1993.

Colish, Marcia L. *Medieval Foundations of the Western Intellectual Tradition, 400–1400*. New Haven, CT: Yale University Press, 1997.

Collina, Beatrice. "Moderata Fonte e *Il merito delle donne*." *Annali d'Italianistica* 7 (1989): 142–64.

Comparato, Vittor Ivo. *Giuseppe Valletta. Un intellettuale napoletano della fine del Seicento*. Naples: Istituto Italiano per gli Studi Storici, 1970.

Conti Odorisio, Ginevra. *Donna e società nel Seicento: Lucrezia Marinelli e Arcangela Tarabotti*. Rome: Bulzoni, 1979.

Conti, Vittorio. *Paolo Mattia Doria: Dalla repubblica dei togati alla repubblica dei notabili*. Florence: Olschki, 1978.

Cox, Virginia. "Moderata Fonte and *The Worth of Women*." In *The Worth of Women: Wherein Is Clearly Revealed Their Nobility and Their Superiority To Men*, by Moderata Fonte. Edited and translated by Virginia Cox. Chicago: University of Chicago Press, 1997.

Dalton, Susan. *Engendering the Republic of Letters: Reconnecting Public and Private Spheres in Eighteenth-Century Europe*. Montreal: McGill-Queen's University Press, 2003.

Davis, Natalie Zemon. "Gender and Genre: Women as Historical Writers, 1400–1820." In *Beyond Their Sex: Learned Women of the European Past*, edited by Patricia Labalme, 153–82. New York: New York University Press, 1980.

DeJean, Joan. *Ancients and Moderns: Culture Wars and the Making of a Fin de Siècle*. Chicago: University of Chicago Press, 1997.

De Smet, Ingrid. "In the Name of the Father: Feminist Voices in the Republic of Letters." In *La Femme lettrée à la Renaissance/De geleerde vrouw in de Renaissance*. Louvain: Peeters, 1997.

De Blasi, Jolanda. *Antologia delle scrittrici italiane*. Florence: Nemi, 1931.

Dictionary of Scientific Biography. Edited by Charles Coulston Gillispie. New York: Scribners, 1970–90.

Dizionario Biografico degli italiani. Rome: Istituto della Enciclopedia Italiana, 1960– .

Dzielska, Maria. *Hypatia of Alexandria*. Translated by F. Lyra. Cambridge, MA: Harvard University Press, 1995.

Elena, Alberto. "In lode della filosofessa di Bologna: An Introduction to Laura Bassi." *Isis* 82 (1991): 510–18.

Farnham, Fern. *Madame Dacier: Scholar and Humanist*. Monterey: Angel Press, 1980.

Ferrone, Vincenzo. *The Intellectual Roots of the Italian Enlightenment: Newtonian Science, Religion, and Politics in the Early Eighteenth Century*. Translated by Sue Brotherton. Atlantic Highlands, NJ: Humanities Press, 1995.

Fido, Franco. "Italian Contributions to the Eighteenth-Century Debate on Women." *Annali d'Italianistica* 7 (1989): 216–25.

Findlen, Paula. "Becoming a Scientist: Gender and Knowledge in Eighteenth-Century Italy." *Science in Context* 16 (2003): 59–87.

———. "A Forgotten Newtonian: Women and Science in the Italian Provinces." In *The Sciences in Enlightened Europe*, edited by William Clark and Jan Golinski, 313–49. Chicago: University of Chicago Press, 1999.

———. "Historical Thought in the Renaissance." In *Companion to Historical Thought*, edited by Lloyd Kramer and Sarah Maza, 99–120. Oxford: Blackwell, 2002.

———. "Ideas in the Mind: Gender and Knowledge in the Seventeenth Century." *Hypatia* 17 (2002): 183–96.

———. "Imaginary Graduates: Women and the Universities in Medieval and Early Modern Italy," forthcoming.

———. "Science as a Career in Enlightenment Italy: The Strategies of Laura Bassi." *Isis* 84 (1993): 441–69.

———. "The Scientist's Body: The Nature of a Woman Philosopher in Enlightenment Italy." In *The Faces of Nature in Enlightenment Europe*, edited by Gianna Pomata and Lorraine Daston, 211–36. Berlin: Berliner Wissenschafs-Verlag, 2003.

———. "Translating the New Science: Women and the Circulation of Knowledge in Enlightenment Italy." *Configurations* 3 (1995): 184–91.

Fisch, Max H. "The Academy of the Investigators." In *Science, Medicine and History*, edited by E. Ashworth Underwood, 1: 521–63. Oxford: Oxford University Press, 1953.

Fraschetti, Augusto, ed. *Roman Women*. Translated by Linda Lappin. Chicago: University of Chicago Press, 2001.

Galasso, Giuseppe. *La filosofia in soccorso de' governi. La cultura napoletana del Settecento*. Naples: Guida, 1989.

Garin, Eugenio. "Cartesio e l'Italia." *Giornale critico della filosofia italiana* 4 (1950): 385–405.

Gentile, Giovanni. *Studi vichiani*. 3rd ed. Florence: Sansoni, 1968.

Gill, Joseph, S.J. *The Council of Florence*. Cambridge: Cambridge University Press, 1959.

Giordano, Antonella. *Letterate toscane del Settecento*. Florence: All'Insegna del Giglio, 1994.

Giorgetti Vichi, Anna Maria. *Gli Arcadi dal 1690 al 1800. Onomasticon*. Rome: Arcadia—Accademia Letteraria Italiana, 1977.

Giuli, Paola. "Corilla Olimpica improvvisatrice: Toward a Reappraisal of Her Life and Work." In *Corilla Olimpica e la poesia del Settecento: Atti del Convegno Internazionale*, edited by Moreno Fabbri, 155–72. Pistoia: Maschietto e Musolino, 2002.

———. "Enlightenment." In *The Feminist Encyclopedia of Italian Literature*, edited by Rinaldina Russell, 79–82. Westport, CT: Greenwood Press, 1997.

———. "The Poetics of Seconda Arcadia and Literary History." *NEMLA Italian Studies* 19 (1995): 51–68.

———. "Querelle des femmes." In *Feminist Encyclopedia of Italian Literature*, edited by Rinaldina Russell, 273–75. Westport, CT: Greenwood Press, 1997.

———. "Traces of a Sisterhood: Corilla Olimpica as Corinne's Unacknowledged Alter Ego." In *The Novel's Seductions: Stael's Corinne in Critical Inquiry*, edited by Karyne Samurlo, 165–84. Lewisburg, PA: Bucknell University Press, 1999.

———"Women Poets and Improvisers: Cultural Assumptions and Literary Values in Arcadia." *Studies in Eighteenth-Century Culture* 32 (2003): 69–92.

Govoni, Paola. *Un pubblico per la scienza: La divulgazione scientifica nell'Italia in formazione.* Roma: Carrocci, 2002.

Graziosi, Elisabetta. "Arcadia femminile: presenze e modelli." *Filologia e critica* 17 (1992): 321–58.

Green, Monica. "In Search of an Authentic Women's Medicine: The Strange Fates of Trota of Salerno and Hildegard of Bingen." *Dynamis* 19 (1999): 25–54.

———. *Women's Healthcare in the Medieval West.* Aldershot: Ashgate, 2000.

Grillo, E. "Giuseppa Eleonora Barbapiccola," In *Dizionario biografico degli italiani*, 6:39. Rome: Istituto della Enciclopedia Italiana, 1964.

Guerci, Luciano. *La discussione sulla donna nell'Italia del Settecento.* Turin: Tirrenia Stampatori, 1987.

———. *La sposa obbediente: Donna e matrimonio nella discussione dell'Italia del Settecento.* Turin: Tirrenia Stampatori, 1988.

Harth, Erica. *Cartesian Women: Versions and Subversions of Rational Discourse in the Ancien Regime.* Ithaca, NY: Cornell University Press, 1992.

Hawley, Richard. "The Problem of Women Philosophers in Ancient Greece." In *Women in Ancient Societies*, edited by Léonie J. Archer, Susan Fischler, and Maria Wyke, 70–84. London: Macmillan, 1994.

The Interpreter's Bible: The Holy Scriptures in the King James and Revised Standard Versions with General Articles and Introduction, Exegesis, Exposition for Each Book of the Bible. 12 vols. New York: Abingdon-Cokesbury Press, 1952–57.

Israel, Jonathan. *Radical Enlightenment: Philosophy and the Making of Modernity 1650–1750.* Oxford: Oxford University Press, 2001.

Jardine, Lisa. "Isotta Nogarola: Women Humanists—Education for What?" *History of Education* 12 (1983): 231–44.

Jordan, Constance. *Renaissance Feminism: Literary Texts and Political Models.* Ithaca, NY: Cornell University Press, 1990.

———. "Renaissance Women Defending Women: Arguments against Patriarchy." In *Italian Women Writers from the Renaissance to the Present: Revising the Canon*, 55–67. University Park: Pennsylvania State University, 1996.

Jordanova, Ludmilla. "Sex and Gender." In *Inventing Human Science*, edited by Christopher Fox, Roy Porter, and Robert Wokler, 152–83. Berkeley: University of California Press, 1995.

Kelly, Joan. *Women, History, and Theory: The Essays of Joan Kelly.* Edited by Catherine Stimpson. Chicago: University of Chicago Press, 1984.

Kelso, Ruth. *Doctrine for the Lady of the Renaissance.* Foreword by Katharine M. Rogers. Urbana: University of Illinois Press, 1956, 1978.

Kennedy, George. *Quintilian.* New York: Twayne, 1969.

King, Margaret L. *Women of the Renaissance.* Chicago: University of Chicago Press, 1991.

———. "Book-Lined Cells: Women and Humanism in the Early Italian Renaissance." In *Beyond Their Sex: Learned Women of the European Past*, edited by Patricia Labalme, 66–90. New York: New York University Press, 1980.

———. "The Religious Retreat of Isotta Nogarola (1418–1466): Sexism and Its Consequences in the Fifteenth Century." *Signs* 3 (1978): 807–22.

Kristeller, Paul Oskar. "Learned Women of Early Modern Italy: Humanists and University Scholars." In *Beyond Their Sex: Learned Women of the European Past*, edited by Patricia Labalme, 91–116. New York: New York University Press, 1980.

Labalme, Patricia H. "Women's Roles in Early Modern Venice: An Exceptional Case." In *Beyond Their Sex: Learned Women of the European Past*, edited by Patricia Labalme, 129–52. New York: New York University Press, 1980.

Laqueur. Thomas. *Making Sex: Body and Gender from the Greeks to Freud*. Cambridge, MA: Harvard University Press, 1990.

Lefkowitz, Mary R., and Maureen B. Fant. *Women's Life in Greece and Rome*. 2nd ed. Baltimore: John Hopkins University Press, 1992.

Lindberg, David. *The Emergence of Western Science*. Chicago: University of Chicago Press, 1992.

Lojacono, Ettore. "Cenni sulle lingue di Descartes e considerazioni sulla traduzione dei *Principia* in lingua italiana." In *Descartes: Principia Philosophiae (1644–1994)*, edited by Jean-Robert Armogathe and Giulia Belgioioso, 531–75. Naples: Vivarium, 1996.

Maggiolo, Attilo. "Elena Lucrezia Cornaro Piscopia e le altre donne aggregate all'Accademia patavina dei Ricovrati." *Padova e la sua provincia* 24, no. 11–12 (1978): 33–36.

———. *I soci dell'Accademia patavina dalla sua fondazione (1599)*. Padua: Accademia Patavina di Scienze Lettere ed Arti, 1983.

Malpezzi Price, Paola. "A Woman's Discourse in the Italian Renaissance: Moderata Fonte's *Il merito delle donne*." *Annali d'Italianistica* 7 (1989): 165–81.

Maschietto, Francesco Ludovico. *Elena Lucrezia Cornaro Piscopia (1646–1684) prima donna laureata nel mondo*. Padua: Editrice Antenore, 1978.

Maylender, Michele. *Storia delle accademie d'Italia*. 5 vols. Bologna: L. Capelli, 1926–30.

Mazzotti, Massimo. "Maria Gaetana Agnesi: The Unusual Life and Mathematical Work of an Eighteenth-Century Woman," *Isis* 92 (2001): 657–83.

Mazzucchelli, Giovanni Maria. "Maria Gaetana Agnesi." In *Gli scrittori d'Italia*, vol. 1, part 1, 198. Brescia, 1753–63.

Meissner, W. W., S.J. *Ignatius of Loyola: The Psychology of a Saint*. New Haven, CT: Yale University Press, 1992.

Meli, Elio. "Laura Bassi Verati: Ridiscussioni e nuovi spunti." In *Alma Mater Studiorum: La Presenza Femminile*, 71–79. Bologna: CLUEB, 1988.

Messbarger, Rebecca. *The Century of Women: Representations of Women in Eighteenth-Century Italian Public Discourse*. Toronto: University of Toronto Press, 2002.

———. "Barbapiccola, Giuseppa Eleonora (Eighteenth-Century)." In *The Feminist Encyclopedia of Italian Literature*, edited by Rinaldina Russell, 27–29. Westport, CT: Greenwood Press, 1997.

———. "Double-Crossing: Female Impersonation in Gasparo Gozzi's *Gazzetta veneta*." *M/MLA Journal* 35, no. 1 (2002): 1–13.

———. "Re-membering a Body of Work: Anatomist and Anatomical Designer Anna Morandi Manzolini." *Studies in Eighteenth-Century Culture* 32 (2003): 123–54.

———. "Waxing Poetic: The Anatomical Wax Sculptures of Anna Morandi Manzolini." *Configurations* 9 (2001): 65–97.

Napier, Henry Edward. *Florentine History: From the Earliest Authentic Records to the Accession of Ferdinand the Third*. Vol. 5. London: Edward Moxon, 1847.

Natali, Giulio. *Il Settecento*. Milan: Casa Editrice Dr. Francesco Vallardi, 1929.

New American Bible. Washington, DC: United States Conference of Catholic Bishops, 2001.

Nicolini, Fausto. "G. B. Vico nella vita domestica." *Archivio storico per le province napoletane* 50 (1925): 227–98.

Nye, Andrea. *The Princess and the Philosopher: Letters of Elisabeth of the Palatine to René Descartes*. Lanham, MD: Rowman & Littlefield, 1999.

O'Malley, John, S.J. *The First Jesuits*. Cambridge, MA: Harvard University Press, 1993.

Osbat, Luciano. *L'Inquisizione a Napoli: Il processo agli ateisti*. Rome: Edizioni di storia e letteratura, 1974.

Pancino, Claudia. "Donne e scienza." In *La memoria di lei: Storia delle donne, storia di genere*, edited by Gabriella Zarri, 89–94. Turin: Società Editrice Internazionale, 1996.

———. "L'ostetricia del Settecento e la scuola Bolognese di Giovanni Antonio Galli." In *Ars obstetricia bononiensis*, 24–31. Bologna: CLUEB, 1988.

Panizza, Letizia, and Sharon Wood, eds. *History of Women's Writing in Italy*. Cambridge: Cambridge University Press, 2000.

Parabiago, Giuliana. "Clelia Borromeo del Grillo." *Annuario dell'I.P.S.I.A. "Cesare Correnti"* 1 (1998): 36–60.

Pastor, Ludwig. *The History of the Popes*. Vol. 12. Edited and translated by Ralph Francis Kerr. 2nd ed. London: Kegan Paul, Trench, Trubner, 1923.

Per il Centocinquantesimo Anniversario 1900 dalla Fondazione della I. R. Accademia di Scienze, Lettere Ed Arti degli Agiati in Rovereto. Rovereto: Tipografia Grigoletti, 1899.

Pomata, Gianna. "Donne e Rivoluzione Scientifica: verso un nuovo bilancio." In *Corpi e storia: Donne e uomini dal mondo antico all'età contemporanea*, edited by Nadia Filippini et al., 165–92. Rome: Viella, 2002.

———. "Gender and the Family." *Short Oxford History of Italy: Early Modern Italy, 1550–1796*, edited by John Marino, 69–86. Oxford: Oxford University Press, 2002.

———. "Risposta a Pigmalione: Le origini della storia delle donne alla London School of Economics." *Quaderni Storici* 110, no. 2 (2002): 505–544.

Ricaldone, Luisa. "Aurelio de' Giorgi Bertola e la gentildonna." In *Un europeo del Settecento: Aurelio De' Giorgi Bertola riminese*, edited by A. Battistini, 119–50. Ravenna: Longo, 2000.

———. "Il dibattito sulla donna nella letteratura del Triennio (1796–1799)." *Italienische Studien* heft 7 (1984): 23–46.

———. "Diodata Saluzzo e la sua attività nell'Accademia delle Scienze." *Atti del Convegno. I primi due secoli dell'Accademia delle Scienze di Torino* (November 1983): 10–12.

———. "Immagini di donne di lettere nel teatro goldoniano." *Italienische Studien* (1993): 75–82.

———. "Letterate e immagini di letterate nel Settecento italiano: proposte per una ricerca." In *Literatur ohne Grenzen: Festschrift für Erika Kanduth*, 339–50. Wein: Peter Lang, 1993.

———. *La scrittura nascosta. Donne di lettere e loro immagini tra Arcadia e Restaurazione*. Paris-Fiesole: Champion-Cadmo, 1996.

Ricaldone, Luisa, ed. *Le avventure del poeta*, by Luisa Bergalli. Rome: Vecchiarelli, 1997.

Ricaldone, Luisa, and Adriana Chemello, eds. *Geografie e genealogie letterarie. Erudite, biografe, croniste, narratrici, "épistolières," utopiste tra Settecento e Ottocento*. Padua: Il Poligrafo, 2000.

Riccardi, Pietro. *Biblioteca matematica italiana dalla origine della stampa ai primi anni del secolo XIX*. Modena: Tipografia Dell'Erede Soliani, 1870.

Sama, Catherine M. "Becoming Visible: A Biography of Elisabetta Caminer Turra (1751–1796) during Her Formative Years." *Studi Veneziani* (2002): 349–88.

———. "Liberty, Equality, Frivolity! An Eighteenth-Century Critique of Fashion Periodicals in Italy." *Eighteenth-Century Studies* 37, no. 3 (2004): 389–414.

———. "Verso un teatro moderno: La polemica tra Elisabetta Caminer Turra e Carlo Gozzi." In *Elisabetta Caminer Turra: Una letterata veneta verso l'Europa*, edited by Rita Unfer Lukoschik, 63–79. Verona: Essedue Edizioni, 1998.

Sama, Catherine, ed. and trans. *Selected Writings of an Eighteenth-Century Venetian Woman of Letters*, by Elisabetta Caminer Turra. Chicago: University of Chicago Press, 2003.

Sanna, Manuela. "Un'amicizia alla luce del cartesianesimo: Giuseppa Eleonora Barbapiccola e Luisa Vico." In *Donne, filosofia e cultura nel Seicento*, edited by Pina Totaro, 173–78. Rome: Consiglio Nazionale delle Ricerche, 1999.

Sawday, Jonathon. *The Body Emblazoned: Dissection and the Human Body in Renaissance Culture*. New York: Routledge, 1995.

Schiebinger, Londa. *The Mind Has No Sex? Women in the Origins of Modern Science*. Cambridge, MA: Harvard University Press, 1989.

Sheriff, Mary. *The Exceptional Woman: Elisabeth Vigée-Lebrun and the Cultural Politics of Art*. Chicago: University of Chicago Press, 1996.

Showalter, Elaine. "Feminist Criticism in the Wilderness." In *The New Feminist Criticism: Essays on Women, Literature and Theory*, edited by Elaine Showalter, 243–70. New York: Pantheon Books, 1985.

Snyder, Jane McIntosh. *The Woman and the Lyre: Women Writers in Classical Greece and Rome*. Carbondale: Southern Illinois University Press, 1989.

Solerti, Angelo. *Autobiografie e Vite de' maggiori scrittori italiani*. Milan: Albrighi, Segate & C. Editori, 1903.

Stewart, Pamela. "Rosaura, the Blue-Stocking Heroine of Goldoni's Donna di Garbo." *Annali d'Italianistica: Women's Voices in Italian Literature* 7 (1989): 242–52.

Stone, Harold. *Vico's Cultural History: The Production and Transmission of Ideas in Naples, 1685–1750*. Leiden: Brill, 1997.

Tilche, Giovanna. *Maria Gaetana Agnesi*. Milan: Rizzoli, 1984.

Torre, Giovanni Maria. *Scienza della Natura*. Naples: Serafino Regio Stampatore, 1748–49.

Toschi Traversi, Lucia. "Verso l'inserimento delle donne nel mondo accademico." In *Alma Mater Studiorum: La presenza femminile dal XVIII al XX secolo*, 23–30. Bologna: CLUEB, 1988.

Totaro, Pina, ed. *Donne, filosofia e cultura nel Seicento*. Rome: Consiglio Nazionale delle Ricerche, 1999.

Unfer Lukoschik, Rita, ed. *Elisabetta Caminer Turra (1751–1796): Una letterata verso l'Europa*. Verona: Essedue, 1998.

Usher, M. D. *Homeric Stitchings: The Homeric Centos of the Empress Eudocia*. Lanham, MD: Rowman & Littlefield, 1998.

Valeri, Diego. *L'Accademia dei Ricovrati Alias Accademia Patavina di Scienze Lettere ed Arti*. Padua: Sede dell'Accademia, 1987.

Van Damme, Stéphane. *Descartes: Essai d'histoire culturelle d'une grandeur philosophique*. Paris: Presses de Sciences Po, 2002.

Venesoen, Constant. *Études sur la littérature féminine au XVIIe siècle: Mademoiselle de Gournay Madame de Scudéry Madame de Villedieu, Madame de Lafayette*. Birmingham, AL: Summa Publications, 1990.

Waithe, Mary Ellen, ed. *A History of Women Philosophers*. 3 vols. Dordrecht: Martinus Nijhoff, 1987.

Weaver. Elissa. "Suor Arcangela Tarabotti (Galerana Baratotti, Galerana Barcitotti) (1604–52)." In *Italian Women Writers: A Bio-Bibliographical Sourcebook*, edited by Rinaldina Russell. Westport, CT: Greenwood Press, 1994.

Woodbridge, Linda. *Women and the English Renaissance: Literature and the Nature of Womankind, 1540–1620*. Urbana: University of Illinois Press, 1984.

Zarri, Gabriella, ed. *La memoria di lei: Storia delle donne e storia di genere*. Turin: Società Editrice Internazionale, 1996.

I

GIUSEPPA ELEONORA BARBAPICCOLA

TRANSLATOR'S INTRODUCTION

In 1722 Giuseppa Eleonora Barbapiccola (ca. 1700–ca. 1740) translated René Descartes's *Principles of Philosophy* (1644), working primarily from the 1647 French edition rather than the Latin original. Allegedly published in Turin by Giovan Francesco Mairesse, it was in all likelihood one of many books published in Naples under false imprimatur in the late seventeenth and eighteenth centuries. The fact that a Neapolitan artist, F. De Grado, engraved Barbapiccola's portrait for the translation makes it even more probable that it was both written and published there. Like many philosophical works published in Naples, including a number of books that Barbapiccola cited in her preface, it may have been part of the semiclandestine circulation of books in the capital city of the Kingdom of Naples. Another case in point is the 1710 edition of Galileo's works, whose title page advertised it as being published in Florence when, in actuality, it was the work of a Neapolitan lawyer, Lorenzo Ciccarelli.[1]

More than simply a translation of Descartes's important work, Barbapiccola's Italian edition was also a manifesto of women's right to learn. In her preface, entitled "The Translator to the Reader," she presented Descartes as the creator of a philosophy that celebrated the female mind.[2] Descartes's

1. The clandestine printing of books in Naples is discussed, among other places, in Vincenzo Ferrone, *The Intellectual Roots of the Italian Enlightenment: Newtonian Science, Religion, and Politics in the Early Eighteenth Century*, trans. Sue Brotherton (Atlantic Highlands, NJ: Humanities Press, 1995), 51, 80–81, 186; and Harold Samuel Stone, *Vico's Cultural History: The Production and Transmission of Ideas in Naples, 1685–1750* (Leiden: Brill, 1997), 58, 64, 214, 215, 279–80. For a general discussion of the intellectual climate in eighteenth-century Naples, see Giuseppe Galasso, *La filosofia in soccorso de' governi: La cultura napoletana del Settecento* (Naples: Guida, 1989).

2. The fundamental study of this subject is Erica Harth, *Cartesian Women: Versions and Subversions of Rational Discourse in the Ancien Regime* (Ithaca, NY: Cornell University Press, 1992). See also

famous dedication of his *Principles of Philosophy* (1644) to princess Elisabeth of Bohemia, one of his important correspondents, was the primary basis for this judgment. "You are the only person I have so far found who has completely understood all my previously published works," he wrote, marveling at the fact that his best reader was not "some aged pedant who has spent many years in contemplation" but a youthful Minerva.[3] Barbapiccola was among the readers of Descartes's works who took his praise of Elisabeth to be praise of women in general. She found further proof of women's special affinity for Cartesian philosophy when she recalled the patronage that Queen Christina of Sweden had offered him in the final year of his life.

Barbapiccola demonstrated that one did not need to be of royal blood to understand Descartes or, more generally, to reflect on important philosophical questions. But she did far more than this, since her preface was simultaneously a history of women's learning, a history of philosophy, and an autobiography. She self-consciously presented herself as an heir to the seventeenth-century tradition of Cartesian women and celebrated its arrival in the city of Naples, where she was one of several women known for their philosophical erudition by the early eighteenth century. Another leading female Cartesian, the duchess of Limatola, Aurelia d'Este (1683–1719), had recently died, making it possible for a younger, less noble woman to claim the place that d'Este had occupied as the preeminent Cartesian woman in the city.

Barbapiccola offered her own tribute to d'Este when she praised Paolo Mattia Doria for writing his *Dialogues in Which It Is Demonstrated That Woman, in Almost All the Important Virtues, Is Not Inferior to Man* (1716), a work he addressed to his famous aristocratic pupil, Aurelia d'Este, while he was still enamored with Cartesian philosophy. D'Este, he wrote, "had applied her mind so seriously to the science of metaphysics that she knows it equally as well as any man who has been better educated in that subject, and she knows how to

---

Paula Findlen, "Translating the New Science: Women and the Circulation of Knowledge in Enlightenment Italy," *Configurations* 2 (1995): esp. 174–85. Most recently, Jonathan Israel includes a few remarks on Barbapiccola's translation in his *Radical Enlightenment: Philosophy and the Making of Modernity 1650–1750* (Oxford: Oxford University Press, 2001), 55, 93–94.

3. René Descartes, *The Philosophical Writings of Descartes*, trans. John Cottingham, Robert Stoothoff, and Dugal Murdoch (Cambridge: Cambridge University Press, 1985), 1:192. The most recent study of their relationship is Andrea Nye, *The Princess and the Philosopher: Letters of Elisabeth of the Palatine to René Descartes* (Lanham, MD: Rowman & Littlefield, 1999), but readers who want to consult the original documents should also use René Descartes, *Correspondance avec Elisabeth et autres lettres*, ed. Jean-Marie Beyssade and Michelle Beyssade (Paris: Flammirion, 1989). For a general introduction to Descartes, the best starting point is Stéphane Van Damme, *Descartes: Essai d'histoire culturelle d'une grandeur philosophique* (Paris: Presses de Sciences Po, 2002).

deduce useful conclusions from it."[4] Her poetic interpretations of the *Meditations*, like Barbapiccola's translation of the *Principles of Philosophy*, played a visible role in the diffusion of Cartesian thought in Naples. More ambitious in her goals, Barbapiccola offered her readers a more comprehensive engagement with Descartes by making herself a central interpreter of Descartes in print, as his translator, and by claiming the right to speak for other women regarding their capacity to learn.

The passion for Descartes among the Neapolitans was well known in Europe by this time, despite or, more likely, because of the fact that his works had been put on the Index of Prohibited Books in 1663. As early as 1671, the Neapolitan clergy had been warned to pay attention to the appearance of the works of "a certain René Descartes" in their city. Growing tensions over the revival of the ancient doctrine of atomism and the emergence of a new corpuscularean philosophy associated with Cartesian thought in the late 1680s made it even more controversial. Of course, this only made reading Descartes more popular. The great Neapolitan philosopher Giambattista Vico (1668–1744) recalled the 1690s as a period in which "Cartesian physics was most in vogue."[5] Yet the specter of atheism lingered over Descartes even when his intellectual significance was decidedly on the wane in the era in which Isaac Newton's natural philosophy increasingly made Cartesian vortices and geometry seem obsolete. Ten years after Barbapiccola's translation appeared, the papal nuncio in Naples reported in 1732 that he was certain "that young people are reading French and other foreign books," especially works that contained those "new Cartesian opinions."[6] But this was hardly news, because reading Cartesian books had been a staple of intellectual life since the late seventeenth century. Rather than seeing Barbapiccola's translation as the introduction of Cartesian thought to her city, we should see it instead as the culmination of a long and contested tradition. From this

4. Paolo Mattia Doria, *Ragionamenti di Paolo Mattia D'Oria indirizzati alla Signora D'Aurelia D'Este Duchessa di Limatola: Ne' quali si dimostra la donna, in quasi che tutte le virtù più grandi, non essere all'uomo inferiore* (Frankfurt, 1716), sig. a.4v. For further discussion of Aurelia d'Este, see her eulogy in the *Giornale de' letterati d'Italia* 32 (1719): 506–13. The fundamental work on Doria remains Vittorio Conti, *Paolo Mattia Doria: Dalla repubblica dei togati alla repubblica dei notabili* (Florence: Olschki, 1978).

5. Vittor Ivo Comparato, *Giuseppe Valletta: Un intellettuale napoletano della fine del Seicento* (Naples: Istituto Italiano per gli Studi Storici, 1970), 140; Giambattista Vico, *The Autobiography of Giambattista Vico*, trans. Max Harold Fisch and Thomas Goddard Bergin (Ithaca, NY: Cornell University Press, 1944), 130.

6. Raffaele Ajello, "Cartesianismo e la cultura oltremontana al tempo dell' 'Istoria civile,'" in *Pietro Giannone e il suo tempo*, ed. Raffael Ajello (Naples: Jovene, 1980), 1:1–181, esp. 102, 151, 163 (quote on 163). See also Eugenio Garin, "Cartesio e l'Italia," *Giornale critico della filosofia italiana* 4 (1950): 385–405.

perspective, it raises a fundamental question: what was the purpose of translating Descartes in 1722?

We know very little about Barbapiccola.[7] She was probably born in Naples around 1700 and seems to have been from a family originally from Salerno. This is surely the reason she knew about the medieval history of women such as Trota of Salerno, who were an important part of Salerno's reputation as an early center of medical learning renowned for their women healers.[8] Her uncle Tommaso Maria Alfani (1679–1742), a well-known Dominican preacher in Naples, had been appointed as the official theologian of the city by the Emperor Charles VI. Alfani also founded the Accademia degli Inquieti in Naples in 1709 and was a correspondent of Vico.[9] While we know nothing of Barbapiccola's parents, it is evident that her uncle's intellectual interests and contacts played some role in her own formation. Sometime prior to the publication of her translation of Descartes, for example, she became associated with Vico's intellectual circle and developed a particular friendship with his daughter Luisa, who was also renowned for her learning.[10]

Barbapiccola's preface brought together several different strands of intellectual debate then preoccupying scholars in Naples. On the one hand, it responded to the growing anti-Cartesianism of important philosophers such as Vico and Doria, who increasingly felt that a modern metaphysics that emphasized the mathematical certainty of reason limited the possibili-

7. E. Grillo, "Giuseppa Eleonora Barbapiccola," in *Dizionario biografico degli italiani* (Rome: Istituto della Enciclopedia Italiana, 1964–), 6.39. For further biographical information, see also Rebecca Messbarger, "Barbapiccola, Giuseppa Eleonora (Eighteenth-Century)," in *The Feminist Encyclopedia of Italian Literature*, ed. Rinaldina Russell (Westport, CT: Greenwood Press, 1997), 27–29; and Manuela Sanna, "Un'amicizia alla luce del cartesianesimo: Giuseppa Eleonora Barbapiccola e Luisa Vico," in *Donne, filosofia e cultura nel Seicento*, ed. Pina Totaro (Rome: Consiglio Nazionale delle Ricerche, 1999), 173–78.

8. Monica Green, *The Trotula: An English Translation of the Medieval Compendium of Women's Medicine* (Philadelphia: University of Pennsylvania Press, 2001).

9. Sanna, "Un'amicizia alla luce del cartesianesimo," 176. I have found the following publications by Tommaso Maria Alfani: *Istoria degli anni santi, dal di loro solenne cominciamento per insino a quello del regnante Sommo Pontefice Benedetto XIII* (Naples, 1725); and Pietro Antonio Corsignani, *Reggia Marsicana, ovvero Memorie topografico-storiche di varie colonie e città antiche e moderne della provincia de i Mari e di Valeria*, ed. Tommaso Maria Alfani (n. p., 1738). On his academy, see Michele Maylender, *Storia delle accademie d'Italia* (Bologna: L. Capelli, 1926–30), 3:386. The Inquieti, also known as the Irrequieti, promoted the mathematical sciences; it may have existed prior to this date and seems to have ended shortly after 1719.

10. Antonio Cirillo, *Napoli ai tempi di Giambattista Vico* (Naples: Edizioni Tempo Lungo, 2000), 233, 244. Unfortunately Cirillo's information about Barbapiccola is somewhat inaccurate, but the book in general offers an interesting overview of Neapolitan cultural life in this period. For more on Vico's family, see Fausto Nicolini, "G. B. Vico nella vita domestica," *Archivio storico per le province napoletane* 50 (1925): 227–98.

ties for other kinds of discussions about the nature of knowledge.[11] On the other hand, it sought to integrate some of the new philosophical insights of Neapolitan scholars into a fresh reading of Descartes. Her preface, for example, invoked Vico's *On the Most Ancient Wisdom of the Italians* (1710), a controversial book dedicated to Doria that presented his new historical consciousness about the origins of knowledge as an implicit alternative to Cartesian epistemology.[12] Within a decade, both philosophers would turn away from Descartes, leaving others to defend his philosophy. Barbapiccola, for example, would argue that these different approaches to knowledge were not incompatible.

The intersection of the debates over the value of Cartesian philosophy with renewed discussion about the value of women's education forms the background to Barbapiccola's project to translate the *Principles of Philosophy*. While telling her readers that she had no intention of defending Cartesianism, this was exactly what Barbapiccola did. She did not openly criticize any contemporary philosophers, though she knew that Francesco Spinelli was in the process of writing a defense of Descartes that directly responded to Doria, and she advertised its imminent appearance. Instead, Barbapiccola offered a more subtle response that reflected the long and difficult history of Cartesian philosophy in Naples during the past century. She argued that her desire to make his writings more accessible was an essential step in demonstrating his compatibility with Christianity.

Any Neapolitan reader of Barbapiccola's preface, and many others outside of Naples, would immediately have recognized the significance of Barbapiccola's decision to wed the history of women's participation in philosophy with the history of philosophy's relation to Christianity. It allowed her to draw extensively on some of the most important philosophical writings of the previous decades in Naples while displaying her own erudition regarding the vexed issue of the relationship between human and divine knowledge. The bulk of her discussion came directly from the writings of one of the great philosophers of the previous century, the lawyer Giuseppe Valletta (1636–1714). Valletta was perhaps the most well-known intellectual figure in late seventeenth-century Naples. Beginning in the 1680s, he corresponded with

11. See, for example, Paolo Mattia Doria, *Dissertazione di Paolo Mattia Doria intorno alla nuova geometria di Cartesio* (Venice, 1721); and Doria, *Discorsi critici filosofici intorno alla filosofia degli antichi e dei moderni ed in particolare intorno alla filosofia di Renato Des Cartes* (Venice [Naples], 1724). Note that Doria's second work is another example of a Neapolitan book on Cartesianism with a false imprimatur.

12. Giambattista Vico, *On the Most Ancient Wisdom of the Italians*, trans. Lucia M. Palmer (Ithaca, NY: Cornell University Press, 1988).

scholars all over Europe and assembled a library of approximately sixteen thousand volumes, a veritable encyclopedia of ancient and modern learning that he generously shared with other scholars. His contacts in other parts of Europe made the most recent developments in French and English philosophy more readily available to the Neapolitans. In the period when Barbapiccola completed her translation of Descartes, his library was in the process of being dispersed by his heirs.[13] The death of Valletta marked an important transition in Neapolitan intellectual life. What would replace his library as the center of that world? Who would speak with his learning and passion about the reasons to pursue modern knowledge?

One of the most important results of Valletta's contributions to Neapolitan debates about knowledge was his *Letter in Defense of Modern Philosophy and Those Who Cultivate It* (1691–97). Written in the course of the famous trial of the "atheists" that occurred in Naples between 1688 and 1697, it mustered all of the learning that Valletta compiled in his fabled library to defend the freedom to philosophize.[14] While the trial had focused specifically on the revival of the ancient doctrine of atomism as a prime example of atheism, the fact that most of the philosophers interrogated were also Cartesians was not unimportant. Immediately prior to these events, in fact, a Neapolitan preacher had openly attacked Cartesianism as another form of atheism. Valletta worked tirelessly to have the Roman Inquisition removed from Naples during this period.[15] He wrote his *Letter* in order to demonstrate the problems with presenting Aristotelianism as the preeminent Christian philosophy. Instead, he argued that a historical investigation of the writings of the early Church Fathers revealed their more positive assessment of Platonism as the philosophy most compatible with Christianity. He demonstrated the subversive uses of erudition in a manner worthy of humanistic predecessors such as Lorenzo Valla.

Valletta offered a historical perspective on the place of philosophy in Christian society in order to argue that modern philosophies of knowledge could also be compatible with Christianity. He considered the early debates about the relationship between faith and knowledge to be an important

---

13. Comparato, *Giuseppe Valletta*, 91–92. The Congregazione dell'Oratorio in Naples acquired a significant part of Valletta's library and his collections in 1726. Doria was among the generation who used books in Valletta's library for research toward his publications; Conti, *Paolo Mattia Doria*, 46.

14. Luciano Osbat, *L'Inquisizione a Napoli: Il processo agli ateisti* (Rome: Edizioni di storia e letteratura, 1974); Max H. Fisch, "The Academy of the Investigators," in *Science, Medicine and History*, ed. E. Ashworth Underwood (Oxford: Oxford University Press, 1953), 1:544–46; and Ferrone, *Intellectual Roots*, 2–4.

15. Comparato, *Giuseppe Valletta*, 141, 147, 162.

reminder that Christianity had not chosen a single philosophical perspective
as its intellectual orthodoxy until the Middle Ages and even then not without
controversy. The dominance and institutionalization of Aristotelian scholasticism in one period did not preclude the choice, or the reasonableness, of
alternative philosophies of knowledge at other moments in time.

While a few unauthorized copies of Valletta's *Letter* appeared in print in
1704, lacking such basic features as a title page and an imprimatur, no full
edition was published until 1732. In all likelihood, Barbapiccola used one of
the many manuscript copies in circulation.[16] She cites it so copiously and so
literally in her preface to Descartes that we must, in part, see her own manifesto as an attempt to publish a summary of his famous defense of modern
philosophy. Undoubtedly, the new threat that Doria's intellectual critique of
Cartesian philosophy posed, in relationship to a lingering theological suspicion of all modern philosophy among the more conservative members of the
Catholic Church, made Valletta's manuscript meaningful in new ways. The
decision to publish parts of Valletta's unauthorized and controversial *Letter*
was yet another reason to make the book appear to come from Turin rather
than Naples. Among other things, it echoed the central message of Galileo's
Letter to the Grand Duchess Christina (1615), which finally had been published
in Italian in the unauthorized 1710 edition of his works. Barbapiccola concluded her preface to Descartes's *Principles of Philosophy* by arguing that scripture and modern philosophy were compatible because, as she reminded her
readers, God did not intend to describe nature scientifically nor did philosophers wish to interpret matters of faith. Such strong words associated with
the circumstances surrounding the 1633 trial and condemnation of Galileo
belied her frequent protestations that her enterprise of presenting Descartes
to Italian readers was a modest endeavor.

So much of Barbapiccola's text is concerned with these philosophical
issues that it is easy to forget that she also intended her work as a defense
of women's right to philosophize. History gave her inspiration for her pursuit of learning with its numerous examples of learned women. Knowledge
of languages such as Latin gave her the tools for reading and understanding the kind of learning that lay beyond the traditional scope of women's
studies. But it was Cartesian philosophy that gave her the tools to think
critically about knowledge. In her preface, she used Valletta's arguments for
the value of modern philosophy to attack recent critics of Descartes, such
as Paolo Mattia Doria, by arguing that, among modern philosophers, he
was the most Christian. Descartes had famously proved the existence of

---

16. Stone, *Vico's Cultural History*, 58. The extant manuscript versions have been compared and
collated in Giuseppe Valletta, *Opere filosofiche*, ed. Michele Rak (Florence: Olschki, 1974).

humanity with the idea of God. He had also argued for the universality of the human mind—a soul separated from the body—allowing certain readers to interpret it as being beyond sex.

Barbapiccola's declaration that women's ignorance was a product of "bad education more than nature" seemed to respond directly to certain key passages in Doria's *Dialogues*, making her preface a response to his well-known treatise. While Doria had praised the ability of exceptional women to surpass the limits of their sex, he also told his pupil d'Este, "I am not in agreement with the sentiment that many attribute to René Descartes, that is, that God gave everyone an equal ability to understand the sciences." Doria underscored the fact that some men as well as many women were not able to master certain subjects, so it was in theory not a question of gender but of ability. Yet he nonetheless left his readers with the distinct impression that he had not exactly answered d'Este's criticisms of his earlier opinions about women's ability, since subsequent passages in his work emphasized the essential deficiencies of the female sex. "Women are by nature weaker," he affirmed.[17] This weakness of body produced a certain deficiency of mind that limited the extent of women's contributions to knowledge. Women might be capable of understanding knowledge, he concluded, but they rarely created it. He felt that the reasons for this distinction were apparent to anyone who understood the anatomy and physiology of sexual difference.

In other words, Barbapiccola's citation of Doria at the beginning of her preface did not necessarily indicate her agreement with his argument in its entirety. She concurred with his fundamental idea that women could learn. But did she agree with the reasons he offered for women's lack of participation in the most active parts of knowledge? Many of the examples of women's accomplishments she cited—for instance, the ancient women philosophers who instructed men—seem to undercut his argument. Doria had interpreted the past as proof that women rarely made knowledge or law. Barbapiccola looked at the same historical record and concluded that women were capable of everything men can do. Their success in the past century, especially as Cartesians, offered the most recent evidence in support of her perspective. While denigrating her own talents as a translator and philosopher in relationship to the work of male Cartesians, Barbapiccola nonetheless left the reader with a strong sense that she had a great deal more to say on this subject, but restrained herself for reasons of prudence as well as modesty.

After the publication of her translation, Barbapiccola joined the growing community of learned women in the Italian peninsula. However, she did

17. Doria, *Ragionamenti*, 344, 351.

not make further intellectual contributions—at least among those that have survived—that evidence a similar desire to play an important role in public intellectual debates. Instead, she became one of many women writers who participated ephemerally in the cultural life of her city. In 1728 Barbapiccola became a member of Italy's leading literary academy, the Accademia degli Arcadi (founded in 1690), taking the name *Mirista* (Fragrant).[18] Her subsequent publications seem to have been only a few poems, leaving us to wonder what happened to her aspirations to philosophize. In 1729 Vico invited her to contribute a poem for a volume dedicated to Michelangelo da Reggio, a Capuchin preacher associated with the Duomo in Naples. Two years later, she contributed another poem to a collection written for the marriage of Tomaso Caracciolo and Ippolita di Dura. For this occasion, she and Luisa Vico wrote poems addressed to each other on the heroic virtue of women, offering further proof of the intimacy that existed between Barbapiccola and the Vico family.[19] Her last publication seems to have been a poem in 1738 in celebration of the marriage of Charles of Bourbon with Maria Amalia of Savoy.[20]

Through the early 1730s, Neapolitan scholars continued to celebrate Barbapiccola as the woman who had made Descartes glorious in Italy, even as the fascination with Descartes was eclipsed by a new passion for the writings of English philosophers such as John Locke and Isaac Newton. The printer-bookseller Bernardino Gessari advertised Barbapiccola's translation in 1734 as one of the books to be purchased at his shop on Via San Biagio dei Librai. Her book also circulated in other parts of the Italian peninsula. In 1740, for example, when the Sienese cleric Giovan Nicolò Bandiera published his important and controversial treatise on women's education, he knew enough about Barbapiccola's work to include her name in his list of contemporary women engaged in philosophical and scientific pursuits in Naples.[21] At least one of the prominent women philosophers of the next

---

18. Anna Maria Giorgetti Vichi, *Gli Arcadi dal 1690 al 1800. Onomasticon* (Rome: Arcadia—Accademia Letteraria Italiana, 1977), 36, 180. While Barbapiccola's portrait in her translation of Descartes simply calls her *Mirista*, she was recorded as *Mirista Acmena*. I thank the reviewer of the manuscript for suggesting the Greek meaning behind her name.

19. The poems are discussed and reprinted in Giovanni Gentile, *Studi vichiani*, 3rd ed. (Florence: Sansoni, 1968), 200, 203; and Giambattista Vico, *Scritti vari e pagine sparse*, ed. Fausto Nicolini (Bari: Laterza, 1940), 254, 327.

20. Stone, *Vico's Cultural History*, 309.

21. Ibid., 267–71; Giovan Nicolò Bandiera, *Trattato degli studi delle donne* (Venice, 1740), 1:147. Barbapiccola might have appreciated the justice of having her name appear in a book that many wanted to place on the Index of Prohibited Books.

generation, the mathematician Maria Gaetana Agnesi, may have read Barbapiccola's work since a copy existed in her family library.[22] Its presence in other northern and central Italian libraries suggests that it enjoyed a certain success, in part because her translation of Descartes's *Principles* remained the only complete one in Italian until Maria Garin's translation of 1967.[23]

Barbapiccola's translation of Descartes appeared one year before the Accademia de' Ricovrati held its famous debate about women's education in Padua. There is no evidence that it inspired the debate, so we should continue to think of these two episodes in relative isolation from each other. The president of the Ricovrati, Antonio Vallisneri, did have contacts in Naples, most notably through his correspondence with Giacinto Gimma, but they did not discuss the appearance of this publication.[24] Nonetheless, we might consider the dialogue that Barbapiccola established with scholars like Vico and Doria in her preface as the Neapolitan equivalent of the kind of debate that the Sienese noblewoman Aretafila Savini de' Rossi engendered in 1729, when she responded to Giovanni Antonio Volpi's view of women's capacity to learn.[25] The fact that it occurred as part of the dissemination of Cartesian philosophy is one of the things that makes Barbapiccola's contribution to the debates about women's education distinctively Neapolitan, since no other part of Italy embraced so fully the writings of this French philosopher. The fact that it involved a young woman, barely out of her teens, who aspired to become a philosopher, makes it part of a much larger story about the relationship between gender and knowledge in the early eighteenth century, when many men and women debated the desirability of education for women as a means of understanding their role in society.[26]

Paula Findlen

22. See the introduction to Agnesi's treatise in this volume for further discussion of Barbapiccola's preface in relation to her own defense of women's education.

23. Ettore Lojacono, "Cenni sulle lingue di Descartes e considerazioni sulla traduzione dei *Principia* in lingua italiana," in *Descartes: Principia Philosophiae (1644–1994)*, ed. Jean-Robert Armogathe and Giulia Belgioioso (Naples: Vivarium, 1996), 532.

24. Giacinto Gimma's correspondence with Antonio Vallisneri is preserved in the Biblioteca dell'Accademia dei Concordi, Rovigo, *Conc.* 37/6.

25. Both texts have been edited and translated by Rebecca Messbarger in this volume.

26. See Luciano Guerci, *La discussione sulla donna nell'Italia del Settecento* (Turin: Tirrenia, 1987); and Rebecca Messbarger, *The Century of Women: Representations of Women in Eighteenth-Century Italian Public Discourse* (Toronto: University of Toronto Press, 2002). For a broader view of these developments and their seventeenth-century background, see Totaro, *Donne, filosofia e cultura nel Seicento;* and Findlen, "Ideas in the Mind: Gender and Knowledge in the Seventeenth Century," *Hypatia* 17 (2002): 183–96.

THE TRANSLATOR TO THE READER:
PREFACE TO RENÉ DESCARTES'S PRINCIPLES
OF PHILOSOPHY (TURIN,[27] 1722)

I would not like it if you, first encountering the title of this book and seeing
that it is the work of a woman, were to consign it to the distaffs, spindles,
and linens, as is the custom of Homer in more than one place, in particular
when he has Hector say to his wife Andromache: "Go do your ordinary
tasks, that is, your linens and spindles . . . ."[28] This is what Madame Dacier
expressed great concern about in her footnote on this passage in Homer, as
a result of her translating it into French, as something she undertook that
greatly surpassed her powers.[29] As confirmation of this, she relates a story
that Herodotus reports of the Princess of Cyrene, Pheretima, with the King
of Cyprus, Evelthon, which leads to the same conclusion.[30] Now, at first
glance it seems that womanly occupations should be nothing more than
"learning the catechism, sewing, and other small tasks, singing, dancing,
doing one's hair up in the latest fashion, curtsying finely, and conversing
politely," considering that Abbé Fleury protests them in his learned *Treatise
on the Selection and Method of Studies* in chapter 36 where he discusses "Women's
Studies."[31] He almost seems to say that women are not capable of study,

27. It is quite probable that the book did not appear in Turin, since many books in Naples were
published under false imprimatur. I thank Luciano Guerci for consulting with me on this detail.

28. Homer, *Iliad*, 6.515–18. When Hector found his wife Andromache on the high wall of
Ilius in the heat of battle, he told her that "war is the work of men." Homer, *Iliad*, trans. Stanley
Lombardo (Indianapolis: Hackett, 1997), 126.

29. Barbapiccola slightly misread what Dacier actually said. In her footnote to this passage,
Dacier comments that Homer always consigned women to their domestic duties and then tells
the story of Pheretima from Herodotus as a prelude to remarking that some of her readers
may want to ask her to do the same after they have seen her translation. *L'Iliade d'Homere, traduite
en françois, avec des remarques par Madame Dacier*, 4th ed. (Amsterdam, 1731), 1:298n83: "Homere
renvoie toujours les femmes à leur fuseaux & à leur laines. . . . J'ai bien peur que beaucoup de
gens en lisant cet Ouvrage & le trouvant fort audessus de mes forces, ne me renvoyent aussi à
mes fuseaux."

30. Herodotus, *Histories*, trans. J. Enoch Powell (Oxford: Clarendon Press, 1949), 1:337–38
(IV.162). Pheretima asked Evelthon for an army in order to rule Cyrene again after the death
of her son. When he refused, sending her a golden spindle and distaff instead, she eventually
raised her own army to avenge her son's death. Barbapiccola's point might be that men can
refuse women the things they desire but the women will find a way to do them on their own.

31. Claude Fleury (1640–1723) was the abbot of Loc-Dieu, a friend of Bossuet and Fénélon, and
the tutor of the prince of Conti. See his *Traité du choix et de la methode des etudes* (Paris, 1687), 264–70.
Barbapiccola's reading of Fleury's treatise seems far more generous than the actual text suggests,
because, while Fleury recognizes the abilities of educated women, he does not encourage them
to pursue the kinds of learning that Barbapiccola herself had mastered.

because their minds have qualities different from and inferior to those of men. But then if one looks carefully and clearly, women should not be excluded from the study of the sciences, since their spirits are more elevated and "they are not inferior to men in terms of the greatest virtues." For this reason, the most learned Signor Doctor Paolo Mattia Doria in his *Dialogues* dedicated to Lady Aurelia d'Este, Duchess of Limotola, managed to demonstrate this with solid reasoning as have many other writers who have spoken of the excellence and dignity of the female sex.[32]

Indeed, even without paging through Boccaccio's book of famous women, or others that have made learned women their subject, who, provided that he has even a mediocre knowledge of history, does not know how many women in every age have distinguished themselves in various literary pursuits?[33] When poetry flourished among the Greeks, famous women included Corinna of Thebes, who five times beat the prince of lyric poets, Pindar; Corinna of Lesbos; and Erinna of Telos, a girl whose verse, when she was only thirteen years old, is said to have attained Homer's majesty. Propertius praised all of them.[34] There was also Daphne, who composed many books of poetry whose verses Homer used afterward, as Diodorus Siculus affirms.[35] Sappho of Lesbos, inventor of the Sapphic verses that bear her name, whom Strabo judged incomparable in poetry;[36] Iambe, inventor of Iambic verse; Charixene, the author of many verses, whom Aristophanes mentions in his

32. The reference is to Doria's *Ragionamenti*. Barbapiccola's phrase, "eccellenza e dignità del Sesso femminile," recalls the title of Lucrezia Marinella's *The Nobility and Excellence of Women* (1600), among other works written on this subject in sixteenth- and seventeenth-century Italy. Since Doria cited Marinella's work, it was evidently known in Naples.

33. Barbapiccola is referring to Giovanni Boccaccio's *De claris mulieribus*, which can now be consulted in an excellent bilingual edition: *Famous Women*, ed. and trans. Virginia Brown (Cambridge, MA: Harvard University Press, 2001).

34. Sextus Propertius (ca. 50–16 BCE) was a Roman poet of the Augustan era whose *Elegiae* (2.3) is the probable source of this information. Barbapiccola is surely referring to Corinna of Tanagra (fl. 500 BCE), whom we know today only through her poetry fragments in Boeotian dialect and for reports of her besting the Greek poet Pindar in competition. See Plutarch, "On the Fame of the Athenians," *Moralia* 347F. Erinna (late fourth century BCE) was a Greek poet from the island of Telos who was known for her poem *The Distaff* and considered the equal of Homer though she reputedly died at the age of nineteen. I have been unable so far to find a reference to Corinna of Lesbos, but for the general context of this material, see Jane McIntosh Snyder, *The Woman and the Lyre: Women Writers in Classical Greece and Rome* (Carbondale: Southern Illinois University Press, 1989).

35. For Diodorus Siculus's discussion of Daphne, see his *Bibliotheca Historica*, 4.66.5–6 (ed. and trans. C. H. Oldfather [Cambridge, MA: Harvard University Press, 1933–67], vol. 3 (1939), 29–31).

36. On Sappho of Lesbos (end of seventh/beginning of sixth century BCE), see Snyder, *The Woman and the Lyre*, 1–37.

comedies;[37] and Telesilla, who is praised by Pausanias.[38] Among the Latin poets, we find Polla Argentaria, the wife of the poet Lucan, who helped him amend the first three books of the Pharsalia, as Statius informs us.[39] Leaving aside numerous others, it suffices to remember Proba Falconia, whose name was not Faltonia and who was from Horta and not from Rome, nor should she be mistaken for Anicia Faltonia Proba or Valeria Proba, as some have done erroneously.[40] (The most erudite Monsignor Giusto Fontanini demonstrates this clearly in book eleven of *On the Antiquities of the Horta Colony*.)[41] Among her other works of poetry, she composed the Virgilian cento in which she used Virgil's lines to describe the deeds of Jesus Christ and the principal mysteries of our faith. Similarly, the empress Eudocia, wife of Theodosius the Younger, wanted to do the same thing with the verses of Homer, using them to describe a great part of evangelical history, although Saint Jerome recalls other Homeric centos before hers.[42] (The most erudite Signor Doctor Niccolò Gallio has marvelously imitated both of them, stealing those hours of repose from serious studies to compose an eloquent cento from the entirety of Ovid's poetry. It is divided into three books with the title *Of God the*

---

37. Charixene appears briefly in Aristophanes, *Assemblywomen*, 943, and seems to have been a learned courtesan (*hetaira*) who lived before the emergence of the Athenian republic.

38. Pausanias, *Description of Greece*, 2.20.8–10. Only one fragment and three single-word quotes remain of the poetry of Telesilla of Argos (fl. 494 BCE), though she was praised by a number of ancient writers, including Herodotus, *Histories*, 6.77–83. Snyder, *The Woman and the Lyre*, 59–62.

39. Polla Argentaria was the wife of Lucan (39–65 CE), Seneca's nephew and author of the unfinished *De bello civili* (*Pharsalia*). Polla supposedly helped her husband compose the first three books of his unfinished epic.

40. Proba Falconia, also known as Faltonia Betitia Proba (fourth century CE), was the Christian daughter of a Roman consul and the wife of a pagan prefect of Rome: Snyder, *The Woman and the Lyre*, 136–39. Boccaccio also mentions the confusion over her origins that a local antiquarian, Giusto Fontanini, seems to have clarified: Boccaccio, *Famous Women*, 413.

41. Giusto Fontanini (1666–1736), professor of eloquence at La Sapienza in Rome, bishop of Ancira, and abbot of Sesto, was a well-known and polemical author of a number of important religious and historical works and an adversary of Muratori. Barbapiccola praised his *De antiquitatibus Hortae coloniae Etruscorum* (Rome, 1708), a work of archaeology and antiquarianism. D. Busolini, "Giusto Fontanini," *Dizionario biografico degli italiani* (Rome: Enciclopedia Italiana, 1964–), 48.747–52.

42. A cento (literally a patchwork quilt) is a poem in hexameters that combined the poetic form and language of Greek and Latin poetry with Biblical content. Proba Falconia's Virgilian cento became a standard text for medieval schoolboys. Eudocia (d. 460 CE), daughter of the philosopher Leontius and wife of Emperor Theodisius II (401–450), was known for expanding a Homeric cento begun by bishop Patricius in the late fourth century CE. Saint Jerome wrote that he disliked the form of the cento because it emphasized private interpretation of scripture rather than the reading of the original text. See M. D. Usher, *Homeric Stitchings: The Homeric Centos of the Empress Eudocia* (Lanham, MD: Rowman and Littlefield, 1998).

Redeemer.[43] Beginning with the mystery of the Holy Trinity and the eternal generation of the Word, it follows the entire life of Jesus Christ according to what the Holy Apostles have narrated. Some pages have been printed and circulated by his friends so far.) If we wish to look closer to home, Vittoria Colonna, Marchesa of Pescara, and Veronica Gambara—both of them mentioned with honors by Ariosto—as well as Tullia d'Aragona and many others were most famous in Italy.[44] In our times, there are quite a few who play a distinguished role in the renowned Academy of Arcadia,[45] without even mentioning those women beyond the Alps, especially in France, where the intelligence of women is cultivated no less than that of men.[46]

If we turn from poetry to more weighty subjects, and especially to philosophy, which encompasses many sciences and where it seems that there is a need for something other than simply a woman's mind, we discover Cleobulina, daughter of Cleobulus, one of the seven wise men in Greece highly praised by Suidas and by Athenaeus.[47] Pythagoras dedicated some of

43. The original text describes him as "Niccolò Gallio de' Duchi di Alvito"; since his relationship to the dukes of Alvito is unclear, I have omitted his descriptor. No printed copies of Gallio's *De Deo redemptore* seem to exist in any standard bibliographies, but perhaps a manuscript version can be found in Naples. Since it seems to have been only partially printed at the time Barbapiccola finished her preface, it may never have fully made it into print.

44. Vittoria Colonna (1492–1547), Veronica Gambara (1485–1533), and Tullia d'Aragona (ca. 1508–56) were among the most well-known women poets of the Renaissance. Barbapiccola may have particularly liked canto 37 of Ludovico Ariosto's *Orlando Furioso* (1516), where he predicted that women writers would become more famous than men and singled out Colonna as an example of this new kind of literate woman (37.16). In the final canto, Ariosto described his poet reaching the end of the journey and seeing friends waiting for him on the shore, including Gambara (46.3) and Colonna (46.9).

45. Founded in 1690 under the nominal patronage of Christina of Sweden, who died in Rome the same year, the Accademia degli Arcadi quickly became the most important literary academy in Italy in the late seventeenth and eighteenth centuries. While Roman in origin, it established colonies throughout Italy in an early attempt to unify Italian culture through a loose network of institutions. One of the striking features of Arcadia was the number of women, mostly Italian but also foreign, admitted as members. See Elisabetta Graziosi, "Arcadia femminile: presenze e modelli," *Filologia e critica* 17 (1992): 321–58. Barbapiccola was not yet a member when she praised it.

46. This is the first of a number of occasions in which Barbapiccola discusses the *spirito* of women. This complex word can alternately be defined as soul (literally: spirit), mind, and intelligence, and I have alternated among these options depending on what seems most appropriate in English in a particular context. It is important to keep in mind the context in which this word is introduced, because it had been less than fifty years since the publication of Poullain de la Barre's Cartesian treatise on *The Equality of the Sexes* (1674), in which he famously declared: *L'esprit n'a point de sexe* (The mind has no sex). It is unclear whether Barbapiccola read this work, but she uses *spirito* in the same fashion.

47. On Cleobulina, who reputedly remained a virgin to devote herself to learning, see Plutarch, "Dinner of the Seven Wise Men," *Moralia* 148C–E. The probable source Barbapiccola has in mind is Athenaeus, *Banquet of the Learned* (*Deipnosophistai*) 4.171, 10.448. For a general discussion

his works to Themistoclea and Damo, sometimes called Damone, one his sister and the other his daughter. They were so well versed in the philosophical disciplines that the first helped her brother a great deal, while the second succeeded her father as head of his school.[48] Diotima and Aspasia were so learned in these sciences that Socrates did not blush to call the first his teacher and did not hesitate to participate in the lessons of the second, as Plato informs us.[49] Leontion, a young woman with great intelligence and much valor, did not hesitate to write against Theophrastus, an otherwise eminently learned philosopher, to the glory of her name.[50] Even if we omit Hipparchia,[51] whom Laertius mentioned, Amphikleia,[52] discussed by Porphyry in his life of Plotinus, Axiothea,[53] described by Apuleius and Plutarch, and many others, there is Hypatia, whom Suidas and Socrates in book seven mention by saying that she advanced beyond all the philosophers of her time in knowledge. She succeeded in teaching in the Platonic School in Alexandria that the praiseworthy Plotinus began, and she had an astonishing group

---

of ancient women philosophers, a good starting point is Richard Hawley, "The Problem of Women Philosophers in Ancient Greece," in *Women in Ancient Societies*, ed. Léonie J. Archer, Susan Fischler, and Maria Wyke (London: Macmillan, 1994), 70–84.

48. Damo was the most well-known of Pythagoras's daughters who continued his school at Croto (now Crotone in southern Italy) and the one to whom he reputedly entrusted all his writings with the provision that she not sell them. See Diogenes Laertius, *Lives of Eminent Philosophers*, trans. R. D. Hicks (1925; rpt., Cambridge, MA: Harvard University Press, 1979–80), 2:359 (VIII.42). Themistoclea is most often described as a Delphic priestess of Apollo and occasionally described as Pythagoras's sister.

49. Diotima and Aspasia are the only women described as philosophers in Plato's dialogues: *Symposium*, 201d–212b; *Menexenus*, 235e, 236ab, 249d. Diotima (fifth century BCE) of Mantinea allegedly taught Socrates the philosophy of love. Aspasia (470–410 BCE), the most famous of the Athenian women philosophers, was a rhetorician who became the teacher and later wife of Pericles. She reputedly enjoyed the company of philosophers such as Socrates in her home. Mary Ellen Waithe, ed., *A History of Women Philosophers*, vol. 1, *Ancient Women Philosophers, 600 BC–500 AD* (Dordrecht: Martinus Nijhoff, 1987), 75–81.

50. Barbapiccola refers to a debate between the Athenian courtesan Leontion, mistress of the Epicurean Metrodorus of Lampsacus, who objected to Theophrastus's (ca. 370–288 BCE) arguments in favor of marriage and female virtue. See Diogenes Laertius, *Lives*, 2:534–35 (X.6). Theophrastus was one of Aristotle's most famous disciples and his successor at the Lyceum. His writings on marriage were primarily known through their description by Saint Jerome in *Against Jovinianus*. Boccaccio presented Leontion as a morally indecent woman who had besmirched philosophy's reputation; see his *Famous Women*, 251–52.

51. Hipparchia, wife of the Cynic Crates, allegedly dressed as a man in order to study philosophy. She is the only woman deemed worthy of a biographical entry in Diogenes Laertius, *Lives*, 2:98–103 (VI.96–98).

52. Amphikleia studied with Plotinus and married the son of Iamblichus, as discussed by Porphyry in his *Life of Plotinus*, 9.3. Gillian Clark, *Women in Late Antiquity: Pagan and Christian Lifestyles* (Oxford: Clarendon, 1993), 132.

53. Axiothea of Philesia (fourth century BCE) repeatedly dressed as a man in order to become one of the two women whom Plato admitted to his academy. She later taught in Corinth.

of listeners in attendance that came from many places to hear her.[54] Other women also flourished in this school at different times.

Closer to our own age were Abella, Mercuriadis, Rebecca, Trotta or Trotila, Sentia Guarna, and Constanza Calenda in the Salernitan School.[55] They were famous because they taught publicly and because they brought forth many worthy works. So as not to recall only those things that are long past, the memory of the most learned Christina, Queen of Sweden, is fresh. Among her many other virtues, she not only cultivated the philosophy of René Descartes, but also protected and promoted it.[56] Among us, there is still another even more recent, the Duchess of Limatola, praised above, who inherited her profound knowledge of poetry and philosophy from Lucrezia d'Este, Duchess of Urbino, and was marvelously well versed in philosophy, "taking such delight in Cartesian physics and metaphysics that she called it the only science," as one reads in the eulogy of her in volume 32 of the *Journal of Italian Scholars*.[57] Monsignor Doctor Filippo degli Anastagi, then archbishop of Sorrento and now Patriarch of Antioch composed a most eloquent oration of her intellectual and moral virtues on her death, which was published along with other writings by this learned prelate.[58]

54. Hypatia of Alexandria (ca. 355–415 CE), daughter of the mathematician and astronomer Theon and wife of the philosopher Isidore, was the most famous woman philosopher of antiquity. A neoplatonic philosopher and mathematician who was also interested in astronomy, she taught publicly in the city of Alexandria until her murder on October 15, 415, at the hands of angry Christians who had been encouraged to see her as a witch. See Maria Dzielska, *Hypatia of Alexandria*, trans. F. Lyra (Cambridge, MA: Harvard University Press, 1995); and Waithe, *History*, 1:169–95.

55. The source for these comments on the famous *mulieres Salernitanae* is evidently Antonio Mazza, *Historiarum Epitome de rebus salernitanis* (Naples, 1681), 128–29: "Floruere igitur in Patrio Studio docendo, ac in Cathedris disceptando Abella, Mercuriadis, Rebecca, Trotta, quam alii Trotulam vocant, miris sanè encomiis celebrandae, ut notant Tiraquellus, ac Sentia Guarna, ut ait Fortunatus Fidelis." Since the physician Mazza was prior of the College of Physicians in Salerno (1684–92), it is not unlikely that there was some personal contact between Barbapiccola and Mazza, who both shared an interest in reclaiming the tradition of learned Italian women for southern Italy. Thanks to Monica Green for providing me with the exact citation. See Monica Green, *Women's Healthcare in the Medieval West* (Aldershot: Ashgate, 2000); and Green, "In Search of an Authentic Women's Medicine: The Strange Fates of Trota of Salerno and Hildegard of Bingen," *Dynamis* 19 (1999): 25–54.

56. Christina of Sweden invited Descartes to her court in Stockholm in 1649. He died there on February 11, 1650, just four months after his arrival. See Susanna Åkerman, *Queen Christina of Sweden and Her Circle: The Transformation of a Seventeenth-Century Philosophical Libertine* (Leiden: Brill, 1991), 44–69; and Van Damme, *Descartes*, 308–12.

57. *Giornale de' letterati d'Italia*, 32 (1719): 506–13.

58. Unfortunately this publication does not seem to have survived, though further research in the Neapolitan libraries might eventually shed further light on it.

Nor should other women furnished with different kinds of erudition be forgotten if we are to discern clearly that their minds are capable of every-thing men can do. There were a great number of them. Aspasia of Milesia, a sharp sophist and a most skilled rhetorician, was Pericles's teacher and then his wife.[59] The foolish Gentiles believed that Sosipatra, wife of the sophist Aedesius, was educated by the Gods because of her many and varied kinds of learning.[60] Zenobia, Queen of the Palmyrines was so well versed in speaking Greek and Egyptian that she abridged the Oriental history of Alexandria, as Trebellius Pollio writes.[61] Phemonoe was so famous in different kinds of writing that she was worthy of being mentioned honorably by Lucan, Statius, Pliny, Strabo, Eusebius of Cesarea, and others.[62] Cornelia the Roman, mother of the Gracchi and daughter of Africanus the Elder, was praised by Valerius Maximus because, compared to a matron of Campania who showed Cornelia her beautiful and costly ornaments, Cornelia did not display gems and gold, or noble and beautifully bedecked garments at their meeting, but showed the woman her sons, instructed by her in the sciences, in which she was well equipped.[63] They are truly the greatest and most important ornaments that matrons can have.

The Roman noblewomen Fabiola and Marcella were both so learned in sacred studies that Saint Jerome rightfully esteemed them enough to dedicate some of his works to them, because he knew well that they would read and consider his work. Only this kind of esteem should matter in the

---

59. See above, note 22, for more on Aspasia.

60. Barbapiccola makes a mistake in this passage, since the neoplatonic philosopher and mystic Sosipatra (mid-fourth century CE) was actually the wife of Eustathius. After her husband's death, her friend and fellow philosopher Aedesius (called "Ardesio" in the original Italian text) helped her raise her three sons and enjoyed a rivalry with her as a philosophy teacher in Pergamum. The probable source is Eunapius, "Lives of the Philosophers," 466–70, in *Philostratus and Eunapius: The Lives of the Sophists*, ed. and trans. Wilmer Cave Wright (Cambridge, MA: Harvard University Press, 1952), 399–417. Mary R. Lefkowitz and Maureen B. Fant, *Women's Life in Greece and Rome*, 2nd ed. (Baltimore: John Hopkins University Press, 1992), 333–34; and Clark, *Women in Late Antiquity*, 130, 133.

61. Queen Zenobia of Palmyra was defeated by the Emperor Aurelian in 274 CE and forced to live the remainder of her life in Rome. See *Tyranni triginta*, 30, in *Scriptores historiae Augustae;* André Chastagnol, ed., *Histoire auguste* (Paris: Éditions Robert Laffont, 1994), 904–9.

62. Phemonoe was the daughter of Apollo alleged to have invented the hexameter.

63. Cornelia (second century BCE) was the daughter of Scipio Africanus who, after being widowed by Tiberius Gracchus, refused to remarry and devoted herself to the education of her two sons, Tiberius and Sempronius Gracchus. The specific source for Barbapiccola's anecdote is Valerius Maximus, *Memorable Deeds and Sayings*, 4.4. See Corrado Petrocelli, "Cornelia the Matron," in *Roman Women*, ed. Augusto Fraschetti, trans. Linda Lappin (Chicago: University of Chicago Press, 2001), 34–65.

dedication of books, as opposed to the vain pomp of putting a name adorned with many titles of nobility on the front of a book. Eustochium, also Roman and learned in Latin, Greek, and Hebrew, was no less dear than the others to this praiseworthy saint.[64] He called her the prodigy of her time. So also were Ginevra and Isotta Nogarola, both from Verona, prodigies of their time.[65] Poliziano made Costanza, wife of Alessandro Sforza, renowned when he said that she continually had in her hands the works of saints Jerome, Augustine, and Gregory and the two Ciceros, pagan and Christian, by which he meant Lactantius in the latter case.[66] Battista, the eldest daughter of Galeazzo Malatesta, prince of Pesaro, and wife of Guido, duke of Urbino, debated the most learned men many times to her greatest glory, gave an oration that was a marvel in the presence of the highest pontiff Pius II, and composed several eloquent works.[67] Poliziano said that the Venetian Cassandra Fedele treated a book as her wool, a pen as her spindle, and a stylus as her needle.[68] And in more recent times, among those of the female sex who cultivate learning, there is no one who appears more splendid than Anna Maria Van Schurman of Maastricht.[69] Beyond her knowledge of the sciences, she knew

64. Saint Jerome (342–420) was noteworthy among the early Church Fathers for his female disciples and for the religious letters he wrote to pious and learned women. The wealthy Roman widow Marcella, who led a spiritual community on the Aventine in which Fabiola and Eustochium participated, was the recipient of more of his letters than any other woman (*Letters* 38, 40, 43, 44) and the subject of a lengthy eulogy following her death in 412 CE (*Letters* 127). He also eulogized the Roman widow Fabiola, who visited him in Palestine in 394 (*Letters* 77). Eustochium (d. 418/419), the third daughter of Paula (d. 404), accompanied Saint Jerome to the Holy Land around 385 and was the recipient of his famous defense of virginity (*Letters* 22). See Saint Jerome, *Selected Letters*, ed. and trans. F. A. Wright (London: William Heinemann, 1993), esp. 483–97.

65. Isotta Nogarola (1418–66) and her sister Ginevra (1417–61/68) were two of the most well-known women humanists of the fifteenth century. On the works of Isotta, see now in this series, Isotta Nogarola, *Complete Writings: Letterbook, Dialogue on Adam and Eve, Orations*, ed. and trans. Margaret L. King and Diana Robin (Chicago: University of Chicago Press, 2003). For a discussion of her life and work, see King, "The Religious Retreat of Isotta Nogarola (1418–66): Sexism and Its Consequences in the Fifteenth Century," *Signs* 3 (1978): 807–22; and Lisa Jardine, "Isotta Nogarola: Women Humanists—Education for What?" *History of Education* 12 (1983): 231–44.

66. Costanza Varano (1426–47) was already well-known for her Latin erudition by the time of her marriage to Alessandro Sforza, lord of Pesaro, in 1444. A number of her works survive; see Margaret L. King and Albert Rabil Jr., eds., *Her Immaculate Hand*, rev. ed. (Binghamton, NY: Medieval and Renaissance Texts and Studies, 1992), 42–44, 53–56.

67. Battista Sforza (1446–72) was the daughter of Costanza Varano. Barbapiccola confused her son, Guidobaldo, with her husband, Federico da Montefeltro (1422–82).

68. The well-known Florentine humanist Angelo Poliziano (1454–94) wrote a letter in praise of the Venetian humanist Cassandra Fedele (1465–1558) in 1491; see King and Rabil, *Her Immaculate Hand*, 126–29.

69. The German-born scholar Anna Maria van Schurman (1607–78) spent most of her life in Utrecht. Her erudition in ancient languages, history, and theology, her publications on women's

Latin, Greek, Hebrew, Italian, French, Spanish, and German as if they were her native tongue. She has made herself as famous as Madame Dacier, who is praised above for her many beautiful translations of Latin authors into French and for the learned and erudite notes that she has added to them.[70] Let us leave aside for further study the many other ancient women, as well as those modern ones still living, because the list of their names alone would be enough to make quite a fine volume about them.

I have been greatly inspired by the example of these famous women. They have led me to believe that I could one day overcome the weakness of my sex, which only studies in order to know how to play games and to speak knowledgeably of fashionable clothes and hair ribbons. Bad education, not nature, encourages this defect. I began first by cultivating languages and then, as much as my ability permitted, the sciences. Among the latter, I studied philosophy because its moral part makes us civil, metaphysics because it enlightens us, and physics because it informs us about the beautiful and wonderful architecture of this great palace of the world that God made as our home, since it is most indecent to live in it like brute animals. I heard it said that Cartesian philosophy was based on solid reasoning and certain experience, and proceeded with a clear method, deriving one thing from another, for which it had acquired endless followers. For these reasons, I was more inclined to this philosophy than to any other. I wanted to study it from the original source, doubtful of the tiny rivulets that usually do not conserve the original clarity of the water.

Thus I obtained the French translation done by a friend of René, who approved and praised the translation in one of his letters. Since he "hoped that it would be read by more people in French than in Latin, thereby making it better understood," I yearned to translate it into Italian in order to share it with many others, particularly women who, as the same René says in one of his letters, are more apt at philosophy than men.[71] He experienced this with

---

learning, and her correspondence with many important members of the Republic of Letters made her perhaps the most celebrated learned woman of the seventeenth century. She first met Descartes in 1635. See, in this series, Anna Maria van Schurman, *Whether a Christian Woman Should Be Educated and Other Writings from Her Intellectual Circle,* ed. and trans. Joyce L. Irwin (Chicago: University of Chicago Press, 1998).

70. Anne Lefèvre Dacier (1651–1720) was a worthy model for Barbapiccola to emulate, since she was the most celebrated and controversial French woman of letters in the early decades of the eighteenth century, well-known for her 1699 translation of Homer's *Odyssey,* her 1711 translation of the *Iliad,* and numerous other translations and critical works that emanated from her position as France's most noted and prolific Greek scholar in the late seventeenth and early eighteenth century.

71. The French translation of the *Principles* by Abbé Claude Pico (ca. 1601–68) was published in Paris in 1647 and made substantial changes to the text. Barbapiccola quotes from the preface

his great patron Elisabeth daughter of King Frederick of Bohemia, to whom he deservedly consecrated these *Principles of His Philosophy* because she alone, from the time she discovered his philosophy, understood his works, among others, perfectly.

Due to both the gravity and gracefulness of its expressions, our language can render a version of this work that conforms even more closely to the Latin text. I have examined it so that the *Translation* will succeed in being more accomplished and faithful to the author's meaning.[72] Let me mention an additional stimulus to this project. In every age it has been customary to translate books into contemporary languages. Thus, the Romans transposed into Latin the most noteworthy Greek works, both histories and works of doctrine. Once the common people no longer used the Latin language, books written in it were transferred into other languages that succeeded it, in particular, into Italian during the flowering of the sixteenth century, and into French in the past century when more than ever reading was established.[73] This has been a great advantage for those who know no other language than their mother tongue and yet desire to learn. This way the path is open to them, not only to enjoy reading books but also to extract that profit from them that the sciences, which are attached to the study of things rather than words, contain. In every language one can explain things well using their own characteristics, but only concerning those terms of art that were first introduced with sound so that we might have the power to recall them.[74] This principle is observed seriously in this translation.

Therefore, all the beauty of spoken Italian is not discernible here. You should know that I have thought more about how to explain sentiments than how to capture the spoken word. Besides, I cannot avoid a few particular vices in translating one tongue into another, because one always loses the elegance, grace, characteristics, and quality of the original language in which authors have written with such distinction. This is why a copy of a picture

---

to the French edition, entitled the "Author's Letter to the Translator of the Book Which May Here Serve as Preface," while also alluding to the original 1644 dedication to Princess Elisabeth of Bohemia. See Descartes, *Philosophical Writings*, 1:179, 192.

72. On linguistic grounds, Barbapiccola is arguing that an Italian translation of Descartes will capture his intent better than the French version because Italian is closer to Latin.

73. Barbapiccola indicates a good understanding of the evolution of vernacular prose in her comments on its arrival in Italy and France. She also suggests an awareness of literacy as a key factor in the transformation of the goals of knowledge.

74. In this somewhat obscure passage, Barbapiccola seems to be espousing a philosophy of language that suggests the difficulty of capturing the phonetic qualities of language in translation. She also makes a Baconian distinction between words and things, which suggests that her theory of language emanated from her reading of modern philosophy.

by an excellent painter, even if it is made by a masterful hand, never retains the original vivacity.

Given what is required to explain the characteristics of philosophical things, which are difficult to understand, I truly did not feel obliged to bring this *Translation* forth in haste, without having it seen by some learned and esteemed man, just as the French translator did who wanted the judgment of René himself. Since antiquity, it has been usual to do this with books that were meant to be delivered to the public. The *Compendium of the Theodosian Codex*, among others, had the most respectable Anianus as its reviser.[75] But having mustered up the courage to print my translation, I induced myself to do this because I persuaded myself that I had the kind compassion of good men. I hope that others who follow after me in the use of my talent will make a better version, since the works of famous authors usually are brought into another language by more than one translator.

I intended to add here a few small notes and brief reflections in order to show step by step how badly and wrongly people have ascribed many things to this philosophy that its author never dreamed of.[76] I also planned to include a brief but complete summary of the life of René at the front of the book to clarify his approach to his studies and the order he followed to philosophize well, with an additional section on the history of his philosophy. But then I found out that Signor Francesco Spinelli, prince of Scalea, was ready to bring forth a most learned work in which he warns against some falsehoods for which Descartes is held responsible, especially in metaphysics (where he has had his strongest critics).[77] Furthermore, the eloquent translation of the *Brief Life* of our praiseworthy author, composed in French by Monsieur Baillet and translated into a noble Tuscan vernacular by Signor Paolo Francone, Marchese di Salcito, fell into my hands.[78] These knights know how to pair different and profound kinds of learning in the

---

75. Perhaps the text of Anianus (fl. 1300) that Barbapiccola consulted was *Codicis Theodosiani lib. xvi. Quam emendatissimi adiectis quas certis locis fecerat Aniani interpretationibus* (Lyon, 1566).

76. Barbapiccola clearly was inspired by the power and influence of Dacier's notes to her editions of Homer in suggesting that she should do the same with Descartes.

77. Francesco Spinelli (1686–1752) was Paolo Mattia Doria's main adversary in the debate over Cartesian philosophy in Naples. See his *Riflessioni . . . su le principali materie della prima filosofia fatte ad occasione di esaminare la prima parte d'un libro intitolato Discorsi critici filosofici intorno alla filosofia degli antichi e de' moderni & di Paolo Mattia Doria* (Naples, 1733). Evidently Barbapiccola knew about this work long before its publication, so we must see her translation as appearing at the beginning of the exchange between him and Doria.

78. See Adrien Baillet, *Ristretto della vita di Renato Descartes: altramente detto Cartesio, ò Sig. delle Carte: in cui si descrive la storia della sua filosofia, e dell'altre sue opere* (Basilea, 1713). The translation is dedicated to Doria, and in all likelihood the place of publication is actually Naples.

most marvelous fashion, which brings splendor to their lineage. I decided that I should abstain from doing it.

But I am not obliged to abstain in order to free myself from some new kind of bad reputation that this can give me, beyond the one I received from the start and from which I have had to defend myself enough.[79] Some believe that I want to make a science vulgar, which is as sublime as the whole of philosophy, and that I want to communicate it to the ignorant. The ancients, who did not have the veil of another language under which to hide their moral precepts and subtle speculations on natural things, studiously obscured them with enigmas and symbols so that they were not exposed to the common people, who were incapable and badly disposed to understanding them. And then, what's worse, they say that I want to make common a philosophy that corrupts the most solid principles of antiquity and is not well adapted to our holy religion.

Regarding the first point, we know well from scholars that it was not the goal of the ancients to keep things secret, obscuring them with characters and formulas understood by few so that they were not made common. Giambattista di Vico has treated this subject with great erudition and learning.[80] Furthermore, we know that one continually hears complaints deploring the unhappiness of our times. The talented minds of today are no less able to learn the sciences than those of antiquity, but in every respect there are very few who achieve some eminence in these subjects, achieving the glory of the theologians, philosophers, mathematicians, historians, and others in many different areas of knowledge who were greatly renowned in ages long past. Among the reasons for this ill state of affairs, the first is the more powerful because it is well reasoned: the ancients did not consume years and years learning foreign languages to understand the sciences, as we do. Rather, they devoted themselves to knowledge in their own, natural languages from the moment of infancy when they sucked milk from their wet nurses.[81]

79. Unfortunately, no documentation of the controversy to which she alludes survives, but presumably Barbapiccola felt under attack by critics of the Cartesian project in Naples and possibly by others who questioned her ability to undertake such an ambitious project.

80. Giambattista Vico's *De antiquissima Italorum sapientia* (Naples, 1710) was dedicated to Doria. Readers can consult the following modern edition: *On the Most Ancient Wisdom of the Italians*, trans. Lucia M. Palmer (Ithaca, NY: Cornell University Press, 1988). Note that Barbapiccola's spelling of Vico's name, "Giambattista di Vico," gives him a nobility that he did not actually possess.

81. This is another instance in which we see Barbapiccola discussing the relationship between language and knowledge. Like a number of her contemporaries, she took the position that knowledge should be acquired in one's own language, hence Italian rather than Latin or French.

Regarding the other point, even though making a good defense of Descartes's philosophy is neither my subject nor am I worthy to undertake this task, since many eminent men have openly defended every line of his philosophy, in particular, Signor Costantino Grimaldi in his *Response to the Third Letter of Aletino*, yet it is necessary to justify myself in this task with a few brief words.[82]

As far as the idea that Cartesian philosophy wants to betray the solid principles of antiquity by leaving them behind, this seems to have been invented by some people who are extremely committed to this idea. First, it is necessary to keep in mind what Lamindo Pritanio (the pen name of the most learned Ludovico Antonio Muratori) says in chapter 5 of part one of his *Reflections on Good Taste in the Sciences and the Arts*. He demonstrates the great damage that those whom he calls "Premature Judges" inflict on the truth and good taste. He considers one aspect more universal and harmful than the others and it is "the esteem that men conceive for some author or master without the necessary discernment, since they believe him to speak the truth simply because they know that he does."[83] From this error it often happens that they succeed "in making a genius out of something vile and insisting on it. Swearing by the words of their master, they treat his statements as Sacraments, and his opinions as Oracles. In this fashion, they agree to confess to Christ that they have neither contradicted Plato nor Aristotle, thereby keeping philosophy and evangelism in balance," as the most learned Father Bartoli reflects in part two of his little book entitled *Man of Letters*.[84] On this subject, the famous Melchior Cano of Spain also complains in book 10, chapter 5 of his *Theological Commonplaces*. He says that "knowing that there were those in our Italy who were as faithful to their masters and to Aristotle as they were to the Apostles and the Evangelists, those of Christian doctrine were more religious and devout."[85]

After having considered all of this, one thing is certain: when one reads

---

82. Costantino Grimaldi, *Risposta alla terza lettera apologetica contra il Cartesio creduto da piu d'Aristotele di Benedetto Aletino [pseud.] Opera, in cui dimostrasi quanto falda, e pia sia la filosofia di Renato delle Carte* (Cologne [Naples], 1703). This work was part of a heated debate in print between Grimaldi and the Jesuit Giovanni Battista Benedetti, who initiated it with the publication of his *Lettere apologetiche in difesa della teologia scolastica e della filosofia peripatetica* (Naples, 1694) under the pseudonym of Benedetto Aletino.

83. Ludovico Antonio Muratori, *Riflessioni sopra il buon gusto nelle scienze e nelle arti* (Venice, 1708), 70.

84. Danielo Bartoli, *Dell'huomo di lettere difeso et emendato* (Venice, 1655 ed.), 195.

85. Melchior Cano, *Locorum theologicum libri 12* (Cologne, 1585). Unfortunately, I have not been able to locate a copy of Cano's work to check Barbapiccola's translation of his Latin.

and learns things without anticipating anything bad or sinister, things appear completely different than one thinks. And when a bad prejudice interferes, they appear completely different from what they are. Thus, we should read Descartes's philosophy in the way he wants it to be read, that is, from the start as if it were a fable.[86] Step by step we consider the knotting of his arguments. Certainly one will never find novelties outside of those ideas one already esteems greatly, if one does not deduce things by following well-established principles like a continuous chain. Perhaps it may seem to some people that Descartes has a few obscure passages. In order to see their origins, we need only reflect that Descartes appreciated nothing more than thinking carefully about everything he said and saying it in a manner that left his readers thinking even more.

Otherwise, the Author, in part four of article 200, confessed that this philosophy "is nothing new, but is about the most ancient and common as it can be, containing no other principles than those which have been received in every time by everyone."[87] Truly, when one wants to observe things attentively, it is necessary to acknowledge the justice of this statement. Since Aristotle was the first to enter into metaphysical speculations, the Doubt for which Descartes has been criticized came from this wonderful beginning. Jacques Rohault in his book of *Conversations* makes the observation that Aristotle also resolves a few questions regarding the size, shape, and movement of the particles of bodies, and also the pores found between them. He advances a proof of this in the second chapter of book two of his *Analytics*.[88] Many others have considered this problem, but mentioning them here would take us too far away from our main subject. But they have profited from the light of the ancients and their reception by modern philosophers. It is good that this gets out to everyone, because the *Search for Truth* should not be impeded by whim or obligation.[89]

Finally, let us consider the point that Cartesian philosophy is not well adapted to our holy religion. This is just a lot of noise that its opponents—for their own particular ends more than for the love of truth—are spreading

---

86. Barbapiccola certainly expected her readers to be familiar with the famous introductory passages of the *Discourse on Method*. Descartes, *Philosophical Writings*, 1:112.

87. Descartes, *Principles of Philosophy*, 4.200, in Descartes, *Philosophical Writings*, 1:286.

88. While Barbapiccola translates the title of Rohault's book as "Trattenimenti," the French is *Entretiens sur la philosophie* (Paris, 1672).

89. Readers would recognize this passage as a reference to Descartes's *The Search for Truth by Means of the Natural Light*, which appeared in Latin in his *Opuscula posthuma*, ed. P. and J. Blaeu (Amsterdam, 1701).

daily among the ignorant and prejudiced. We must, as the saying goes, strike from the start.

Whenever human wisdom has been founded on weak principles, does it not need the assistance of faith, which proceeds from high and established principles that are revealed by God? There are two equally great evils, as the praiseworthy Father Bartoli informs us in the place I cited, "searching for faith with philosophical curiosity and believing in philosophical things with the certainty of faith."[90] Thus, our first Christians were forbidden to read the works of the Gentiles according to apostolic rule, especially philosophical works because of the sophistries that were found there. The Apostles wanted them to apply themselves only to the Gospel and the other books of the Sacred Bible. This was also true for women and is the reason why the holy maidens produced so many responses to the tyrants that were taken from sacred letters.

As the number of the faithful grew and many Gentile philosophers joined the ranks of those following our Christian religion, philosophy began to be used by Christians as well, either to defend the faith or to impugn those who offended it. And the Fathers knew that Platonic rather than Aristotelian philosophy was more suitable to this purpose, since Plato had famously discussed Divine Providence and the Immortality of the Soul clearly. The same was not true of Aristotle, who did not speak of these things with dignity. His logic was also too confused and his moral philosophy was too human, as Saint Gregory of Nazianzus said in judgment of him in the letter he wrote to Dioscorus.[91] Indeed, on the contrary, he was filled with dogmas opposed to our Holy Faith. Ugo of Siena noted the contrast with those ideas of Plato in the Council of Ferrara.[92] They are collected in a learned and erudite piece of writing by the most eminent Giuseppe Valletta for the defense of modern philosophy addressed to the most holy Pope Innocent XII.[93] He maintains that since the sixth century, the Fathers have embraced and sustained no other philosophy than the Platonic one. Many Greeks—the majority of

90. Bartoli, *Dell'huomo di lettere*, 195.

91. In all likelihood, Barbapiccola had access to the works of Saint Gregory of Nanzianzus through Valletta's *Lettera in difesa della moderna filosofia*. She may also have consulted the most recent edition of his works: Gregory of Nanzianzus, *Opera . . . quo Poemata omne Graece et Latine* (Cologne, 1690). See Valletta, *Opere*, 104, 563.

92. For more on the significance of this council, see Joseph Gill, S.J., *The Council of Florence* (Cambridge: Cambridge University Press, 1959). It is discussed in Valletta, *Opere*, 93–95.

93. Since the second half of Barbapiccola's preface is a reworking of Giuseppe Valetta, *Lettera in difesa della filosofia moderna* (1691–97), this passage serves to remind readers that defending modern philosophy is not incompatible with faith.

them great philosophers like Saint Justin the Martyr, Clement of Alexandria, Origen, and Saint Basil, the praiseworthy Saint Gregory Nazianzus, and others—have happily availed themselves of it both to refute the errors of Gentiles and to establish the truth of the Christian religion. So did the Latins, among whom one counts principally Saint Augustine, a perspicacious genius of profound reflection with an inimitable way of speaking. However it may give strength to Manichaeism or many other heresies, Platonism also knows how to Christianize, so to speak, in such a way that it greatly has helped to sustain Catholic dogmas.

The same thing later happened to Aristotle's philosophy. From the beginning, it was seen as promoting the Arian error.[94] Indeed, Saint Jerome wrote that it was the origin of many heresies. In one place he says that "those heretics leave the Apostle to line up behind Aristotle." In his book against Eunomius, who said that he tried to fell and destroy Christ with Aristotle's weapons, Saint Basil the Great responds to him, "For pity's sake, o crazy man, leave behind Aristotle's wicked and harmful twittering, leave it behind. I warn you against his poisonous and pestilential words."[95] Other most holy Greek and Latin Fathers of that era, and in the period until the age of Saint Bernard, always rail against Aristotle's philosophy in similar ways. Launoy makes a list of them in chapter 2, number 33, of the *Varied Fortune of Aristotle,* detailing the problems this philosophy suffered in the Paris Academy.[96]

The Sacred Councils of those times as well as the Church Fathers vigilantly examined this philosophy, especially a famous Arab council in the

---

94. Arianism was named after its founder, Arius (ca. 260/280–336), who, around 319, came forth with the view that Christ was not eternal with the Father but the first creation of God. In this view Christ was a creature, subordinate to God. Athanasius (ca. 296–373), bishop of Alexandria, strongly opposed Arius, holding persistently to the equality of the Son with the Father. The Council of Nicea was convened by the Emperor Constantine in 325 to resolve the dispute but failed to do so. It was finally settled at the Council of Constantinople in 381, where the orthodox Trinitarian Christian view of God emerged, proclaiming the equal divinity of each of the Three Persons of the Trinity (Father, Son, Spirit). Arianism thereafter gradually lost favor and disappeared after the Franks were converted to Catholicism in 496, though it is worth noting that it enjoyed a certain revival among an educated minority in Barbapiccola's day; Isaac Newton was perhaps the most famous Arian of this period. See F. L. Cross and E. A. Livingstone, eds., *The Oxford Dictionary of the Christian Church,* 3rd ed. (Oxford: Oxford University Press, 1997), 99–100, 104, and sources cited therein.

95. Saint Basil's *Contra Eunomium* is not the source of this quotation. Perhaps she was thinking of Saint Gregory of Nyssa's treatise against Eunomius? Valletta makes the same mistake; *Opere,* 104.

96. Barbapiccola seems to have been confused about the title, since she calls it the "varia fortuna da Aristotle." See Jean de Launoy, *Theologia de varia Aristotelis in Academia Parisiensi fortuna, extraneis hinc inde adornata praesidiis liber* (Paris, 1662). Also cited in Valletta, *Opere,* 354, 373.

time of pope Fabian that forbade the Aristotelian sect that had begun to diffuse widely among the Christians of Alexandria, as well as the Dahuiti one that made its followers swear by the words of Aristotle.[97]

But toward the end of the eighth century and the beginning of the ninth century, Aristotelian philosophy was transmitted from Africa to Europe as Arabs infested many regions, bringing with them the fame of their scholars.[98] It was first introduced to Spain and then France, where the School of Paris began to cultivate it. And even here at different times it suffered diverse fortunes, as Launoy tells us (beyond the problems that Johannes Hermann notes in the Protestant Schools).[99] The Council of Paris in 1209 ordained that Aristotle's books be consigned to the flames and reading them was prohibited. This decree was then confirmed in 1215 by the Cardinal of Saint Stephen in Monte Celio, whom pope Innocent III sent as his legate, and again in 1231 by Gregory IX, who sent a bull addressed to the Parisian scholars.[100] But then Aristotle found shelter there because he was Christianized by Alexander of Alexandria, by the blessed Albertus Magnus, by Saint Bonaventure, and above all by the angelic Saint Thomas Aquinas.[101] Knowing that Aristotle could not be eradicated from the schools, Saint Thomas's intent specifically was to write at least as a Peripatetic in order to refute the errors of his great commentators, Averroes and Avicenna, who caused no small harm to our religion.[102]

Therefore, Aristotle was Christianized but not despoiled entirely of the

---

97. Valletta further elaborates on the "Dahuiti" as an Islamic sect that abandoned the Qu'ran for natural reason. He alternatively spells their name "Da[r]vi[s]i." Valletta, *Opere*, 309, 338. His source seems to have been the works of Abraham Echellensis.

98. Barbapiccola uses the word *scienziati* but the modern term *scientist* doesn't fully capture what she means.

99. I have yet to identify the work by Johannes or Johann Hermann that Barbapiccola mentions.

100. Robert de Courçon, cardinal of Saint Stephen, was a leading church reformer during the papacy of Innocent III and played an important role in preparing the way for the Fourth Lateran Council of 1215. During his trip to Paris in 1215 as papal legate, Courçon reaffirmed the bishops' decree of 1210 forbidding the teaching of Aristotle's natural philosophy in the university. In 1231 Gregory XI had the official regulations of the University of Paris reflect the continuing suspicion of Aristotle by insisting that it not be taught unless it had been purged of all error. David Lindberg, *The Emergence of Western Science* (Chicago: University of Chicago Press, 1992), 216–17.

101. These developments are well discussed in Marcia L. Colish, *Medieval Foundations of the Western Intellectual Tradition, 400–1400* (New Haven, CT: Yale University Press, 1997), 265–315.

102. Barbapiccola's remarks on the great Islamic jurist and medical commentator Avicenna (980–1037) and the great Islamic commentator on Aristotle, Averroes (1126–98) reveal her own prejudice toward the Christian recuperation of antiquity.

barbarism in which the Arabs had clothed him. He began to have a universal following in the Schools that gradually were divided into four types—Thomists, Scotists, Nominalists, and Neutrals[103]—due to the various interpretations they made of him, or based on the different translations of him from his original Greek, or according to the different thoughts of his advocates. Thus, they made him responsible for many falsehoods, either because they didn't understand him or because they didn't even read him or because they believed in the power of lies to increase his significance.

But this did not occur simply because Aristotle was introduced into the Schools. At the same time, some people began to abuse sacred studies, profaning them by excessively intermingling their sophistic vanities with the simplicity and innocence of Holy Doctrine, which also caused no little harm. They raised new questions about the Mysteries of Faith. They made it conform to the rules of dialectic and no longer resolved their questions by respecting the opinion of the Church Fathers, as had been the custom. Thus, horrible errors and execrable judgments emerged from this that forced Catholic scholars to labor greatly to combat them.

Not even Plato's and Aristotle's philosophies were esteemed enough to become Christian and the basis for our Holy Religion. Epicurus's philosophy has been interpreted in a better fashion. The most learned Kunhius did this, according to what Jacques du Rondel says in the life of this philosopher that he wrote for us, in which he says that Epicurus not only explained the existence of God through numbers, like Pythagoras, but also taught that he was purely spiritual and incorporeal.[104] Francis Bacon defended him from the infamy of Atheism in his *Moral Essays*.[105] What's more, Saint Augustine praised him greatly in his book *On the Utility of Believing to Honoratus* and preferred him over all other ancient philosophers in *The City of God*, because, in another life, Epicurus had believed in punishments and rewards.[106]

---

103. Among the four groups, the first three are well-known as the followers of Thomas Aquinas (1224/25–1274), Duns Scotus (1265/66–1308), and William of Ockham (ca. 1285–1347). Who the "Neutrals" are is less evident, though the name suggests that they were those who chose not to take a strong position.

104. Jacques du Rondel, *De vita et moribus Epicuri autori Iacobo Rondello* (Amsterdam, 1693). This passage is also reproduced in Valletta, *Opere*, 240.

105. Francis Bacon, "Of Atheisme," in *The Essays or Counsels, Civill and Morall*, 2nd ed., ed. Michael Kiernan (Oxford: Clarendon, 2000), 51 (essay 16). Also cited in Valletta, *Opera*, 240. In the original text, Barbapiccola identifies Bacon simply as "Verulamio."

106. Augustine's *De utilitate credendi* (ca. 390s) was an attack on Manichaeanism addressed to his friend Honoratus. Barbapiccola seems deliberately to misread the point of Augustine's descrip-

Now much has been made of other Gentile philosophies where one perceives clearly their impiety. But why don't you, who read this work, receive favorably the philosophy of a Catholic, as René Descartes was, who spread his metaphysics following the beliefs of Saint Augustine, and who wanted his physics to be coupled with experience? He did not depart from the principles laid down by other ancient philosophers and submitted everything he wrote down "to the judgment of the wisest men and to the authority of the Catholic Church," according to the sentiments and words that he expresses here in the end.[107]

I do not wish to say anything more on this subject, leaving the rest to the sagacity and knowledge of my readers. As a crowning point, I estimate that it is well worth adding that which the most learned Father Hyacinthe Serry of the truthful Order of Preachers (Dominicans), who to his highest honor is a professor at Padua, presented as a theory in one of his *Opening Lectures* for the beginning of classes in 1718 and happily proved. A short version of it appeared in the *Journal of Italian Scholars*, tome 31, article 12, page 431, reported with these following words: "that is, that the discoveries of modern philosophers should not be immediately rejected as contrary to the truths of our Holy Faith. Rather they should first be considered and examined carefully to see if they can agree with them, since many things which seem contrary to the Holy Faith at first glance really are not opposed to it. The Holy Documents often adapt their ways of speaking to the intelligence of the common people. But if we take them in their deepest sense, they agree with the Moderns. We can introduce many examples. Finally the spirit of God did not dictate Scripture to teach physics or mathematics but

---

tion of the third kind of error, which uses the example of a man who misread Epicurus to make the point that we perceive what we want to in the words we read (Augustine, "The Advantage of Believing," trans. Luanne Meagner, in *Writings of Saint Augustine*, vol. 4 of *The Fathers of the Church*, ed. Ludwig Schopp [New York: Cima Publishing, 1947], 2:403–4). Similarly, Augustine does not express admiration of Epicurus in the *City of God*. He critiques materialists for placing too much faith in the reality of corporeal things (8.5; 14.2) and argues against an Epicurean worldview as both doubtful and deceitful (8.7), while noting that the Athenians admired the Epicureans (18.41). In 1722 the trials of the "atheists," accused of atomism and other philosophical heresies, had been put to rest for little more than a decade after almost thirty years of conflict between the Holy Office and those who upheld the freedom to philosophize in Naples. All this is to say that Barbapiccola raised some controversial issues that had not been entirely resolved. See Osbat, *Inquisizione*.

107. In the final passage of his *Principles of Philosophy*, Descartes underscored his obedience to the Catholic Church by submitting his views to its judgment, telling his readers: "And I would not wish anyone to believe anything except what he is convinced of by evident and irrefutable reasoning." Descartes, *Principles*, 4.207, in *Philosophical Writings*, 291.

to demonstrate how to perfect our habits and to show us the pathways to Heaven, and not natural phenomena."[108]

This is what I was able to say in a brief letter about things that in order to be discussed fully would need more than a few pages and require more than my lowly talent.

Translated by Paula Findlen

108. The author in question was Jacques Hyacinthe Serry (1659–1738). Possibly, the text in question became his *Praelectiones theologicae: theologicae, dogmaticae, polemicae, scholasticae habitae in cele-berrima Patavina Academia* (Venice, 1742). The language of Serry's article in the *Giornale de' letterati* clearly invoked the sentiments expressed by Galileo in his *Letter to the Grand Duchess Christina* regarding the proper relationship between knowledge and faith. Barbapiccola's decision to end her preface with an eighteenth-century French theologian's paraphrase of Galileo's argument was, to say the least, controversial. It seems quite clear that she did not share Descartes's caution in presenting her views, because she was, among other things, a disciple of Valletta.

THE DEBATE OF THE ACADEMY
OF THE RICOVRATI

TRANSLATOR'S INTRODUCTION

The year was 1722. Newly elected to head the prestigious Ricovrati Academy in Padua, Antonio Vallisneri (1661–1730), the natural philosopher and chair of theoretical medicine at the University of Padua, dispatched a letter to his friend Antonio Muratori, the historian and Ducal librarian at Modena Ludovico. In it he unveiled his plan to begin a radical reform of the academy's intellectual aims and exchange.[1] The frivolous scholastic disputes that had become a standard practice of the Ricovrati were, he averred, unworthy of these "grave men" and of the academy itself, which, after all, had been founded in 1599 by, among others, that master of "the new science" Galileo Galilei.[2] Vallisneri planned to abandon archaic academic games for more pragmatic and scientific intellectual discourse, beginning, he tells Muratori, with a critical examination of the question of educating women. In light of Vallisneri's instrumental work to advance modern scientific methods and theories in and beyond Italy, his desire to inaugurate a new analytic age of the academy with a debate about women would seem remarkable.

By the time he wrote his letter to Muratori, the sixty-one-year-old Vallisneri had achieved international acclaim as a vigorous advocate and practitioner of Galileian experimental philosophy. Born to patrician parents in the city of Trassilico, near Modena, where his father was papal governor, Vallisneri was educated first by his father and then by the Jesuits in Modena.

---

1. On Ludovico Antonio Muratori, see Angelo Solerti, *Autobiografie e Vite dei maggiori scrittori italiani* (Milan: Albrighi, Segate, & C. Editori, 1903), 535–78; and Sebastiano Brigidi, *Vita di Lodovico-Antonio Muratori: La sua mente e il suo cuore* (Florence: Galileiana, 1871).

2. On Galileo's role in founding the academy, see Diego Valeri, *L'Accademia dei Ricovrati Alias Accademia Patavina di Scienze, Lettere, ed Arti* (Padua: Sede dell'Accademia, 1987), 10.

He attended a Catholic college in Reggio Emilia, where he took a degree in Aristotelian philosophy. It was his subsequent training at the University of Bologna under the founder of microscopic anatomy, Marcello Malpighi, however, that was to steer his intellectual trajectory. Under Malpighi's guidance and the influence of writings by the physician and scientist Francesco Redi (1626–97), Vallisneri came to espouse a "philosophy of facts,"[3] drawing general laws from meticulous and extensive scrutiny of natural phenomena. From his early studies of comparative anatomy and entomology at Reggio and Bologna, he developed a keen interest in embryology. Among his first and most influential publications was a series of *Dialogues on the Curious Origin of Many Insects* (1696), in which he extended Redi's findings against prevailing theories of the spontaneous generation of insects.[4] This work led to his appointment as Chair of Modern Experimental Philosophy at the University of Padua, which was later redesignated the first Chair of Practical Medicine. Vallisneri's intellectual interests greatly exceeded the bounds of medicine, however. His prolific publications and correspondence reflect an expansive range of scientific inquiry, from the earth and planetary sciences to zoology, anatomy, archaeology, and hydraulics. In his *History of the Generation of Man and Animals* (1721) can even be discerned protoevolutionary biology and genetics. His scholarship won international recognition, as evidenced by his induction into prestigious European academies, including the Institute of Sciences in Bologna in 1707 and the Royal Society in London in 1703.[5]

What then explains his determination to confront the "grave men" of the Ricovrati with the question of women's education rather than a more explicitly scientific problem? Perhaps better than any other event during the early Settecento, his proposal reflects the transformative effect of burgeoning Enlightenment thought and ethics on the treatment of the "woman question" among members of the Italian Republic of Letters. For Vallisneri, as for the rising class of modern experimental philosophers like him, a prime object of scientific inquiry was the practical enhancement of the public good.

---

3. Nicola Badaloni uses this expression to describe the experimental philosophical principles adhered to by such followers of the Galileian heritage as Vallisneri and his compatriot and colleague Antonio Conti. Badaloni, *Antonio Conti: Un abate libero pensatore tra Newton e Voltaire* (Milan: Feltrinelli, 1968), 10.

4. Redi stopped short of disputing the spontaneous generation of insects in all cases. He upheld the belief that insects were spontaneously generated in plant galls.

5. On Vallisneri, see Dario Generali, introduction to *Epistolario*, by Antonio Vallisneri, ed. Dario Generali (Milan: Franco Angeli, 1991), 9–72; G. A. di Porcia, *Notizie della vita e degli studi del Kavalier Antonio Vallisneri*, ed. Dario Generali (Bologna: Patron, 1986); and American Council of Learned Societies, *Dictionary of Scientific Biography*, ed. Charles Coulston Gillispie, vols. 13–14 (New York: Scribners, 1970–90), 562–64.

As historian Dario Generali has observed, Vallisneri saw himself as part of a "single international scientific community" collaborating to discover and to write the natural history of the world and to spread this new scientific knowledge, ultimately in order to improve the human condition.[6] In his work as editor, with Apostolo Zeno and Scipione Maffei, of the *Giornale de' letterati d'Italia*, Vallisneri can be seen working toward all of these ends by disseminating new texts and ideas in Italy and promoting Italian modern scientific theories and methods both at home and abroad. His decision to write all of his major treatises in the vernacular rather than Latin is further indication of his commitment to the *bene pubblico* (public good). In keeping with the Galilean tradition, he sought to make the "new science" known to a broad literate public and not just the learned. The efficacy of science (understood as both knowledge as well as critical empirical analysis) for the good of society and the modern state lay at the heart of the question of women's education and was for this reason of special interest to Vallisneri. He, like increasing numbers of eighteenth-century *lumi*, advocated rational examination of this age-old issue, which was seen to have new relevance in the contemporary "critical age." If the *common masses* of women were formally instructed in the arts and sciences, these *accademici* asked, would they better fulfill their primary functions as guardians of the nation's young and managers of the domestic economy, functions essential to the well-being of the domestic sphere, society, and the modern state?

This was not the first time that the Ricovrati had broached the "woman question," however. Indeed, women had been eagerly discussed before 1723, as in debates over "Whether It Is Better for Those Who Serve Women to Win Their Hearts by Enduring or by Resenting Women's Amorous Injuries"; "What Would Be More Laudable, to Exclude Women from Government as the Romans Did, or to Admit Them as Did the Greeks?" and "Which Would Be More Desirable Given a Reign of Government Led by a Woman, a Woman Dedicated to Arms or to Letters?"[7] But by comparison with the debate on the education of women held in 1723, these arguments had been rhetorical and without genuine practical or political merit. They were, as Vallisneri wrote to Muratori, unrealistic and therefore irrelevant issues that needed to be supplanted by such real problems for pragmatic academic disputation as the question of women's learning.

Thus, in accordance with Vallisneri's command as Prince of the Ricovrati, at nine in the evening of June 16, 1723, the intellectual and social elite of Padua gathered in the green room of the Prefect's Palace to hear a debate on the question: "Should Women Be Admitted to the Study of the Sciences and the Liberal Arts?" Music played, hot drinks were served, and Guariento's refulgent frescos of the hierarchy of the angels set the mood as the hall filled with academicians, notable citizens, and, according to notes taken at the time, "ladies, who had come there in marvelous numbers."[8]

In his introduction to the proceedings, Vallisneri explained that he had selected the topic in response to the "bitter complaints, blunt rebukes, and . . . harsh disputes against men" by "illustrious, noble, and spirited women" for their having been generally denied admittance to the study of the arts and sciences.[9] Eloquently, and somewhat hyperbolically, Vallisneri declared the academy's intention to submit a well-worn subject to a modern, analytic critique and underlined the debate's historic importance: "The case, therefore, O most Noble Listeners, is grave and most worthy of your attention; its outcome is awaited by the governments of every well-regulated Republic, and it conveys consequences of great weight."[10]

Despite Vallisneri's claims about the rational method and the magnitude of the debate, however, the reform of the Ricovrati's academic discourse was, in fact, more conceptual than it was practical. The debaters, Guglielmo Camposanpiero (1691–1765), poet, scholar, and chief librarian at the University of Padua,[11] and Giovanni Antonio Volpi (1686–1766), a noted scholar, publisher, and professor of philosophy, Greek, and Latin at the University,[12]

---

8. Accademia patavina, MS B, *Giornale delle adunanze*, 275. For a detailed overview and analysis of this event and its implications for the representation of women in Italian Enlightenment discourse, see Messbarger, *The Century of Women: Representations of Women in Eighteenth-Century Italian Public Discourse* (Toronto: University of Toronto Press, 2002), 20–48.

9. Antonio Vallisneri, "Introduzione," in *Discorsi accademici di vari autori viventi intorno agli studi delle donne* (Padua: Giovanni Manfrè, 1729), 1.

10. Vallisneri, "Introduzione," 4.

11. According to Attilio Maggiolo in *I soci dell'Accademia Patavina dalla sua fondazione, 1599* ([Padua: Accademia patavina di scienze, lettere, e arti, 1983], 59), Camposanpiero was a frequent speaker at reunions of the Ricovrati. His discourse on women, was, however, his most famous. He was heavily involved in the administration of the academy, holding the posts of secretary (1717–19); prince (1725–31); censor (1740–51); and counselor-treasurer (1754–56). He was a member of other prestigious academies, including the Crusca and the Agiati of Rovereto.

12. On Volpi, see Marco Callegari, "'Tipografi Umanisti' a Padova nel '700: I fratelli Volpi e la Stamperia Cominiana," *Archivio Veneto* 145 (1995): 31–63; Marco Callegari, "La tipografia Volpi-Cominiana (1717–56): Gestione dell'azienda ed attività commerciale," *Bollettino del Museo Civico di Padova* 80 (1991): 279–301; and Maggiolo, *I soci dell'Accademia Patavina*, 359. As regards administrative posts held by Volpi in the Ricovrati Academy, he was secretary (1716–17) and prince (1743–45).

generally adhered to the conventions of the *querelle des femmes*, the formal controversy about woman's nature and abilities dating from Boccaccio's *De mulieribus claris* (ca. 1350). Traditionally, the "woman question" had served more as a pretext for male academicians to display ingenious rhetorical variations on a set of standard arguments than as a serious inquiry into women's capabilities.[13] This held true, by and large, for the participants in the 1723 debate, which was as stage-managed as any theatrical production.[14]

Camposanpiero rested his defense of women's education on a catalog of celebrated and accomplished women already conventional to the genre, from Aspasia to Isabella Andreini, a noted sixteenth-century poet and *commedia dell'arte* actor, and cited arguments that he deemed sympathetic toward women made by patriarchs of the Western cultural canon from Plato to Bembo. Volpi, by contrast, relied heavily on ancient humoralism and reiterated the customary argument that the "inordinate" fluids women require to perform their primary reproductive function leave their physical fibers too weak and flaccid to sustain concentrated activity in the brain, thereby precluding women from serious thought and analysis. In order to appeal to the elite women in his audience, however, each of the participants also inserted reformist and prowoman arguments and in places even disavowed his more masculinist positions, thus producing an internally divided discourse that would contribute importantly to the evolution of the question as the Italian Enlightenment progressed. As so many male intellectuals had done before them, the academicians of the Ricovrati met in an arena of entrenched male

13. On the controversy as genre, see Linda Woodbridge, *Women and the English Renaissance: Literature and the Nature of Womankind, 1540–1620* (Urbana: University of Illinois Press, 1984); Joan Kelly, *Women, History, and Theory: The Essays of Joan Kelly*, ed. Catherine Stimpson (Chicago: University of Chicago Press, 1984); Ruth Kelso, *Doctrine for the Lady of the Renaissance* (Urbana: University of Illinois Press, 1956); Constance Jordan, *Renaissance Feminism: Literary Texts and Political Models* (Ithaca, NY: Cornell University Press, 1990); Albert Rabil Jr., "Agrippa and the Feminist Tradition: The Other Voice in Agrippa's Declamation on Women," in *Declamation on the Nobility and Preeminence of the Female Sex*, by Hernicus Cornelius Agrippa, ed. and trans. Albert Rabil Jr. (Chicago: University of Chicago Press, 1996); Margaret L. King, *Women of the Renaissance* (Chicago: University of Chicago Press, 1991); Margaret King and Albert Rabil Jr., *Her Immaculate Hand: Selected Works by and about the Women Humanists of Quattrocento Italy*, rev. ed. (Binghamton, NY: Medieval and Renaissance Texts and Studies, 1992). For a conflicting though thoughtfully argued study that treats the formal controversy about women of the Italian and English Renaissance, see Pamela Joseph Benson, *The Invention of the Renaissance Woman: The Challenge of Female Independence in the Literature and Thought of Italy and England* (University Park: Pennsylvania State University Press, 1992).

14. Vallisneri selected Volpi and Camposanpiero for participation in the debate and assigned their roles.

privilege to engage in a debate about women. But the nature and tone of their proceedings were influenced by the advance of Enlightenment ethics and, even more palpably, by the presence of the women before them.

In each case, that appeal to the female audience began by separating women into the ordinary and the extraordinary (intellectual as well as economic) and restricting their arguments to the common mass of women, not to those of high rank and quality. Camposanpiero even went so far as to claim that, in fact, the debate was not about whether all women should be educated—an absurd idea—but about whether the female elite worthy of the privilege should be taught. Even Volpi qualified his remarks by instructing his female listeners to exempt themselves from his antifeminist comments. And Vallisneri, in his role as judge, concluded by allowing an education to only those women "in whose veins flow clear and illustrious blood, and in whom burns and sparkles a spirit outside of the norm, surpassing that which is common to the masses, exactly that which I recognize in you, O noble, and by your many titles, most esteemed Ladies." Ambivalence and inconsistency thus mark this disputation, which is traditional and self-consciously and reluctantly revisionary at once. The incongruities that characterized the debate, unorthodox within the rhetoric of the *querelle des femmes*, derived unmistakably from the growing recognition by elite and intellectual men that upper-class women constituted an influential interest group whose existence and attitudes in themselves contested the conventional constructions of femininity.

This uneasy awareness of women's interests, desires, and growing public authority revealed itself even more starkly in the version of the debate published six years later, in 1729. In response to the outcry that arose from women in and outside of Padua at the publication of Volpi's argument against the education of women in 1723,[15] the original arguments of the debate participants were supplemented with apologies for women's education, including *Oratio qua Ostenditur Artium liberalium studia a femineo sexu neutiquam*, a Latin oration in defense of the education of girls by the nine-year-old prodigy Maria Gaetana Agnesi (translated in this volume);[16] an oration on

---

15. Giovanni Antonio Volpi, *Discorso Accademico, Che non debbono ammettersi le Donne allo Studio delle Scienze, e delle Belle Arti; da lui recitato in Padova nell'Accademia de Ricovrati il dí 16 Giugno 1723 sopra il Problema proposto dall'Ill. Sign. Antonio Vallisneri, Pubblico Primario Professore di Medicina Teorica nello Studio di Padova, e Principe di essa Accademia* (Padua: Giovanni Manfrè, 1723).

16. On Agnesi, see Paula Findlen's introduction to the translation of Agnesi's oration in this volume; Paula Findlen, "Translating the New Science: Women and the Circulation of Knowledge in Enlightenment Italy," *Configurations* 3.2 (1995): 184–91; and Giovanna Tilche, *Maria Gaetana Agnesi* (Milan: Rizzoli, 1984).

the importance of educating noblewomen in moral philosophy that had been delivered to the Ricovrati by Guiseppe Salìo, one of its number; and the forceful rebuttal of Volpi's arguments written by the Sienese noblewoman Aretafila Savini de' Rossi, with her disparaging footnotes appended (rebuttal and notes are translated in this volume).[17] Moreover, the text of the debate now included disclaimers (also translated here) undoubtedly aimed at a female readership by the editor of the edition, Volpi himself, who now disavowed the adversarial stance he had taken six years before.

Volpi's ambivalent voice of male authority in the 1729 text, more poignantly than any other contribution to the debate, reflects the changing, often conflicted views about women among eighteenth-century *accademici*. His approval of a traditional social order in which men occupy the world and women the home is plain from his argument against women's learning. Yet he is also acutely mindful of the expanding public presence and authority of women that threatens the old order. His frequent direct appeals to the women in attendance at the debate and his multiple apologies to his female reading public in the 1729 volume, in which he both defends and disclaims his argument against women's education, reflect a struggle to reconcile old and new paradigms of femininity. Although the few known details of Volpi's life fail to explain his ambiguous response to the question of women's education and, more generally, women's place and function in contemporary society, they do shed some light on his conservative ideological disposition.

One of four lettered brothers from a wealthy bourgeois Paduan family, Volpi and his brother Gaetano directed an esteemed, though commercially unsuccessful, press that opened in 1717 on the first floor of the family home. An affiliated bookstore under the management of Giuseppe Comino, from whom the bookstore and press took their name (Stamperia Cominiana), opened in the Volpi residence the following year. The Volpi brothers also published the aforementioned *Giornale de' letterati d'Italia* edited by Vallisneri, Maffei, and Zeno, which advertised texts forthcoming from their press. The express aim of the press was the publication of superior quality literary classics in Italian and Latin, as well as refined devotional texts that reflected the Volpis' conservative Catholic views. Their specialized catalog

---

17. On Savini de' Rossi, see Messbarger's introduction to the translation of her rebuttal to Volpi in this volume; Messbarger, chap. 1 of *The Century of Women*; Antonella Giordano, *Letterate toscane del Settecento* (Florence: All'Insegna del Giglio, 1994), 146–48; and Maria Bandini Buti, *Poetesse e scrittrici: Enciclopedia biografica e bibliografica italiana*, vol. 6 (Rome: Istituto Editoriale Italiano Carlo Tosi, 1941), 219–20.

of books was designed for an elite reading public from the academic and ecclesiastic classes. Giovanni Antonio was in charge of compiling the list of literary texts for publication, which centered narrowly on master Italian narratives, including Poliziano's *Stanze*, Castiglione's *Cortegiano*, Della Casa's *Galateo*, Dante's *Divina Commedia*, Torquato Tasso's *Aminta* (not *Gerusalemme Liberata*), morally sound selections from Boccaccio's *Decameron*, and Petrarch's *Canzioniere*. Although they also published contemporary historical, philosophical, and scientific works by such authors as Ludovico Antonio Muratori, Scipione Maffei, Marcello Malpighi, and Giovanni Battista Morgagni, the brothers were disdainful of popular literary currents, especially such "sinister" genres as novels, comedies, and collections of poetry "for every frivolous theme."[18] "Dishonesty and profane love are implicit in these . . . obscene and lewd books in prose and verse," wrote Gaetano Volpi, "and vanity, curiosity and indolence are fomented by novels, novellas, and illusory and romantic stories."[19]

The Volpi publishing enterprise thus served an exclusive clientele possessed of extensive academic preparation and the wealth necessary to purchase precious texts. While the Volpi brothers grudgingly recognized the growing number of consumers of popular contemporary literature—women were prominent among these—and the financial success of publishers who catered to the "unrefined" literary appetites of these readers, economic success was for them subordinate to maintaining the material and moral virtue of their products. Theirs was a zealous project of cultural conservation in terms of both the literary canon and social distinctions: by means of exquisite paper, ink, and binding, they preserved the noble verses of Dante, Petrarch, Virgil, and other canonical authors for the cultural and social aristocracy. Discernible in Gaetano's criticism of the "new" reading public is, moreover, a latent masculinist bias. He condemns the "infinite vile and useless" books, produced by less scrupulous presses, for inciting in the unlettered "vanity, curiosity, and indolence," conventional "feminine" vices. Indeed, the "dishonest" genres listed by Gaetano (novels, novellas, occasional poetry, and romantic stories) themselves have more than a whiff of the "feminine" about them.

Despite the brothers' professional allegiance to an old cultural and social order in which erudition—access to Latin and Italian literature—was a privilege of the *noble* few, they were keenly aware that their endeavors were futile. The market soundly rejected their costly editions, on which they took

---

18. Callegari, "Tipografi umanista," 46–47.
19. Cited by Callegari, "Tipografi umanisti," 46.

significant losses. Gaetano Volpi's irate censure of the widening distribution of low-cost editions of canonical texts among the untutored multitude must be read as a nostalgic lament as well as an implicit admission of the irrelevance of their press in the current expanding market for economic cultural goods: "It is truly a great shame to see such rare and admirable art demeaned in the hands of vile and ignorant people, who are barely able to read, and who have no appreciation for the many demands and intricate subtleties of this [art] and, even worse, who are willing to be aided by anyone at all in order to save money."[20]

What applicability do the professional designs of the Volpi brothers have for interpreting Giovanni Antonio's position on the question of women's education? It is reasonable to infer that this conservator of the literary canon exclusively for a male academic elite would have viewed widening the access of women, especially bourgeois women, to learning as a dangerous diffusion of culture. To educate women in the arts and sciences would mean placing "rare and admirable art" in the hands of the uncultivated and the ill-prepared—a dangerous democratization of the Republic of Letters. However, just as the Volpi brothers were forced to acknowledge that, despite their best efforts to preserve the great works for the select few, the diffusion and commercialization of culture was well underway, Giovanni Antonio was faced with an expanding literary republic that included more and more women.

Inciting Volpi's ambivalence in the 1729 text was, therefore, the authoritative presence of women, a presence that signaled a change not only in the culture of the Ricovrati but in the broad cultural landscape of eighteenth-century Italy as well. At the end of the seventeenth century, the Academy of the Ricovrati had been among the small number of academic institutions in Europe to open its ranks to women as honorary associates; these included, in 1678, Eleonora Cornaro Piscopia, the first woman in Europe to receive a university degree;[21] in 1679, Anne Lefèvre Dacier, the French philosopher and translator;[22] in 1685, Madame de Scudéry;[23] and four years later,

20. Cited by Callegari, "Tipografi umanisti," 51.

21. On Cornaro Piscopia, see Attilio Maggiolo, "Elena Lucrezia Cornaro Piscopia e le altre donne aggregate all'Accademia Patavina dei Ricovrati," *Padova e la sua provincia* 24, (1978): 33–36. I am grateful to Paula Findlen for this source.

22. On Anne Dacier, see Fern Farnham, *Madame Dacier: Scholar and Humanist* (Monterey, CA: Angel Press, 1980).

23. On Scudéry, see Constant Venesoen, *Etudes sur la littérature féminine au XVIIe siècle: Mademoiselle de Gournay, Madame de Scudéry, Madame de Villedieu, Madame de Lafayette* (Birmingham, AL: Summa Publications, 1990).

Maria Selavaggia Borghini, the Pisan poet, translator, mathematician, and *salonniere*.[24] As honorary associates, however, these women were prohibited from voting, from holding office within the academy, and, except on rare occasions, from addressing the academy. And of the twenty-five women granted membership during the seventeenth and eighteenth centuries, only four were Italian; the rest were natives of France who never set foot within the academy. Significantly, too, no women had been deemed worthy of induction even as an honorary associate in the twenty years or so before 1723. At the time of the debate, women's presence in the academy was, therefore, essentially symbolic.

But with the inclusion of women's dissenting voices, equal in command to those of the "grave men" of the academy, in the published version of the debate, its text effectively rewrote the events of 1723 and formally recognized women's increasing relevance and authority within the academy and the broader sphere of intellectual discourse generally throughout Italy. As Vallisneri had indicated in his introduction to the debate, a new critical age demanded that old questions, customs, and beliefs be reevaluated and put to the test of reason and disinterested scientific analysis, and the woman question was primary among these. The Ricovrati's literal and literary treatment of the woman question in the debate of 1723 and in the published text of 1729 thus served as a preview to the complex and continuing evolution of the formal controversy about women over the course of the Italian Enlightenment.

In its 1729 version, the Ricovrati debate was an ideologically conflicted text remote from the rhetoric and method of previous entries in the *querelle des femmes* and of academic discourse in general. Its text re-presented and simultaneously repudiated the traditional misogynist arguments of 1723. Conventional notions of women contended with Enlightenment ethics and protofeminist resistance within and among the texts in the collection— effectively opening the traditional discourse of the academy to the cultural and social changes taking place beyond its protective walls. And by so doing, the published version displaced the rehearsal of stock arguments by the designated adversaries, Camposanpiero and Volpi, from centrality. Instead, it foregrounded the spontaneous clash between the dominant male intelligentsia, as represented by Volpi's text, and the group of recalcitrant educated women, as represented by Aretafila Savini de' Rossi's *Apologia* and

---

24. On Borghini, see *Dizionario biografico degli italiani* (Rome: Istituto della Enciclopedia Italiana, 1960–), 12.676–77.

Maria Gaetana Agnesi's *Academic Oration*, with its demand for a turn at the public podium and its assertion of a singular authority over questions concerning women.

Rebecca Messbarger

TO THE GRACIOUS AND LEARNED READER,
FROM GIOVANNI ANTONIO VOLPI

Not long ago, gracious and learned reader, the members of our Academy of the Ricovrati applied their intellects to the curious problem: *Should Women Be Admitted to the Study of the Sciences and the Liberal Arts*, proposed by Cavalier Antonio Vallisneri, Public Professor of Theoretical Medicine at this celebrated university, physician to the reigning Emperor Charles VI, a man greatly renowned throughout Europe for his superior learning and, at the time, Prince of that literary assembly. By my ill fortune, I was called upon to maintain the negative view (as decreed by the Academy, and whose laws I was obliged to obey); and having arrived, as they say, at this slippery slope, I sought to temper my words in some way so as to offend neither the noble female listeners present at my discourse nor any other members of the fair sex, not departing from my custom, since I have always thought that we owe respect and esteem to women. Despite my attempt at rhetorical tempering, as I had feared, my discourse achieved the opposite effect, and thus brought me universal condemnation instead of praise. Moreover, a short time later, after it was published and disseminated in various Italian cities at the request of many reputable individuals desirous of a copy, a great clamor arose along with the suspicion that I, perhaps incited by passion or a wicked genius, had wanted to denigrate the merits of women and, adding insult to injury, to promulgate these slurs everywhere. Those who know my feelings and way of life fully understand how far this is from the truth.

Not all of the defenders of women, however, held such an opinion about me. There were some who sought to refute my arguments fairly, without accusing me either of passion or of malice, and who instead interpreted my statements positively, imagining that I was compelled to write and speak in this way either at someone else's behest, or for some other honest reason. Among these is the Illustrious Signora Aretafila Savini de' Rossi, eminent Sienese lady and resident of Florence, who, jealous of the honor of her sex, wished to take up arms in defense of this common cause and, unsatisfied with glossing my speech with witty and judicious footnotes here and there, also countered it by a very learned letter addressed to a cavalier. She demonstrates that if women devoted themselves to cultivating the sciences, it would not only prove a great benefit to individual families but to human life generally. In this letter the force of her intellect shines no less than her courtesy; she always treats me not beyond hope, but rather as an open-minded adversary, one disposed to cede victory.

When the letter fell into the hands of the aforementioned Signor Vallisneri, he graciously shared it with me, and we agreed that it was necessary to republish my argument, which had been the origin of these disputes, and which was desired by many since copies could no longer be found among the booksellers. We agreed to include the footnotes of the lady in the margins along with her sage letter of reply, which might be called an apology for the education of women. He likewise advised me to take charge of this reprint and to collect in a small volume not only the compositions already mentioned but also the *Introduction to the Problem* that he himself had presented, together with his *Judgment*; as well as the *Argument in Favor of Women's Education* by Signor Guglielmo Camposanpiero, a most noble Paduan cavalier, and most learned in the choicest literature; another similar discourse on the same topic by Signor Giuseppe Sanò, a celebrated and most talented individual; and finally, a brief Latin oration on the same topic, delivered not long ago in Milan by a girl perhaps nine years of age, a true testimony to what women can achieve from the youngest age. He told me that this collection was meant to satisfy fully erudite women and their allies, and to demonstrate openly the sincerity of my intentions to uncover nothing but the truth. I let myself be persuaded by his advice, and by the authority of so great a man. I gladly accepted the task; I collected the essays; I had them printed; and I thought to add my own *Protest* in which I declared the real reasons for my *Argument against the Education of Women*. Having judged that all this should suffice to erase every shadow of suspicion about my character from people's minds and feeling no remorse of wrongdoing, I chose to enhance the prestige of this volume by dedicating it to the ever-venerated name of a great lady, my sole benefactress,[25] and to thereby give her a small sign of my gratitude, and by this clear declaration to demonstrate the certainty of my convictions, since I would never dare to present something that did not honor the fair sex, or her, who by every account is one of the principal glories of this same sex. It seemed necessary to me, gentle Reader, to make you fully aware of this affair. Live happily.

---

25. Volpi dedicated the volume to Elisabetta Cornaro Foscarini, the wife of the Procurator of Saint Mark's.

INTRODUCTION BY SIGNOR ANTONIO VALLISNERI,
PUBLIC PROFESSOR OF THEORETICAL MEDICINE AT THE
UNIVERSITY OF PADUA, PHYSICIAN TO HIS IMPERIAL AND
CATHOLIC MAJESTY, ON THE PROBLEM PROPOSED BY HIM
ON THE 16TH OF JUNE, 1723 WHILE HE WAS PRINCE OF
THE ACADEMY OF THE RICOVRATI: SHOULD WOMEN
BE ADMITTED TO THE STUDY OF THE SCIENCES
AND THE LIBERAL ARTS?

If I had not heard from illustrious, noble, and spirited women, adorned and arrayed with every superior attribute, their bitter complaints, blunt rebukes, and, indeed, their harsh disputes against men for having been generally denied an education in the sciences and liberal arts, I would not dare on so solemn a day, in so venerable a gathering, in a city, by the loftiest signs, greatly renowned for letters and arms, I would not dare, I say, to propose a problem that will seem to some superfluous and, perhaps, even laughable, for the opposite view seems long since to have been validated by custom, by sage teachers, and by legislators who consider themselves advanced in the government of their peoples. But since, most noble listeners, we live in so admirable and prudent a century, a most severe critic of every opinion, of every judgment, of every history, of every action, and of every custom, most successful discoverer of infinite deceptions, of many childish credulities, and of innumerable hidden truths (not to say falsehoods), a century in which everything is put to the test with disinterested and dispassionate rigor, and in which the yoke of authority of writers, even those of the first rank, has been shaken off, nothing is exempt from scrupulous investigation; and nothing is held to be true that clear reason aligned with experience do not make manifest. Therefore, it should be no surprise that I am submitting a question for your wise consideration that appears already to have been decided. It is, however, still greatly in dispute (if I see rightly) and depends, or at least seems to depend, on the decision of the judge.

We have by now refuted the dark centuries whose dreams and fables certain grave men in long robes and venerable beards with marvelous arrogance had taught to the less knowledgeable as regards the sciences and arts of this lowly earth, in the manner done to naive children. To cite the Poet: "Remaining by the fire to weave, the old women"[26] recount strange,

---

26. The citation is from Virgil's *Aeneid*, 8.408–9: "cum femina primum, cui tolerare colo vitam tenuique Minerva in positum, cinerem et sopitos suscitat ignes," ["the hour when a woman might rise for Minerva to earn a living with slender spindle, stirring drowsy sparks at a fireplace," trans.

marvelous things, tedious jokes, and mirthful yarns, and with superhuman credulity, eyebrows raised and mouths open, they gulp these down as truth. But no more are such mundane assumptions accepted, nor should they be, unless proved by reason and experience (although I know antiquated, even false, opinions do continue to hold sway in the minds of men). Wherefore, if experience were to show itself to be united with reason in today's dispute, and the grievances of so worthy, gracious, and lovely a sex to be just, this case would be decided, which is not in itself new, but new would be its common good use, new would be your praise, O most learned academicians, and new would be the glory of all of your kindly austere and honest ladies, celebrated by the followers of Martial, Claudius, Tacitus, and many other authors of the highest virtue, for the honor of the sex and for the example of all women. Adding new praises and virtues to the ancient accolades, these will be extended to all women, who will become the object of every most rare and resounding veneration.

Praise of you will be no less than that given to many other of today's famous living women from various European cities, of whom Italy boasts a great number. Not long ago in Venice a very learned noble Venetian, who honors us today with his presence, brought to light an illustrious collection of Italian poetry composed solely by women, which clearly displays and promotes the ability of their spirit and the litheness of their intellect, and so shames those many men born to be nothing more than part of the herd and a useless burden to the earth they tread.[27] Moreover, the poems demonstrate the great love by which the Muses, who are also female, can more readily and modestly guide other females, just as Athena, the Goddess of Wisdom, with greater ingenuity and justification conceivably favors her own sex with the more somber and more sublime virtues.

The case, therefore, O most Noble Listeners, is grave and most worthy of your attention; its outcome is awaited by the governments of every well-regulated Republic, and it conveys consequences of great weight: it concerns increasing the number of new, great minds dedicated to the letters and sciences, such that these minds may be illuminated and elevated to the highest degree, for the disorder of centuries past, for the example of those to come, and for the decorum owed to your motherland, forever grand, forever revered, tireless cultivator of every science and art.

Edward McCrorie (Ann Arbor: University of Michigan Press, 1995), 180.] A variant of this verse is also found in Petrarch's *Canzoniere*, 33: S.26.5: "Levata era filar la vecchierella."

27. The "noble Venetian" to whom Vallisneri refers is Giovanni Batista Recanati, author of *Poesie italiane di rimatrici viventi raccolte da Teleste Ciparissian Pastore Arcade* (Venice: Sebastiano Coleti, 1716). My thanks to Elisabetta Graziosi and Marta Cavazza for their help in identifying this text.

So, let the problem that we address today be: *Should Women Be Admitted to the Study of the Sciences and the Liberal Arts;* and in this way we shall see if women have reason on their side when they frankly censure and strongly lament the warped and traitorous politics and the pure injustice by which, they say, men condemn them in the flower of their youth to the needle, the spindle, the spinning wheel, and other toilsome domestic cares, when they should instead be learning the foundations of language and the sciences in order one day to be ready and able to penetrate the darkest and thorniest mysteries of the earth and the heavens, and to elucidate all the most obscure and hazy truths.

I will listen therefore, O most learned academicians, to the arguments for and against their cause, in order to rule (I beg your mercy), from my place, as they say, on the judge's bench. I will ponder the merits of each argument without passion, merits no longer influenced by personal considerations, but rather determined by the cold, wrinkled age that, willy nilly, advances at great strides within me, and which renders remote from and alien to me any suspicion of blind adoration or of adulterated reason. And if I should be an inexpert judge of them, I ask you to judge both them and me. To you I grant the glory of supreme judgment, and I will keep for myself the crimson blush at having judged ineptly, and will content myself with the sole merit of having acted in your service.

WOMEN SHOULD NOT BE ADMITTED TO THE STUDY OF THE SCIENCES AND THE LIBERAL ARTS. AN ACADEMIC DISCOURSE BY SIGNOR GIOVANNI ANTONIO VOLPI

Translator's note: The original manuscript included an unnumbered note by Volpi, reproduced below,* as are notes written by Aretafila Savini de' Rossi criticizing Volpi's arguments, which are marked by symbols.

As my gentle and learned adversary was undertaking to defend with sound and ingenious arguments that side of the debate that would be most acceptable to the noble womanly sex (whose honor he has always defended loyally, as is required of such a cavalier), he thought that N. N. had burdened me with a harsh and arduous a task.[28] I was assigned the difficulty of sustaining

---

*This is Sig. Guglielmo Camposanpiero, Paduan patrician, a young man much revered and esteemed by me, who, in keeping with the nobility and generosity of his birth, conjoins courtesy, prudence, and learning—*Giovanni Antonio Volpi.*

28. "N. N." signifies "the unnamed."

the weaker part, and of thus assuming the distinct risk of rendering myself loathsome to those whom I least desired to offend. By this act, however, N. N. firmly believed that he had honored me, not the opposite. Perhaps too magnanimously judging that I might have something worthy to say, he wanted me to take up the less plausible argument so that I would acquire the name and the reputation of a brilliant man. On these points I recognize his generosity toward me as well as the great regard he has shown me. And, to be truthful, before I began to consider seriously the matter of the present problem,* I believed that my situation was truly as he had claimed. When I came to fully comprehend my role, however, I was quite distressed. I would either have to shame myself by incompetently defending my part, or by constructing false and obvious arguments to support an offensive campaign from which I would garner from those who are wise and knowledgeable not esteem as a good philosopher but censure and reproach as a malicious sophist. Do not ask how much these things disturbed me. Yet, after examining the question more closely, I found that I had in my hands too facile an argument to treat in the way I had originally thought. I dismissed my fear of incurring the wrath of those persons whose good graces anyone with sense should try to cultivate above all.[I thus possess the courage necessary to prove that denying women knowledge of the sciences and the liberal arts would not only serve republics, but would be a great benefit to women themselves,† from whom I hope through this proposition to gain benevolence rather than any disdain or disfavor.]Furthermore, the illustrious women now listening to me, who are manifestly elevated above the common mass of women by the splendor of their blood, by their education and by the greatness of their spirits and intellects, should in no way apply to themselves what I intend to say about the female populace at large, as they know quite well that there is not a law in the world or a tradition so rigorous as to preclude exceptions for those endowed with singular merit.‡

To begin, I assume that we are not now arguing whether we should reform the custom followed since ancient times by nearly every nation calling for the education of males in arduous exercises of the body and mind, but which has spared females these dangers and toils as that more delicate portion of humanity, assigning to them instead the peaceful management of the family under the command either of fathers, brothers, or husbands, and keeping them in activities and work appropriate to their delicacy and to the

*He was right to believe this; the first ideas are always the best—*Aretafila Savini de' Rossi.*
†Here is the deceit—*A. S.*
‡Overblown adulation that destroys the argument—*A. S.*

comeliness of their visages. For if this were the argument, then all who came before would be thought to have had very little judgment; and it would be almost as if, after the passage of so many centuries, the heavens suddenly selected us to be the first among men to use reason conversely;* and we would at the same time see the most stable foundations of civilization collapse. I therefore judge that the current question centers on a praiseworthy desire to know whether ancient men acted rightly or wrongly by first introducing such a tradition and then passing it, generation after generation, to their successors, and what the reasons were that incited them to act in this way. Despite my adversary's assertion that there is no law that explicitly prohibits the education of women, he is nonetheless forced to admit the existence of this tradition that outweighs the most stringent of laws;† and if it were otherwise, our question would be pointless. Now, disregarding the question of how much respect is owed so ancient a custom, that has been rendered ever stronger by the approbation of nations and the abiding experience that has made its utility manifest, a utility which no one can reasonably doubt at this point, and assuming, but not conceding, that the ancients were motivated to keep women out of academies and schools by their tyrannical desires and violent spirit of domination, I ask, then, why women acquiesced in so unjust a situation and subjugated themselves to so great a wrong without otherwise protesting.‡ I will be told—I can see it clearly—that deficiencies of physical strength rather than of intellect prompted women's patience and accommodation of this condition. But I aver that this is a baseless retort. As we can plainly see, even the greatest physical force is subordinate where intelligence abounds; of this, lions, tigers, elephants, and many other fierce and muscular animals, disarmed and domesticated by human industry, offer the fullest and most obvious proof. It is therefore necessary to conclude that whosoever shoulders the yoke and allows himself to be led by another's judgment and discretion (when this is not done for that most noble end of pleasing God) is not only wanting in and poorly endowed with physical strength, but lacks intelligence as well. It is for these reasons that primitive and robust peoples more willingly endure their subjugation, in contrast to those possessed of subtler intellects and natural superiority. Moreover, it proves that tyrants owe their place on the throne more to the stupidity of their subjects than to their own sagacity. Let no one reply that intelligence conjoined with physical force necessarily will prevail over intelligence alone, and that precisely

---

*It would not be the first idea of the ancients that the moderns have corrected—*A. S.*

†Not a tradition, in fact, but an abuse—*A. S.*

‡And to whom should they protest?—*A. S.*

for this reason women are unjustly oppressed by men—despite ceding nothing to men in prudence or wisdom—because among the human species we
frequently observe that the vigor of the brain marvelously agrees with the
temperature of the body, and where the body has abundant humidity, such
that the fibers are rendered weaker and to a certain extent relaxed, the brain
is deprived of the strength sufficient to ponder sublime notions. Small children, whose excessive humidity* leaves them intellectually wanting, validate
my claims.

That the same is true of women, those will judge who are much more
learned in natural science than I. When Aristotle wrote that "the softer of
flesh are the more intelligent" (*Physiognomics*, chap. 6), he was not speaking
about the young or the female, but was instead referring to men who are
excessively coarse or dry, in whom the opposite cause, that is, the excessive rigidity of the fibers,[†] resulted in the infirmity of their minds and their
stupidity.[29] But why, my lords, am I dealing with these false suppositions? I
wished to say all of this not because I believe it, but to better defend my
cause, rebutting every possible counterargument in this way.[‡] In addition,
I aver that neither were those men tyrants who introduced the aforementioned tradition, nor were women without judgment when they devoted
themselves primarily to the needle, the spindle, and their other domestic
duties and put aside the study of letters. On the contrary, these women were
moved by wisdom and judgment and knew themselves so well (in this they
were more advanced than men) that they did not want to be put to the test,[§]
and instead took up those activities they knew to be appropriate to their

---

*Rather, it is for a lack of spices that they are this way—A. S. [Here Savini de' Rossi is punning
on the dual meang of "spezie": species and spices.]

[†]Women, who are in fact naturally possessed of fibers neither too lax nor too rigid, will therefore
be without one or the other exception—A. S.

[‡]I don't know how falsehoods can bolster an argument that one truly wants to defend—A. S.

[§]The deal made by women referred to here is an ingenious supposition on the part of Signor
Volpi, who will never find record of our community's rejecting the right to an education—A. S.

29. The brief argument of *Physiognomics*, whose attribution to Aristotle is in question, seeks to
supplant pervasive unscientific physiognomic methods with a comprehensive systematic and
scientific analysis of bodily signs. Volpi's reference to this text, and book 6 in particular, is
clearly disingenuous. The author of *Physiognomics* is concerned throughout the treatise, and
especially in book 6, with proving female inferiority. Indeed, book 6, which ends the treatise,
concludes with the statement, "the male sex has been shown to be juster, braver, and, speaking
generally, superior to the female." (Aristotle, *Minor Works*, trans. W. S. Hett [London: William
Heinemann, 1936], 137.) Moreover, although the meaning of bodily signs is influenced by
placement, genus, and general disposition, soft flesh (associated with the female) is predom-
inantly an indicator of poor character and intelligence, while muscular flesh (associated with
the male) reflects greatness of mind and character.

delicacy, as that excellent tutor nature instructed them. And by this same infallible law, they understood that beauty was the real endowment of their bodies, as modesty and reticence were the ornaments of their spirit. They began to cultivate these two noble qualities with great care (I am speaking of the wise and discreet), in this way gaining dominion over that proud animal known as man, subjugating the fiercest warriors with their sweet and cherished violence, and skillfully incapacitating the most antagonistic and severe philosophizers with beautiful and gentle artifice.

→Indeed, it seems to me that the great attributes bestowed upon women render them more fortunate in some ways than men. A little thought will suggest how much, for example, a young man, even one of high birth, must sweat, toil, and wrack his brain in order to please the woman he loves; and how little time and effort, by contrast, a woman requires to win the love of whoever sees her. Men must know how to speak well, play cards, fight, dance, ride horseback, and a hundred other things on pain of seeming boors and fools if they do not. But a woman is born equipped with everything she needs to subjugate the will of men. Without moving a muscle, without uttering a word, simply with a modest glance, a smile, a gesture, a small sigh slowly suspired from her breast, a woman is often more persuasive than the most eloquent orator. If, then, the health of the whole gives balance to the parts of which it is composed, so that the one is not subjugated by the other, women, who are also a principal part of the republic, can never fairly lament that they remain subordinated to men because they have been denied learning and science,* when, even without these, they have been furnished such fine weapons in the form of charm and beauty, which are found everywhere; and for them to ask for that which was given to us by heaven so that we could resist them, would be asking for too much, indeed would amount to a desire to oppress us.†

I admit that it would be a lovely thing to see young maidens together with boys, in the manner of ancient Sparta, attending classes at the university and lower schools;‡ and perhaps in that case we would find that boys would no longer flee their teachers, as now happens, but would instead more willingly attend class, even without a snack. But I'm not convinced that either boys or girls would benefit from study in these circumstances. It seems to me that there is some reason to believe that their eyes would often stray

---

*To maintain the balance of the parts of the republic in this way, it would be necessary to deny the most intelligent an education so that they would not subjugate the others—*A. S.*

†A fine fulfillment of their roles!—*A. S.*

‡If this was the custom of the Spartans, it is not an ancient tradition to deny women an education—*A. S.*

from their books and would wander during recitations. And if someone were to say to me that females could be educated separately from males, I would ask how, in that case, the tutor could be supervised to insure that he did not teach them more than was necessary, without their being deprived of the stimulus of emulation, which in comparison to men could have the force of inciting in them a greater desire for knowledge.*

[But, jokes aside,† if women began to philosophize, either they would want to remain perpetual virgins, or they would submit themselves to the yoke of matrimony. I intend to prove that, in either case, learned women, should their numbers become great, would cause grave damage to the human species and to civil society.]Dwelling upon the first stage of life, who does not understand that nature produced women for that sole end, that through her the species is preserved, she who has been destined to conceive offspring, to nourish it with her own substance, enduring (as punishment for original sin) the tedium of nine long months of pregnancy, during which she is afflicted with feeble limbs, stomach pains, fainting, boredom, and irritation. Then, suffering atrocious pain and evident risk of death, she gives birth to this off-spring, and afterward nourishes it with her own milk, and cares for it until it leaves infancy; burdens all troublesome, if not intolerable, which that union between man and woman called *matrimony* has assigned to her rather than to him. If women devoted themselves to scientific speculation instead and so wanted to preserve the flower of their virginity intact, what woe for human affairs. Nature would not realize the presumed end of bringing women into the world. Moreover, the knowledge of the miseries to which every woman is subject who takes a husband, knowledge that would become more acute in learned women, would make it more likely that they would abhor marriage, while, on the other hand, the pleasure of an education would prompt them to live more independently, following in that way the example of famous ancient women‡ and some modern women as well, who, in their love of learning, care nothing for their "other" spouse. If time permitted, I could list several dozen of these women without the least fear of betraying my cause, since I never intended to deny absolutely that women are occasionally born virile and exceptional and are admired as a consequence. However, I would argue only that such regard should not be given the common mass of women. We see, moreover, that many philosophers are interested only in nourishing their spirits with beautiful and rare ideas, and give no thought to marrying.

---

*That same form of emulation would be found among women that is now present among men —A. S.

†Jokes that destroy—A. S.

‡Another confirmation of the wisdom of ancient women—A. S.

I believe it was for this reason that the ancient storytellers cast the Muses as virgins living in the woods and the mountains far from the common din.*

But let us also grant that erudite spinsters would not disdain the marital yoke. Even then, the affairs of the world would go very poorly. Aristotle in his books on economy and Plato in those on law, especially in the *Alcibiades*[30]—but why need I cite them when the thirty-first Proverb of Divine Scripture itself assigns to the married woman, as her explicit vocation, the care of the family, the sound discipline of the servants, responsibility for food and clothing, exercise of the distaff and the needle, and finally the happiness of the entire household, as she was created by God to be neither a spendthrift nor too animated in her spending, but rather to be restrained and discriminating.[31] Studies, by contrast, naturally make people negligent

---

*Virgins with children—*A. S.*

30. Of the distinct roles of men and women, Aristotle states in the *Oeconomica*:

> Thus the nature both of the man and the woman has been preordained by the will of heaven to live a common life. For they are distinguished in that the powers which they possess are not applicable to purposes in all cases identical, but in some respects their functions are opposed to one another, though they all tend to the same end. For nature has made the one sex stronger, the other weaker, that the latter through fear may be the more cautious, while the former by its courage is better able to ward off attacks; and that the one may acquire possessions outside the house, the other preserve those within. In the performance of work, she made one sex able to lead a sedentary life and not strong enough to endure exposure, the other less adapted for quiet pursuits but well constituted for outdoor activities; and in relation to offspring she has made both share in the procreation of children, but each render its peculiar service toward them, the woman by nurturing, the man by educating them. (Aristotle, Oeconomica, book 1, 343b, trans. E. S. Forster, in *The Works of Aristotle*, ed. W. D. Ross [Oxford: Clarendon Press, 1921], vol. 10)

Plato's *Alcibiades* has been called a "drama of philosophical seduction," in which Socrates attempts to convert to philosophy the young Alcibiades, a simultaneously heroic and notorious general and statesman of fourth-century BCE Athens and Sparta. See Nicholas Denyer, introduction to *Alcibiades*, by Plato, ed. Nicholas Denyer (Cambridge: Cambridge University Press, 2001), 1–29. One section specifically treats the question of the distinct areas of expertise of men and women. In chapter 21, on "Friendship and Oneness," Socrates prompts Alcibiades to conclude that women, and not men, know wool-spinning, while men, not women, know politics as their natural sphere of accomplishment.

31. Chapter 31 of Proverbs defines the virtues of the good wife. These contrast in striking ways with the feminine attributes of beauty and idleness fervently praised by Volpi earlier in his argument. The proverb reads:

> When one finds a worthy wife, her value is far beyond pearls. Her husband, entrusting his heart to her, has an unfailing prize. She brings him good, and not evil, all the days of her life. She obtains wool and flax and makes cloth with skillful hands. Like merchant ships, she secures her provisions from afar. She rises while it is still night, and distributes food to her household. She picks out a field to purchase out of her earnings and she plants a vineyard. She is girt about with strength, and sturdy are her arms. She enjoys

and careless, inattentive to income and all that is esteemed by society, neither elegant nor prompt in the least and often in need of reminders to eat,
go to bed, change their clothes, and so on.* To echo the teachings of the
poet Horace (the comments of whom are much less severe than those of the
philosopher): "The heart of a poet is not blindly set on gain; he loves verses
and studies those alone. . . . [He does not contrive to defraud an associate or
an orphan boy.] He lives on pulse and a loaf of bread"† (epistle 1, book 2),[32]
we would deem that family sad where a learned woman, ever desirous to
know more, had set her foot, because, as Petrarch states: "How can one hold
others dear, who holds himself so vile?" (Canzoniere 29).[33]

I will concede that a discreet matron should be educated in everything
that is appropriate to her office, even by means of books, but she should
not want to reach for the stars by abandoning her home to the will of her
servants in order to remain in abstract thought, contemplating things useless
to her and detrimental to the other members of her family.‡ But the potential
outrage would not only lie here, my lords; worse would be to come. I believe
that all of you will gladly agree with me that the happiness of a household
depends in large part upon the unity between the husband and the wife.

---

the success of her dealings; at night her lamp is undimmed. She puts her hands to the
distaff, and her fingers ply the spindle. She reaches out her hands to the poor, and
extends her arms to the needy. She fears not the snow for her household; all her charges
are doubly clothed. She makes her own coverlets; fine linen and purple are her clothing.
Her husband is prominent at the city gates as he sits with the elders of the land. She
makes garments and sells them, and stocks the merchants with belts. She is clothed
with strength and dignity, and she laughs at the days to come. She opens her mouth in
wisdom, and on her tongue is kindly counsel. She watches the conduct of her household,
and eats not her food in idleness. Her children rise up and praise her; her husband,
too, extols her: "Many are the women of proven worth, but you have excelled them
all." Charm is deceptive and beauty fleeting; the woman who fears the LORD is to be
praised. Give her a reward of her labors, and let her works praise her at the city gates.
("Proverbs Chapter 31," in *New American Bible* [Washington, DC: U.S. Conference of
Catholic Bishops, 2001], 1–2 [database on-line])

*Idiotic stoicism, more often than not feigned—A. S.

†The poet learned these maxims in the school of philosophy, which liberates the spirit in order
to scorn fortune, causes it to abhor vice, and to live frugally. How right for us to achieve this
by means of an education—A. S.

‡Do not claim that women will study so much that they will be thrown into ecstasies—A. S.

32. "Non temere est animus: versus amat, hoc studet unum; . . . Pupillo, vivit siliquis, pane
secundo" The Latin actually reads: "vatis avarus non temere est animus; versus amat, hoc studet
unum. . . . [Non fraudem socio puerove incogitat ullam pupillo]; vivit siliquis et pane secundo."
I wish to thank Albert Rabil Jr. for his careful reading and translation of this citation.

33. "Come / Tien caro altrui, chi tien sè così vile?" This citation actually comes from Petrarch's
celebrated political canzone, "Italia mia," *Canzoniere* 128, that calls for peace from Italy's warring
princes.

→Now, given that a husband, according to natural and divine law, is called upon to govern, and a woman to obey,* imagine what dissension and quarrels would be heard the day long between these two if the woman, grown self-important by knowledge, were no longer willing to obey blindly, and at every opportunity argued with her spouse and demanded an explanation for his orders, even when she did not wish to claim for herself part or all of the authority.† And what should I say about the cruel jealousy that might easily arise in the heart of a stupid husband who, by his misfortune, found himself a female philosopher? How many suspicions (not always unreasonable) would he harbor about her doings, correspondence, malice, and betrayals!‡ How much disquiet and anxiety might be aroused in such a pathetic mind at seeing her courted by erudite youths, applauded by esteemed assemblies, revered, and perhaps desired by many in power? And if the situation were no worse than what has been described here but were merely a case of the breakdown in that harmony produced when men define themselves by their gravity and women by their charm—harmony that would necessarily be put at risk if all women were admitted to the study of the sciences—wouldn't this alone cause considerable disorder? And so it is thus, my lords.

From the beginning, woman was created to serve not only as helpmate to man, but also as a diversion and an innocent delight for him, who, returning home thoroughly exhausted from public or private affairs, would find a comfort to dispel his vexing thoughts and restore him from the pressures he has suffered. But what repose, what respite would he find in a woman who, instead of greeting him benevolently, confronted him with thorny questions without giving him a moment's breath,§ so desirous is she to have an account of the day's business (as if she were capable of understanding it), to discuss with him some new theorems, to have him listen to her narrate some stories, and so determined is she to persist without end in twittering on and in driving him mad, when he would like to amuse himself with other things. If the cords of a zither were all to be grave or acute, or if all the elements in the world wanted to reign regardless of their proper station, all would return to its original chaos. If the parts of the body competed to exercise the most noble functions, disdaining the lower but necessary ones, such sedition

---

*The husband must demand only things that are just, and the woman who is wise will not only recognize these but will anticipate the command—A. S.

†The ignorant often quarrel without knowing why—A. S.

‡Consider how malicious men would be, who are this learned—A. S.

§It would be for lack of judgment and not a lack of wisdom that would prompt her to ask such questions at an inopportune time—A. S.

would destroy the very life of the body by upsetting its operations. I am well
aware, my lords, that having until now spoken about the public good, and
having tried with all my might to demonstrate the wisdom of our ancestors
in dividing the roles of the one and the other sex[I will be accused by some
of my listeners of putting forth deceptive arguments that support men's reputation for intelligence and ambition, and of neglecting my obligation to
sustain the other side as I had promised.]However, in my opinion, whoever
wishes to judge correctly and dispassionately will admit that not only men
but women, too, contribute to the public good that results from maintaining
and observing established conventions and that the good that is enjoyed by
the entire body redounds in each part of the republic[But, while this is most
true, I nevertheless intend to satisfy expectations and keep my promise by
putting forth other arguments]

I am absolutely certain that if this question were to be decided not by
our Academy or by its most worthy and learned Prince, but instead by an
assembly of the most civil and respectable young women found in Padua,
I would be victorious.[†] For if we were to educate those few women whom
nature endowed at birth with a magnanimous and generous spirit, indeed
those most noble women now listending to me,[†] all the others would doubt-
less be loath to hear our intention to deny them the mirror, the spindle, the
skeinwinder, and their life in the shade, in order to bring them to hear philosophical precepts about how the world is made, about the principles that
govern reality, about the essence of the soul, and a thousand similar questions, things which we scholars have long studied but have attained no more
mastery of than idiots—things unimportant, too, to the many men who take
pleasure only in eating, drinking, sleeping, playing cards, hunting, and, in
short, having a good time and amusing themselves, men who wouldn't spend
a dime to be transformed overnight into either a Plato or a Demosthenes.[‡] [34]

In my own experience, I have encountered extremely few women who,
when a conversation about literature began, did not immediately blun-
der,[§] and who did not distort their features by turning a stony face to the
originator of these discourses, which they treat as dry, withered, and taste-
less, only to finally relax and unfurrow their brows when the subject changed
to textiles, fashions, fairs, love, and other interesting and pleasant events.

---

*I greatly doubt it. He appears to be praising Paduan women, but he offends them by considering
them incapable of understanding how he wrongs them—*A. S.*

†Typical adulation—*A. S.*

‡These same Men are those most disdained by anyone possessed of a modicum of sense—*A. S.*

§This happens precisely because they are uneducated—*A. S.*

34. Demosthenes (384–322 BCE) is known as the greatest of the Greek orators.

What need is there, then, for my most noble adversary to labor to defend an education which they don't prize and which, in fact, they amiably mock when they make fun of those excessively studious men as too grave, ill-mannered, and unworthy of their affections. In my opinion, women should not make the same mistake by imitating such men, because, as we often see occur, instead of making people more capable in the management of affairs and at civil conversation, protracted and intense studies usually make them uncouth, taciturn, preoccupied, bizarre, lovers of solitude, and, to a certain extent, hateful of other people.* Indeed, it often happens that natural, pure, and genuine wisdom unadulterated by art or education brings matters to a more favorable end than does wisdom acquired by poring over books until one grows pale. History affords us ample proof: the Romans, in expanding the boundaries of their vast empire, cared nothing for the erudition or the eloquence of the Greeks, who, for all of their syllogisms, had to bow their heads to the majesty of Rome and revere, face down, the fasces of the unkempt, poorly spoken, but strong and disciplined Latin Consuls.†

Women have always been favored by the heavens with a certain intuitive understanding that we men could never acquire were we to study for a hundred years.‡ I remember reading in chapter 15 of Homer's *Ulysses* that, while they prepared to depart from the house of Menelaus, the King of Sparta and their host, Pisistratus, son of Nestor, and Ulysses's son Telemachus, who had gone there for news of his father, upon observing a certain omen, beseeched Menelaus as a man of great wisdom to give them an explanation. While Menelaus mulled over many things in his mind in order to avoid erring in his answer, he was preempted by his wife, Helen, who was also present, and who, with the gods' enlightenment, predicted exactly what, according to the omen, would take place upon Ulysses's return.§ 35

---

*Misanthropes more imaginary than real—*A. S.*

†The literacy of the Greeks and the ferocity of the Romans are attributes too different to be compared. The Greeks, although subjugated by violence, never lost the benefit of their learning. Moreover, when they had conquered the Greeks, the Romans were no longer unkempt and poorly spoken—*A. S.*

‡Was this understanding that is so incompatible with a deficient and poorly-prepared genius instilled by nature or was it cultivated by an education?—*A. S.*

§Even the Ass of Balaam reasons by means of inspiration.—*A. S.*

35. Homer, *Odyssey*, chap. 15, 160–81: "I will read this matter as heaven has put it in my heart, and as I doubt not that it will come to pass. The eagle came from the mountain where it was bred and has its nest, and in like manner Ulysses, after having traveled far and suffered much, will return to take his revenge—if indeed he is not back already and hatching mischief for the suitors." This is one in a series of four bird omens that predict Odysseus's return home and destruction of the suitors (trans. Samuel Butler [Internet Classics Archive by Daniel C. Stevenson, Web Atomics], http://classics.mit.edu/Homer/odyssey.html.

Now, who cannot see that without attending school, the most noble sex
has many natural powers of foreseeing and advising, and that it would be a
wasted effort to compel them to learn by paying for what they are granted
freely by the heavens when the need arises? What would be the point of
subjecting women's delicate complexion and the gentle fabric of their bodies
to the vigils, the fatigue, the sweat, and toil that whosoever goes in search of
knowledge must needs suffer? Let those lovable creatures preserve the fresh
and chaste flower of their beauty, which is cherished (not without great reason) both by them and by men; and let them not risk miserably losing this
by acquiring a wan and washed-out color, a sullen look, a shy manner, un-
gainly gestures, and an affected mode of speaking that reeks of erudition, all
of which would leave them deformed and disagreeable.* Let them envision
the many lettered men who, from their excessive desire for knowledge, have
lost and continue to lose their serenity of spirit, the health of their bodies,
and even life itself. Certainly a number of these men languish, go mad, face
hatred from their superiors, fight viciously with their rivals, and burn with
anger when certain new sprouts grow near them and every day become more
fruitful. And from these rivalries come animosities, rancor, slander, calumny,
and a thousand other ghastly vices and villainies from which it is right that
the humane and lovable womanly sex keep its distance. Let them equally
consider that there is no oriental gem so precious and worthy of such vigi-
lant care and jealousy as that noble shyness and modesty, whether virginal
or matronly, which conjoins with beauty to make woman a most sweet and
marvelous spectacle in the eye of the beholder. This virtue would certainly
be diminished by learned disputes and competitions, wherein it would debase itself with impertinent concerns. Moreover, let women consider that
learning swells and muddles the head. Let them remember that they do not
need to become offensive through ostentatious bearing and manners, by ap-
pending to their beauty the presumption of knowledge.† Finally, let them
reflect that the sweetness of life consists in allowing oneself to be carried
along by the current of popular custom, rather than by becoming entangled
with philosophy and its harsh and nasty disillusionments.‡ Let it be said that
he who is discerning derives pleasure from marveling at the novelties that

---

*Not female pedants, but erudite women are wanted—*A. S.*

†Through an education, the grandeur of beauty would be diminished and understood as something fragile that is not won through merit—*A. S.*

‡He knows the maxims of Epicurus. Lucretius states that philosophy puts man in such a state of
awareness that without the least astonishment he finds pleasure in seeing himself free of those
passions to which the rest of the world is lost, like one who, from a secure vantage point, watches
the waves of the sea batter a fragile boat and the harsh vicissitudes of a relentless battle—*A. S.*

occur every day and from pleasing the senses within the bounds of honesty. All of these sweets turn bitter and taste of absinthe to those who engage in subtly examining each thing, and who discredit, unmask, and, so to speak, peel the lovely, unblemished rind of certain fruits that had seemed beautiful, in order to uncover, as is the custom of agitated philosophers, the ugliness, defects, and displeasures within.

I know this for I feel it and grow angry.
                              Petrarch, *Canzoniere* 31[36]

If, then, among the multitudes of women, some take a contrary position, with praise for their generosity of spirit and loftiness of thought,[*] I will bring my discourse to a close, if not with the confidence of triumphing, at least with the support of a clear conscience, knowing that I faithfully counseled the community of women on how to achieve their best.

PROTEST OF SIGNOR GIOVANNI ANTONIO VOLPI REGARDING HIS ACADEMIC DISCOURSE ON THE EDUCATION OF WOMEN

So that in the future no erudite woman, or one who wishes to devote herself to the study of the sciences and the finest letters should ever complain that in my academic discourse I set out to prove that women are absolutely unable to benefit from such endeavors, I believe it is necessary for me to declare candidly my intentions when I spoke about the education of women in the Academy of the Ricovrati. I say, therefore, that I was led to take up the adverse argument not out of some imagined disdain or aversion for the female sex—"Quorum causas procul habeo" [from the motives of which I am far removed], to avail myself of the words used by Tacitus at the beginning of his *Annals*[37]—but only out of obedience to the Prince of the Academy and, moreover, reluctantly, knowing full well the manifest danger that I would fall into disfavor, if not with all women, at least with some and, by my fate, those most worthy of esteem. It was therefore my duty to obey and to treat my cause with the greatest efficacy, in order to avoid any suspicion of collusion.

---

*If these praises are sincere, they immediately destroy all that was said against women—which I believe was argued contrary to his belief—A. S.

36. I have here cited Mark Musa's elegant English translation of "I'l so, ch'l sento; e spesso me n'adiro," in Petrarch, *The Canzoniere or Rerum vulgarium fragmenta,* trans. Mark Musa (Bloomington: Indiana University Press, 1996), 223. This citation is from Petrarch's confessional canzone, *Canzoniere* 135.

37. Tacitus, *Annals,* 1.1.

I attempted to demonstrate that it would not be generally useful to humanity for women to be universally allowed to study in the academies and in the schools, in the exact terms that the very learned Signor Vallisneri posed the problem, providing, moreover, a right just testimony to the merit and rare value of those most singular women, who in ancient times, and modern as well, have distinguished themselves from the masses by virtue of their learning.

Read my discourse carefully, I pray you, from beginning to end, and you will know that what I say is true. It seems to me that this should satisfy the literary women who adorn our century; indeed, they should, if I do not err, thank me, since an education and erudition will be considered all the more admirable in them to the extent that it is rare. Many times I praised the gentlewomen who were present at the recitation of my discourse, not to flatter them, as I have been accused, but because I believed them to be then, and I continue to believe them to be now, endowed with rare talent, and because equally, I sought to show my civility. Otherwise, they might have perhaps taken offense at my words. Among the arguments put forth by me then, there are those more and less strong, not all certainly of one weight or worth twenty-four carats. This is the custom, if I do not err, of every orator, indeed, of every lawyer. And in the academies probable arguments can most certainly be put forth. And not every thing is treated as genuine philosophy. Even captains and military troops do thus with soldiers more or less valorous in order to achieve victory. And with respect to this subject, Signor Giovanni Boccaccio rightly said at the conclusion of his ten days: "Even Charlemagne, who first created the Paladins, was unable to produce them in numbers sufficient to form a whole army . . ." and that "no field was ever so carefully tended that neither nettles nor brambles nor thistles were found in it along with all the better grass."[38] In the same way, the victor in this case is he who has reason on his side.

I am not opposed to, nor could I oppose, even if I were willing, a new custom that has been introduced by the consensus of the wise. Many of the arguments exploited by me were not of my invention, but obtained from nobler fonts, having been treated many centuries before by the most sage philosophers, who were the masters of all who know best. Even less do I believe that I said everything I might have on the topic. The matter is too vast and fecund. But lord keep me from stirring up the wasp's nest further, and let he who has authority over me in the future charge me with wholly different

---

38. Giovanni Boccaccio, *The Decameron*, trans. G. H. McWilliam (New York: Penguin Books, 1972), 800.

duties. Signor Vallisneri decided the case, as was expected of him, when he divided women into two classes, according to their different inclinations. Therefore, let those women study who are capable, and who appear to be destined by nature to such a vocation. It would be a great cruelty and evident tyranny to deny them so great a good. But let those less capable who do not wish to become learned live in peace and attend to their duties. Experience and time will indicate to us whether or not the size of the first group shall become very great. Very well then, the two sides are agreed, the complainers' mouths are closed to complaints, and so too has my conduct been vindicated.

However, in order that virtuous women will be wholly persuaded of the true esteem in which I hold them, with great goodwill I endorse the sentiments expressed by Signor Ludovico Ariosto in these lovely verses that serve as the beautiful opening of canto 20 of his *Furioso*:

I

Women in ancient times have wondrous things
Performed in arms and in the sacred arts.
Their deeds, their works, their fair imaginings
Resound in glory in all minds and hearts.
Harpàlyce and Camilla Clio sings,
In battle skilled, in strategy experts.
Sappho and Corinna, in whom genius flamed
In splendor shine and are for ever famed.

II

And truly women have excelled indeed
In every art to which they set their hand,
And any who to history pay heed
Their fame will find diffused in every land.
If in some ages they do not succeed,
Their renaissance is not for ever banned.
Envy their merits has perhaps concealed
Or unawareness left them unrevealed.

III

Such talent in this century, I think,
Is seen in women lovely to behold,

That there will be much work for pen and ink
Ere chroniclers the full account unfold.[39]

I can honestly confirm that what Ariosto claims about his age is also true
of our own. Although when he says "women," the meaning is not *de singulis
generum* [of the individuals of the genera], but *de generibus singularum* [of the
genera of the individuals], to borrow a saying of the Scholastics. To the extent that others now do or have previously done, I admire and venerate true
virtue and solid learning in any person in whom these are found, whether
in man or in woman, and indeed, more in woman, because these qualities
are more exotic and rare. And certainly a woman deserves to be regarded
as an inestimable joy who devotes herself to studies neither from a vain desire to appear learned nor because she wishes to argue interminably about
every foolish subject, but rather because she wishes to better herself and
her family and to fulfill more effectively her blessed role by inscribing her
own mark instead of adorning herself with others' plumes. And although I
would never profess that beautiful women should be denied the benefits of
literature, I will nonetheless candidly declare that erudite women, the less
beautiful and charming they are, the more easily they will find acceptance
among cultivated persons.

Now it is time that I briefly explain some parts of my academic discourse
that the most illustrious Signora Aretafila Savini de' Rossi, celebrated and
virtuous Sienese lady residing in Florence, deigned to honor with her acute
reflections. For example, I said in my academic discourse: "what a lovely
thing it would be to see young maidens, together with young men, attending lessons in the academies and the lower schools in the manner of ancient Sparta." Perhaps I did not explain myself adequately with respect to
this custom of the Spartans. Here I sought to allude to the ancient custom
introduced by Lycurgus, Legislator in the city of Sparta, of educating girls
together with boys in all of the most difficult exercises—track, wrestling,
swimming, boxing, discus throwing, and many others besides—in order to
accustom them to discomfort and to prepare them to become the mothers
of strong men. This custom was celebrated by the great poet Propertius in
the twelfth elegy of his book 3, in the following verses:

Sparta, we much admire the rules of your palaestra,
But more its many female gymnastic attractions.
Naked girls and men wrestling together train

39. Ludovico Ariosto, *Orlando Furioso*, trans. Barbara Reynolds (New York: Penguin Books,
1975), 612.

Their bodies in games without dishonor,
When the ball deceives the arms in its swift flight
And the hook clinks on the rolling hoop
And women covered in dust stand at the winning-post
And suffer wounds in the cruel pancratium.
Now they gladly bind their arms with thongs for boxing,
Now wheel the discus' weight in a circle before throwing.
They tread the ring on horseback, belt sword to snow-white thigh
And protect girlish heads with hollow bronze,
And sometimes, with hair frost-powdered, follow their country's hounds
Over Taÿgetus' long ridges.[40]

Marcus Tullius Cicero also makes reference to these customs in the second book of the *Tusculan Disputations*,[41] not to mention many other ancient
sources.

With respect to the annoyance a too-learned wife would cause her husband, I was heeding the example laid down by Juvenal, who, in the Satire
dedicated to this subject, said:

Worse still is the well-read menace, who's hardly settled for dinner
Before she starts praising Virgil, making a moral case
For Dido (death justifies all), comparing, evaluating
Rival poets, Virgil and Homer suspended
In opposite scales, weighed up one against the other.
Critics surrender, academics are routed, all
Fall silent, not a word from lawyer or auctioneer—
Or even another woman. Such rattle of talk,
You'd think all the pots and bells were being clashed together
When the moon's in eclipse. No need now for trumpets or brass:
One woman can act, single-handed, as lunar midwife.[42]

40. Sextus Propertius, *The Poems*, trans. Guy Lee (Oxford: Clarendon Press, 1994), 90–91.

41. In the second book of the *Tusculan Disputations*, Cicero states: "Accordingly those who gave
to Greece the specific form of her governments were in favor of having young men's bodies
strengthened by toil; the citizens of Sparta applied the same rule to women, who in all other
cities lead a luxurious mode of life and are 'sequestered behind the shadow of walls.' The Spartan,
however, wished for nothing of that sort:

  in Spartan maids
  Whose cares are wrestling, sun, Eurotas, dust and toil
  Of drill far more than barbarous fecundity.'"

(Cicero, Tusculan Disputations, trans. J. E. King [Cambridge, MA: Harvard University Press,
1989], 185).

42. Juvenal, *The Sixteen Satires*, trans. Peter Green (New York: Penguin Books, 1967), 144.

And further down, in an attempt to discourage his friend from taking an educated wife, added:

So avoid a dinner-partner
With an argumentative style, who hurls well-rounded
Syllogisms like slingshots, who has all history pat:
Choose someone rather who doesn't understand *all* she reads.
I hate these authority-citers, the sort who are always thumbing
Some standard grammatical treatise, whose every utterance
Observes all the laws of syntax, who with antiquarian zeal
Quote poets I've never heard of. Such matters are men's concern.
If she wants to correct someone's language, she can always
Start with her unlettered girl-friends. A husband should be allowed
His solecisms in peace.[43]

The aforementioned most virtuous lady Aretafila Savini de' Rossi asserts that "when the Romans subjugated the Greeks, they were no longer the badly groomed and poorly spoken" that I made them out to be. In truth, I let myself be deceived by Horace, who in the first epistle of book 2 prayed that the study of eloquence, poetry, and all of the liberal arts would be transported to Rome along with the other spoils taken from conquered Greece. Here are his exact words: "Greece taken took her fierce captor captive and bore her arts to Latium's farms."[44]

Indeed, Velleius Paterculus, in chapter 13 of the first book of his *Compendium of Roman History*, recounts a ridiculous fact which clearly indicates the primitivism of the Romans at the time with respect to the arts cultivated by the Greeks when Lucius Mummius, the great general of the Romans who tamed the people of Achaicus, the greatest province of Greece, conquered the very rich and famous city of Corinth. According to Velleius: "Mummius was so uncultivated that when, after the capture of Corinth, he was contracting for the transportation to Italy of pictures and statues by the hands of the greatest artists, he gave instructions that the contractors should be warned that if they lost them, they would have to replace them by new ones."[45]

---

43. Ibid., 144.

44. Horace, *Satires and Epistles*, trans. Jacob Fuchs (New York: W. W. Norton, 1977), 77.

45. Velleius Paterculus, *Compendium of Roman History*, trans. Frederick W. Shipley (New York: G. P. Putnam's Sons, 1924), 33–34.

JUDGMENT ON THE PROBLEM RENDERED BY SAID
SIGNOR ANTONIO VALLISNERI

If my mind has ever been agitated, sorrowful, and grieved, this, more than any other, is the time, a time when it is bewildered by great dread and hangs irresolute. For I have heard numerous, equally strong arguments by two valiant orators, and like an inexperienced traveler who comes upon two equally large and well-trodden roads and who stops amazed and vacillating, staring now at the one, now at the other, fretting and worrying and puzzling over his uncertain fate, at this time and by my ill-fortune so I find myself, nor did I ever envision such a fate. I was inclined toward your side (naively, I confess), O most gentle and lovable female listeners. To you (for the love of God) I wished to grant the palm of victory, as it seemed to me an offense against your noble sex, an affront to your ability, and a spite against your glory and your good, indeed against the public good, and against the advancement of the liberal arts and the sciences to prohibit universally your education. But (let it be my fault and not yours) these so-called zealots and ponderous arguments caused me to doubt whether such a ruling would be contrary to the law of nature and of nations, indeed, against reason and the public good. To my great embarrassment, I was nearly ready to render no ruling and to resubmit the case to others more sage and less compassionate toward you, when I recalled a prudent observation made by the divine Plato that I had read not long ago in the fifth book of his *Republic*. As if Mercury of the ancient roads had shown me by his pointed finger the right way to reach a coveted end, and the wind had swept clean and erased the fog and every dark mist from my soul, (God's mercy), to reiterate the words of Dante without giving offense to anyone:

Like a man in doubt who then grows sure,
exchanging fear for confidence, once truth
has been revealed to him, so was I changed.
Purgatory, canto 9[46]

The great, illumined mind of Plato believed that women are endowed with spirit and reason, as we are, but that they are neither all endowed with the same organs and intellect we have, nor are they all capable of or suited for onerous duties and momentous undertakings. And in the same way that

---

46. Dante Alighieri (1265–1321), *Purgatorio*, trans. Allen Mandelbaum (New York: Bantam Books, 1982), 78–79.

there is an elite among men, so too is there an elite among women. Some are most tender lovers of virtue and wisdom; others are the most dazzling scorners and virtual enemies of these; some possess lofty and sublime spirits, others have spirits feeble, tormented and wretched.

And, if the matter is thus, O revered Listeners, I hope you will allow the problem to be resolved without great effort. Let there be admitted to the study of the sciences and the liberal arts only those women who are passionate about the same, whose hidden noble genius leads them to virtue and to glory, in whose veins flows clear and illustrious blood, and in whom burns and sparkles a spirit beyond the norm, surpassing that which is common to the masses, exactly that spirit which I recognize in you, O noble and by your many titles most esteemed women who kindly listen to me. In you virtue combined with beauty and noble birth will find its true nesting ground, and since virtue will always be more illustrious for you than other women, in the same way, you will always be more illustrious by means of virtue. The entire world will venerate you as rare and divine, and you will be the genius and the wonder of the most cultured ages. In the past the sweetly severe Paduan honesty and the ancient innocent, serenely majestic Venetian simplicity were held as an exalted sign by the most luminous pens—and so they will always be—and thus united with virtue will appear something suprahuman and a marvel greater than any marvels past.

Because God gave different characters with distinct manners, appearances, and temperaments to different portions of humanity for the right governance of men, it is wrong to censure those women who are led by some mysterious, obscure violence to administer to the economy of the home, to noble toils, or other amiable duties. Rather, they should be held most worthy of praise not only as useful to the right harmonious governance of men, but necessary to it. This vague, uniform deformity and this invariable variety that is eternal, immutable, and, in its inconstancy, constant in the order of the world is and always will be an exceptional marvel, such that, anyone attempting to imagine otherwise, would "unimagine it," as one modern writer states.[47]

In this way, therefore, O revered listeners, is the problem happily resolved without offense to the truth nor to any of you, O most eloquent orators. Without the arrogance of tyranny, let the range of womanly duties be divided. Divide the tasks such that the superior intellect is left free. Let some women attend to household tasks and to their honest and necessary work. Let others follow the Muses most chaste where inclination transports

47. I wish to acknowledge Michael Sherberg's assistance with this passage.

them and, by means most necessary, let them be animated, guided, and filled with delight, so that, unyielding to indolence, ignorance, and envy, they may enhance the sciences and at the same time their own praises; and let virtue, praised and protected in this its ancient refuge by our most serene Prince, and by his most worthy representative of so magnanimous a heart, shine and triumph evermore to the benefit of women's homes, to the glory of their fatherland, and to the jubilation of the entire Republic of Letters.

Translated by Rebecca Messbarger

III

ARETAFILA SAVINI DE' ROSSI

TRANSLATOR'S INTRODUCTION

It is before this image or engraving (of you) that I write. Good that it does not lower its eyes in response to my sincere and deserved praises as, lamentably, humility would prompt you to do. To it I say that which I would not say to you. Indeed, to it I ask for that which it might not provide, but would never refuse me. It would certainly not concede some chance comedy that I know you to have wittily prepared and seasoned with plautine salts. No amorous novella that I know you playfully invented, à la Boccaccio. . . . I bring to the stage that which appears on the back of your own medallion showing Minerva and Venus portrayed together and embracing, the motto: Gratior, et pulchro veniens in corpore virtus, taken from the Aeneid. I represent the union of these two virtues, so rarely combined, in *Elena Casta*.[1]

I n these dedicatory lines to his tragedy *Helen, the Chaste* (1721), the poet and playwright Pier Jacopo Martello (1665–1727), known for his invention of Martellian verse, describes his source of poetic inspiration: Sienese noblewoman and author Aretafila Savini de' Rossi. Contemplating her symbolic representation as Venus and Minerva on a medallion coined by regional officials in 1710 to honor her talents as poet and painter, Martello venerates Savini de' Rossi as a modern Helen, a woman "of beauty, modesty, wisdom, and intelligence."[2] Martello's dedication is significant as one of the few extant primary sources about the Sienese author.[3] Not only does it catalog her

---

1. Pier Jacopo Martello, *Teatro*, ed. Hannibal S. Noce (Rome: Laterza, 1980), 322–23. The Latin quotation on the medallion is from a description of the beautiful youth Eurylus in the *Aeneid*, 5.344. It reads: "Virtue found in a beautiful body is more pleasing." I wish to acknowledge the assistance of Cathy Keane with the translation of this citation.

2. Martello, *Teatro*, 323.

3. On Savini de' Rossi, see Antonella Giordano, *Letterate toscane del Settecento* (Florence: All'Insegna del Giglio, 1994), 146–48; and M. Bandini Buti, *Poetesse e scrittrici*, vol. 6 of *Enciclopedia biografica e bibliografica italiana* (Rome: Istituto Editoriale Italiano Carlo Tosi, 1941), 219–20.

eclectic attributes and confirm her distinction as a poet among her contemporaries, it also mentions that she wrote comedies and novellas, now lost.

Apart from Martello's cursory biographical sketch, we know that Aretafila Savini was born in Siena in 1687 to aristocratic parents, Antonio Savini and Margherita Conte. She married the Florentine nobleman Isidoro Rossi and moved with him to Florence, where she frequented literary salons and became a member of the Arcadia Academy in 1712 under the name Larinda Alagonia, as well as a member of the Florentine Academy of Design. The medallion described above by Martello and its companion representing an eagle gazing into the sun's rays with the motto *mentis acumen* (sharpness of mind), testify to her acclaim as a learned woman in her native Tuscany. She enjoyed friendships with a number of prominent writers and intellectuals aside from Martello, including Anton Maria Salvini (1653–1729), a poet, translator, and professor of classics at the University of Florence. Salvini wrote several discourses on the question of women's virtue and education, one of which he dedicated to Savini de' Rossi, arguing "against the antiquated thesis, which would continually reappear over the entire eighteenth century, that 'literary studies' divert women 'from their principal obligations.'" Salvini's arguments in favor of granting women literary instruction, according to Luciano Guerci, may have served as inspiration for Savini de' Rossi's own writings on the subject in response to Giovanni Antonio Volpi's argument in the 1723 Ricovrati debate against the education of women.[4]

It was Savini de' Rossi's formal rebuttal to Volpi's argument, published in the appended 1729 version of the debate, that brought her wide acclaim. During her lifetime, noted writers and intellectuals cited her apology for women's learning in published and private writings, and she continued to be included in catalogs of illustrious learned women through the course of the century.

Yet the circumstances that prompted her rebuttal are known only vaguely. Giovanni Antonio Volpi recounts, in his prefatory letter "To the Gracious and Learned Reader" in the 1729 volume he edited, that Savini de' Rossi's argument formed part of the "great clamor that arose" among women in response to the original publication of his argument against women's education in 1723. She initially appended retaliatory footnotes directly to his argument, refuting one-by-one each of his misogynist theses. Afterward,

---

4. Anton Maria Salvini, *Discorsi accademici di Anton Maria Salvini, geniluomo fiorentino, lettore di Lettere greche nello Studio di Firenze e accademico della Crusca, sopra alcuni dubbj proposti nell'Accademia degli Apatisti*, 3 vols. (Venice: Pasinelli, 1735). Cited by Guerci, *Discussione sulla donna*, 147n44. See Luciano Guerci's comments on Salvini in *La discussione sulla donna nell'Italia del Settecento* (Turin: Tirrenia Stampatori, 1987), 148.

she composed a traditional academic rebuttal in the form of a letter to an unidentified nobleman. Of the letter, Volpi writes that Signor Vallisneri, "graciously shared it with me, and we agreed that it was necessary to republish my argument, which had been the origin of these disputes, and . . . to include the footnotes of the lady in the margins along with her sage letter of reply, which might be called an apology for the education of women."[5]

Savini de' Rossi thus composed an unprecedented two-part response that served to double her voice of authority in the 1729 volume. She assumed separate literary personae in her footnotes and her formal apology, which employed antithetical language and rhetorical styles. In the footnotes to Volpi's discourse, she is terse, sarcastic, and frequently mocking. Through the presence of her notes in the midst of Volpi's disputation, she is, in effect, able to interrupt her opponent and immediately challenge the legitimacy of his proofs as well as the honesty of his intentions. She repeatedly accuses him of trying to dupe women with flattery and, in her final footnote, even maintains that Volpi "argued contrary to his belief." As I have discussed elsewhere, the footnotes permit Savini de' Rossi to act as a heckler in the back of the room, challenging quite literally from the margins the academician as well as the male academic tradition of the *querelle des femmes*.[6] Speaking from outside the body of the text and as an outsider to the academic disputation and its rhetorical formalities, she spontaneously interjects her radical voice of dissent.

In her formal apology for women's education, however, Savini de' Rossi assumes a very different position. Now acting in accordance with the conventions of academic disputation, her tone is moderate, her language decorous, and her arguments stoical and well-reasoned. Although she continues to insist on her status as outsider to the academy, it is her inexperience in the classic art and artifice of persuasion, she promises, that makes her a more honest and credible disputant on the question of women's education.

Savini de' Rossi's strategy in the apology represents an appropriation of the terms and tenets of the "new" empirical science and philosophy to which Vallisneri laid claim in his introduction to the debate. Where Vallisneri and his cohorts failed to resolve this "old question" as promised, according to the modern intellectual standards of reasoned, dispassionate, and practical analysis, Savini de' Rossi seeks to show herself more capable. The

---

5. Giovanni Antonio Volpi, "Al cortese e dotto Lettore," in *Discorsi accademici di vari autori viventi intorno agli studi delle donne* (Padua: Giovanni Manfrè, 1729), 4.

6. Messbarger, *The Century of Women: Representations of Women in Eighteenth-Century Italian Public Discourse* (Toronto: University of Toronto Press, 2002), 42.

Ricovrati debate participants reiterated roles and stock arguments standard to the *querelle des femmes* genre. To this empty academic gesture, deficient in both analysis and contemporary Enlightenment ethics, Savini de' Rossi opposes the indisputable facts of women's lives, ordinary and extraordinary, including her own, as well as a practical ethics of the public good. Her design is apparent from the opening lines of her defense when she calls attention to her own deficient education that has left her without "the necessary arguments," but not without the will, to defend the interests of women. Here and throughout the apology, she counters Volpi's misogynist and often myth-based constructions of femininity with the real-life stories of women and men. Beyond her own experience, she builds her defense on the examples of various learned contemporaries, including the erudite Pisan noblewoman Maria Selvaggia Borghini (1654–1731), who founded a celebrated literary and scientific academy; the Arcadian poet and artist Faustina Maratti Zappi; the Sienese improvisational poet Emilia Orlandini Ballati; her friend, the Tuscan writer Benedetto Bresciani; and the learned autodidact, Pippo the Peasant, from Fiesole. The mix of male and female, rich and poor among her exemplars reflects Savini de' Rossi's egalitarian notion of human intellectual potential.

Her egalitarianism is indeed a defining characteristic of her apology. Explicitly rejecting the division of women into two categories, the exceptional and the norm, invoked by each of the Ricovrati participants, Savini de' Rossi advocates the education of *all* women, noble and plebeian alike, "each according to her constitution, her circumstances, and, above all, her talent." This unification of women and their interests is effectively expressed by her insistent use of the pronoun *we* to indicate a choral female rejoinder to Volpi's masculinist claims. Savini de' Rossi consistently returns to women's actuality within the home to prove the necessity of this education for the well-being of the domestic and, by extension, the public spheres. In order to competently oversee the early education of their children and the management of their households, for which they are primarily responsible, women, she argues, require formal instruction. Indeed, she offers an exceptional argument for women of the lower classes to collaborate in the formal instruction of "willing young girls." This implicit apology for the usurpation by women of men's traditional roles of authority over the education of women signifies one of the most remarkable propositions to have been made by any author during the Italian Settecento.

Nowhere does Savini de' Rossi advocate women's civil emancipation. She never links instruction to broader roles for women outside of the home. She makes clear that an education would strictly serve to enhance women's competency and happiness inside the home in their roles as wives and mothers. However, this domestic rehabilitation of women by means of formal instruction would necessarily benefit society at large, what she deems the "body of the Republic." Financial ruin, she argues, is that most prevalent hazard posed by unschooled women to the well-being of the family and the state. By succumbing to the myth of feminine beauty propagated by such authors as Volpi, ignorant women threaten to bankrupt their homes in the pursuit of cosmetic remedies and fashionable goods and practices that have nothing to do with genuine virtue. The author demystifies beauty as an arbitrary and ephemeral attribute whose pursuit must be supplanted by "intellectual studies" in order for women to be truly good and happy. Savini de' Rossi also discusses such realistic dangers to family life as the long-term absence or death of the husband, which leaves illiterate and incapable women to oversee the many affairs of the estate. Were women given adequate instruction, she argues, they could capably govern their households on their own, and thus rectify a common social affliction.

Despite the rigid domestic frame in which Savini de' Rossi encloses women's lives, she nonetheless asserts a belief in universal human nature and intellectual potential that transcends categories of sex and class. Indeed, the dominant strategy she employs to expose the absurdity of Volpi's arguments against women's learning based on sexual difference (women's reproductive imperative and their abundant humidity in which is rooted their physical and intellectual irregularity and delicacy) is to apply those same standards and assumptions to men. If learning does not generally make men disobedient, impertinent, misanthropic, pedantic, and, most important, disdainful of the opposite sex and family life, then, she argues, women will be no different. Likewise, knowledge will improve women in the same ways it is said to improve men. They will become, by means of education, more discerning of the truth, more eloquent and thus better conversationalists, less vain, more capable in their management of household affairs, better guardians and educators of their children, and more temperate with respect to material pleasures.

Aretafila Savini de' Rossi thus composed a powerful, rational rebuttal founded on the actual life experiences of contemporary women and men, as opposed to the myths, social customs, ancient humoralism, and irrational fears on which Volpi built his thesis against women's learning. *Esperienza* was the foundational principle of the "new science and philosophy"—it signified the content of an individual's life as well as scientific empirical proof. Savini de' Rossi combines both of these meanings in her argument for women's learning. And while her strategy of "reversing the charges" (applying those same assumptions to men that Volpi applies to women) leaves her, to some extent, entangled in Volpi's logic, she helps establish an effective method of self-defense for women and their interests within and in the terms of the eighteenth-century Republic of Letters.

Rebecca Messbarger

APOLOGY IN FAVOR OF STUDIES FOR WOMEN, AGAINST THE PRECEDING DISCOURSE BY SIGNOR GIOVANNI ANTONIO VOLPI, WRITTEN TO A GENTLEMAN BY SIGNORA ARETAFILA SAVINI DE' ROSSI, SIENESE LADY

I am certain that it was not by chance that you sent me the academic discourse by Giovanni Antonio Volpi, "Women Should Not Be Admitted to the Study of the Sciences and the Liberal Arts," but rather to tempt me to tell you my feelings on the subject. For you know full well that I must perforce feel the great wrong done to our sex when he claims to justify rationally the unfortunate and injurious abuse that prevents women from sharing in so good a thing.

If only it had pleased God that I not be barbarously thwarted from following my penchant for learning, perhaps I would not lack the arguments necessary on this occasion to satisfy your expectations and to defend the justice of our cause. However, despite the risk of compromising my reputation, I will not be silent about what little I know because I believe I can bolster our defense. I hope to persuade you of the truth neither through artistry nor through genius but through my personal observation that we contemplate and scrutinize every detail of those things in which we have a vested interest; the interested party, however ignorant, is drawn to an issue that would leave indifferent someone else possessed of a precise understanding of the same. We tend to pass over things that flatter our intellects without reflecting on them, much less examining them with care.

This clearly appears from the pressure felt by Signor Volpi to publish his academic lesson in opposition to the womanly sex, to which men are so inimical, I don't know if out of natural antipathy or out of disdain at seeing themselves so often subjugated by them. With respect to this antipathy, men consider themselves vindicated when they see women depressed and humiliated. Yet after close examination of the way things truly stand, it is apparent that men find themselves conquered and ruled over by us, not through any violence or tyranny on our part, but because they do not know how to control their passions. For this reason, men were so pleased by the

pretense of Volpi's argument that they did not perceive the degree of artistry
Dr. Declaimer had used in his treatment of it. He did not in fact embrace
this occasion in order to inveigh against women, but rather to correct those
vices that we sometimes see rule over the learned. In this way he obeyed the
Prince of the Academy by defending, though not out of sincere conviction,
his position in the debate. But in the manner of Father Pardies on the souls
of brutes, this author revealed his true feelings through the great allowances
he made for objections and through his references to claims much more
ostensible than true on the proposed subject.[7]

Who does not know that knowledge is neither the immediate nor the
remote cause of the disorders of our passions? Indeed, by means of knowledge shouldn't we be able to correct these more readily? And if correction
does not eventually occur, the failure should be attributed to a substandard
education, to corrupt manners, or to a deficient will. Vice is born with us and
is nourished without distinction by all in such a way that if reason does not
hasten to impede its progress we will very quickly see it predominate. Now,
by what means can reason be most keenly awakened in us to oppose the disorder of the vices, such that through studies that teach us to distinguish the
true from the false and the good from the bad, we attain enlightenment and
clarity which better enables our flight from evil and our search and desire for
good? There is no sound basis for arguing that the result of educating women
will be an incivility of manners, a crudeness of comportment, a disregard for
household duties, infinite damage not only to women themselves but to the
body of the republic and to the domestic economy, boredom for husbands,
the encumbrance of conversations, and the creation of more misanthropes.
The outcome (he claims) will be affected female pedants, whose excessive
studies will also dull the healthy color of their complexions and thus dimin-
ish their natural beauty, which culminates, he says, "with a modest glance, a
smile, a gesture, a small sigh slowly suspired from her breast, . . . in this way
gaining dominion over that proud animal known as man." Let these same arts
be left without prejudice to those women not only ignorant but uncouth.

How miserable we would be if our greatest asset were beauty, which
soon vanishes and with which few women have been endowed. But even to

---

7. Ignace Gaston Pardies (1636–73) entered the Jesuit order at a young age and later became
professor, first of literature, then of mathematics and philosophy, at the University of Clermont.
He was among Descartes's best students; he corresponded with Newton and collaborated on
the *Philosophical Transactions* of London. The Italian translation of his 1672 tract on the souls of
brutes was published in Venice by Andrea Poletti in 1696: *Dell'anima delle bestie, e sue funzioni. Nel
quale si disputa la celebre questione de' moderni se gli animali bruti siano mere machine automate senza cognizione,
ne senso come gli orologi.* In this tract, the author seeks to determine whether animals are more than
biological machines and whether they possess cognition.

those who value this privilege, how greatly beauty would be enhanced and perfected by an education. Certainly much more than by the expensive luxuries of fashion, clothing, and household services in which the majority of women wastefully indulge at the cost of condemning their homes to financial ruin. The origin of this great obsession is in large part that inexplicable allure that these material and sensuous things have, particularly for those unaccustomed to considering something better. Now then, since over an extended period of time these material desires grow and cause trouble, one who does not know better where to turn thus necessarily becomes preoccupied and, moreover, filled with vice. By contrast, intellectual studies give comfort and ever more sweetly lead one to investigate the good and the true, generating scorn for that which is opposed to the temperance of our desires.

Allowing women access to a formal education, each according to her constitution, her circumstances, and, above all, her talent, would be not merely a great but an honest diversion, one which would pose no risk that they might abandon their primary duties. It can be seen from experience that the world abounds with men who hoe the earth and do other things for the maintenance of the republic, yet no one has ever suggested that even one of these remain willingly blind and ignorant. Unfortunately, a certain natural laziness keeps us confined in a state of indolence. But no one tries to repress with fancy reasoning those courageous spirits who, wholly fearless of the difficulties to be met in acquiring knowledge, willingly take on the task. That supreme author God created all of our souls equal, giving them the same powers; and these veils that cover our souls are not biased in their substance; therefore, one cannot justly deny women that assistance that contributes to self-knowledge and a sense of one's own dignity. In distributing its gifts, nature does not demonstrate greater partiality toward the poor man, the rich man, the nobleman, or the plebeian, as has always been proven by people of rare talent who overcome adverse fortune, and who constantly push themselves ahead of those lacking in neither the social rank nor the talent for an education. Let the example suffice for all of the famous peasant Pippo from below Fiesole, who, despite cultivating his native earth for many hours each day for forty years, nevertheless became an excellent mathematician, astronomer, and master of Greek, which he studied with the same felicity as the other subjects. He was a marvel of the learned and a favorite of the very illustrious Benedetto Bresciani,[8] who, for the enjoyment of Pippo's conversation, quite often left beautiful Florence, but who could never persuade Pippo to move to the city and to live a less arduous life.

---

8. Benedetto Bresciani, (1671–1742), Tuscan intellectual who coedited Galileo's complete works.

Do not then scorn so great a gift out of petty fear, but let all women study on whom the heavens have bestowed a strong will and intellect: noblewomen and citizens for their personal benefit and glory; common women, not for themselves alone, but in order to educate willing young women in the sciences. As for the claims about tutors scandalously seducing their students, prudent parents can easily avoid these, since every day we find girls taught music, dance, and other things by paid instructors, and rarely if ever do those things happen that Signor Volpi in jest claims to fear.

We have even less cause to worry that if women's cognition were to be enlivened by the sciences they would lose their desire to marry and would have to be compelled by subjecting their neck to the yoke. If women were allowed to philosophize, what would follow would be no more and no less than what we now have with men. In the same way that philosophy and the arts will never cause men and women not to be men and women, there is no danger that their natural instincts will be taken from them that the Creator instilled to preserve the human species.

And since men continue to study without failing to take a wife, thus sacrificing that freedom much more appropriate to their sex than to ours, even more so would this occur with woman who, in whatever state she chooses to live, is never free because of the harsh laws of our nations, as the famous tragedian Martello states so well:[9]

A daughter serves her father; A wife serves her husband;
A widow her decorum, And they die having only served.

We women do not boast greater wisdom than men. So, if men, with their abundant intelligence and philosophy, seek and desire our love and company, why should they fear virtues too austere for us? Aren't we women, according to Signor Volpi, naturally weak and intellectually deficient? It is therefore improbable that with all of these disadvantages we would succeed in becoming more cultivated than those same very strong, very intelligent, and very grave men. This would not mean great "woe for human affairs." Indeed, there would be the additional advantage that women enamored of studies would seek a mate among educated men—falling in love because of what they share in common—the same bond that we find to be not only frequent but very enduring among men from their own discourse about their studies. And spouses, finding in each other attributes much more estimable

---

9. A martello is a verso of fourteen syllables invented by Pier Iacopo Martello (1666–1727).

and less vulnerable to the injuries of time than those of the body, would forever defy that great sentiment of Lord Chevalier Guarini:

The tedious conversation generates boredom,
Boredom disdain, and hate in the end.[10]

Fortunate, in my view, would be those families and those husbands whose women, enlightened by knowledge, could do what many women desire and attempt in vain because they are without the requisite will and the learning that are, unfortunately, necessary. As things stand, the most grievous deficiency regards the education of children, since ignorant women ignore their duty to curb promptly the first corrupt inclinations in children, sadly a sure prelude to the vice that over time will certainly take hold.

I don't believe that anyone can deny how useful it would be to infuse in tender minds, as easily receptive to first impressions as they are strong to retain them, those first seeds of virtue, free from contamination of falsehoods, and that first horror of vice, chasing from them certain unfounded fears that one will oppose with time the honest freedom of the spirit; and instead of this opposition, instill in them a useful and reasonable fear of all that is truly evil, doing so always in appropriate ways that they can best understand. Nothing could be easier than to convince children of the truth by means of reason, even if they don't completely understand, when it comes from the authority of mother or father.

I can tell you that I myself saw a wise mother reduce to tears her entire brood, several boys and a girl, the oldest of whom had not yet reached the age of fifteen, by the timely reprimand she gave them without altering her voice and without threats. No one can tell me that men of their own volition will attend to the right upbringing of their children, because fathers, who are more often busy in other things, already find little time to dedicate to this critical matter. And paid tutors are by no means equal to maternal affection and diligence. Here it is important to reflect on and to recognize how advantageous and profitable it would be for children if their mothers, instructed in the sciences and the arts, could supervise their studies and their preceptors' method of teaching. And who can tell: some of these mothers might be capable of educating their children themselves, as we have seen in the case of Madame Selvaggia Borghini, the very erudite Pisan lady who schooled her nephews not only in those most delightful humanistic arts, but also in the

---

10. These lines are from the pastoral drama by Giovan Battista Guarini (1538–1612), *Il Pastor Fido*, act 1, scene 3.

most difficult and severe sciences.[11] Such a woman would be no less useful to the household economy, particularly in a household governed by foolish and indiscreet managers. In such a case, she would be able to substitute for her husband to the extent necessary for the protection of their properties. It would also be useful if it happened, as it can so easily, that a wise and prudent husband found himself ill, or far away, or occupied with unrelenting duties to the Republic. Think what a consolation it would be for this man to rest assured of the vigilance of his wife, and to take the necessary repose on his return home, confident that she would give him a brief, fitting, and untedious account of how she took care of this or that affair for the governance of the household. In this way, he would not need to rely on a steward, a butler, or an attorney, who so often very cleverly wait, hoping that their employers won't have the time to attend to and reflect on their own interests, in order better to exploit them to their own advantage.

But let us grant that when men are present women are not permitted to interfere, except in that most ordinary householding familiar even to maidservants. Still, how great a relief would [an educated wife] be to those families who by ill-fortune are left without a father, and where the burden very often lies entirely on women, whose susceptibility to deception increases with the number of agents on whom they must depend to run their households.

Neither should the authority of Scripture dismay us; since if what Signor Volpi cites from chapter 31 is true,[12] what comes after in the same passage that undergirds our cause is also true. He says that the strong woman, who took such great and exact care of her family and domestic affairs and, when necessary, managed the distaff and the needle, was in essence full of wisdom and of sweetness, which one could immediately recognize from her speech.

---

11. Maria Selvaggia Borghini, (1654–1731), was a learned noblewoman of Pisa who founded a noted literary and scientific salon there. She was well-versed in Latin, Greek, logic, philosophy, and was an expert in mathematics, which she studied with Alessandro Marchetti, a noted scholar of literature and mathematics. She wrote numerous poems and a translation of Tertullus published in 1756, and she engaged in extensive correspondence with noted intellectuals, primarily from Tuscany. These included Francesco Redi, Vincenzo Filicaia, Benedetto Menzini, and Lorenzo Magalotti, among others. Redi, with whom she had a prolonged close relationship, compared her in a letter to Vittoria Colonna and called her the "splendor of Europe." She was a member of numerous academies—the Stravaganti of Pisa, the Spensierati of Rossano, the Innominati of Bra, and the Arcadia of Rome as Filotima Innia—and she supervised the education in the arts and sciences of her nieces and nephews. Her niece Caterina Borghini of Pisa, whom she tutored, won renown for her learning and was inducted into the Arcadia Academy as Erato Dionea. On Borghini, see the *Dizionario Biografico degli Italiani* (Rome: Istituto della Enciclopedia italiana, 1960–), 10.676–77.

12. *This is note 1 in Savini de' Rossi's text:* Prv 31:26: "Elle ouvre fa bouche avec sagesse, & la loy de Misericorde est sur la langue."

Since this woman, whom Solomon described in the proverb, was that same Queen, his Mother, let Signor Volpi content himself with returning to the beginning of this chapter, and for proof of Bathsheba's wisdom he will find that she knew enough to teach the wisest of all men and, continuing in his reading, he will know what rewards knowledge bestowed on her such that she was able to understand and correct her son so skillfully with respect to his unruly desire for wanton pleasures and to furnish him with maxims so grave that he wanted to learn them well enough to teach them.[13] These truths serve as sufficient response to the author's claims and make it clear that an education and knowledge will not make women more inattentive to their duties but, on the contrary, will make women know and better fulfill them.

After this, Signor Volpi conjures a woman given to "abstract thought" regarding all things on which she dwells: "devoted to the contemplation of things useless to her and harmful to her family, rendered vain by her knowledge, resolute in her disobedience, antagonistic to her husband, impertinently critical of the logic of his commands, and ready even to lay complete or partial claim to her husband's authority."[14] And he follows this by describing her as troublesome for "confronting her husband, who returns home in search of repose, with thorny questions without giving him a moment's breath, so desirous is she to have an account of the day's business, to discuss with him some new theorems, to have him listen to her narrate some stories, and so determined is she to persist without end in twittering on and in driving him mad."[15] Without a doubt, this character, far from being a woman devoted to learning and adorned by the sciences, is the portrait of a lunatic, of a presumptuous, disrespectful, vain woman and, to speak tactfully, of the most ignorant woman in the world. Since when are the arts and sciences, those purifiers of the spirit, those regulators and very mysterious illuminators of life, considered the source of so many evils? There may exist some women like those described by Signor Volpi, but they will never be so for having studied, or because of knowledge; they will be so because they have never studied anything of worth, and because, being ignorant, they foolishly

---

13. Savini de' Rossi mistakenly indicates that Proverbs 31 refers to Bathsheba's (Savini de' Rossi uses the Latin name of Bersabea) lessons to her son, King Solomon. Instead, this passage concerns "the words of Lemuel, King of Massa, which his mother taught him." Proverbs 31:10–31 is known as the eulogy of the good wife and is written in the form of an acrostic poem following the Hebrew alphabet. Verse 26 states: "She openeth her mouth with wisdom; and in her tongue *is* the law of kindness." See *The Interpreter's Bible: The Holy Scriptures in the King James and Revised Standard Versions with General Articles and Introduction, Exegesis, Exposition for Each Book of the Bible* (New York: Abingdon-Cokesbury Press, 1952–57), 4.953–57.

14. Savini de' Rossi is here paraphrasing Volpi's argument on pp. 37–38 of his discourse.

15. Again, Savini de' Rossi paraphrases Volpi's argument, from p. 39 of his discourse.

believe themselves to be esteemed as learned and wise. Since the number of lunatics is great, I would expect to find many such men. And yet, woman that I am, I would never be so unjust as to deduce that for this reason one should forbid all men to study, with the exception of a very select few whom I have decided to exempt out of supreme benevolence. I will not discuss the question of envy that is said to awaken in men if women should study. A beautiful woman, although ignorant, will always be sought after and courted; it is not necessary for her to be erudite in order to make her husband jealous.

The strangest thing of all, however, is to lead us to believe that an education renders one inept and impotent in social conversations. As punishment for this opinion, I would like to condemn Signor Volpi for a few hours only to attend the conversation of six or seven ignorant persons. As cultivated as he is, I am certain he would vigorously decry the offense that had caused him to endure such a hardship. Yet I esteem him so much, even though he has assumed the role of our adversary, that I pray to heaven to punish him with anything other than this misfortune that would be too great for him to endure. I think that if women were educated, they would greatly improve conversations because, without a doubt, they would resolve to frequent learned men, as we are naturally given to conversing with those with whom we have the most in common. In this way, conversations would not be subject to the current criticism, nor would you hear as much drivel and stupidity as you do now. Moreover, young men, aware that the more they know the more highly regarded they are, would apply themselves much more than they do now to their studies, wanting to present themselves to and be approved by those women who are most knowledgeable and esteemed. There would be no risk that these men would be bored by erudite conversations, even those not ornamented by the beauty of the female conversant, because finally young men would esteem only what is virtuous. I believe that the refined and no less erudite pastoral poet Aglauro Cidonia was moved by this very consideration to close her loveliest sonnet in this way:

O you who praise only the silent Woman,
Tell the one who speaks ill to be silent:
When a sage Woman speaks she was and is pleasing.[16]

---

16. The verses are from a sonnet by Faustina Maratti Zappi (1680–1745), poet, artist, and wife of noted Arcadian poet Giovanni Battista Felice Zappi. Maratti was admitted to the Arcadia Academy in 1704 under the name of Aglauro Cidonia. She took part in a noted debate in the academy on the question of love with Petronilla Paolini Massimi and Prudenza Gabrielli Capizucchi. Her poetry was published with her husband's verses, and she was celebrated in verse and prose by such noteworthy figures as figures as Giovanni Maria Crescimbeni, Gian Pietro

A great proof of this truth is found in Signor Volpi's citation about Helen, when Menelaus entertained Peisistratus and Telemachus. Having returned to Sparta after the long siege of Troy, the Queen was greatly applauded for her sagacity, despite no longer being in the flower of her youth or beauty, which might have compensated for her lack of learning.[17] Thank God Signor Volpi himself, constrained by the truth, finally grants that we women are more clever than men, a thing he had denied many times during the course of his disputation! And even though he undermines the significance of this praise by calling our reasoning "unexpected and passing,"[18] we have proof that the ability and penchant for studies is in as many of us as it is found in the most excellent of men. And I will not contradict what he says about women's humid and flaccid temperament, because everyone knows there is nothing more erroneous than using these humoral systems to deduce the talents of the mind. There is at the Tuscan court a peasant maiden,[19] lately relieved of the hoe by the beneficence and refined discernment of the great Princess Violante.[20] She readily sings improvised poetry with extraordinary brilliance on any subject she knows, without the benefit of any education, being possessed of a discerning genius, extraordinary insight, a stout memory, and all those natural abilities that would render any great poet more laudable. It is incredible with what sincerity, ebullience, and keen wit she has sung so often, always preserving her virginal modesty in her words and comportment, and poetizing with the most erudite poets

---

Zanotti, and Carlo Innocenzo Frugoni. On Maratti see Maria Bandini Buti, *Poetesse e scrittrici: Enciclopedia biografica e bibliografica italiana* (Rome: E.B.B.I., 1942), 6:375–76.

17. In book 4 of Homer's *Odyssey*, Queen Helen is celebrated for her refinement and her insight. She is the first to recognize Telemachus as the son of Odysseus. She then tells him how Odysseus disguised himself as a slave to deceive the Trojans and how, on that occasion too, she was the first to uncover his true identity.

18. Here, Savini de' Rossi paraphrases Volpi's argument on pp. 23–24 of his discourse.

19. Savini de' Rossi is undoubtedly referring to Emilia Orlandini Ballati, a Sienese improvisational poet who allied herself with the renowned improviser of the age, Bernardino Perfetti (see below, note 15). Ballati was inducted into the Arcadia Academy as Eurinda Annomidia. On Ballati, see Maria Bandini Buti, *Poetesse e scrittrici: Enciclopedia biografica e bibliografica italiana* (Rome: E.B.B.I., 1942), 6:56–57.

20. In 1688 Princess Violante of Bavaria married Prince Ferdinand II, son of the Grand Duke of Tuscany, Cosimo de' Medici III. After Ferdinand's death, Violante "assumed the government of Siena" at Cosimo's behest. When Giovanni Gastone became the seventh and last Medici Grand Duke of Tuscany in 1723 upon his father Cosimo III's death, Princess Violante had distinct influence over him and the court of Tuscany. She helped introduce French fashions and manners to the court, was an enthusiastic patron of the arts, and supported such improvisational poets as Perfetti and Ballati of her hometown of Siena. On Princess Violante of Bavaria, see Henry Edward Napier, *Florentine History: From the Earliest Authentic Records to the Accession of Ferdinand the Third* (London: Edward Moxon, 1847), 5:517–83.

and, in particular, with the incomparable Cavalier Perfetti in the presence of the King,[21] of princes, and of an infinity of nobility. If such reticence can be preserved by an uneducated country girl while reciting improvised poetry for long periods of time to gain admiration and secure respect, I don't know why one might fear that an education and learned discourse would make women lose that natural blush and that matronly modesty that Signor Volpi rightly calls more precious than any oriental gem.

Lastly, he would have us be pleased with the admiration born of ignorance, and he would disdain the real pleasure forged by intellectual inquiry and by the unexpected discovery of the truth. He must necessarily retract this claim, since it is futile to contradict the truth and since no argument can convince us that good fortune is that which everyone else understands to be misfortune. Even this truth aside, it will be difficult for an educated man like Signor Volpi to convince us of his argument, as his own example serves to disprove his words.

To conclude, none of the problems enumerated by the author is born of an education. Given this judgment, we should either deny education to all (men and women alike) or to no one. For good reason, the arts and sciences have until now flourished among men. If women were to study, who knows whether given their natural serenity and tranquility they would also be subject to these same "hardships."

There you have my thoughts on the argument that you sent me, which I now return to you with some marginal notes, a great deal of material, if I am not mistaken, to provide you with a full counterargument. Since you determined to tempt me, for my part, you have had to pay the penance of reading my lengthy discourse. In any case, writing this has served to entertain me and now gives me the occasion to send you my regards. I am grateful for both opportunities, but above all, I would be deeply gratified if you would enlist yourself in the defense of our cause.

Farewell. Live happily.

20 December 1723

Translated by Rebecca Messbarger

---

21. Bernardino Perfetti (1681–1747) was a noted improvisational poet from Siena (see above, note 13). In 1725 he was crowned poet laureate on the Capitoline Hill at the behest of Pope Benedict XIII. Although he neither wrote down nor published his poetry during his lifetime, others transcribed his improvisational pieces, and these were published posthumously in Siena in 1747 and 1748 in two volumes. On Perfetti, see *Vita degli Arcadi illustri*, vol. 6 (Rome: Antonio de' Rossi, 1751).

I V

MARIA GAETANA AGNESI

TRANSLATOR'S INTRODUCTION

In the summer of 1727, Maria Gaetana Agnesi (1718–99) gave an oration in defense of women's education before a group of patricians assembled in her father's famous salon in Milan. Agnesi was the oldest daughter of Anna Brivio and Pietro Agnesi (ca. 1690–1752), the socially ambitious son of a prosperous silk merchant who prided himself on his talented children. Indeed, Pietro Agnesi considered the public display of the abilities of his two eldest daughters, Maria Gaetana and her younger sister, the musically talented Maria Teresa, essential ingredients in the social ascent of the Agnesi family into the ranks of the Milanese nobility.[1] By the early 1720s, Milanese patricians and scholars as well as foreign visitors to the city regularly attended the evening academies that Pietro Agnesi sponsored at Palazzo Agnesi on via Pantano. His precocious daughters were often present at these meetings. In 1723 an anonymous poet celebrated the five-year-old Maria Gaetana's marvelous ability in French; at a tender age, she became famous for her linguistic abilities and her "prodigious memory."[2] In all likelihood, this was the first occasion in which Maria Gaetana Agnesi was publicly celebrated for her learning.

While little is known about Agnesi's early years, it seems evident that her role in defending women's education and presenting herself as an example of a young girl capable of erudition was inspired, in part, by several impor-

---

1. Maria Teresa Agnesi (1720–95) first enjoyed fame as a musical prodigy when she played the harpsichord in her father's salon. She continued to play the harpsichord into adulthood and became known as a successful composer of operatic pieces that were performed publicly in Italy and other parts of Europe. In 1752 she married Don Pietro Antonio Pinottini.

2. *Alla nobile fanciulla D. Maria Gaetana Agnesi, Milanese, che nell'età di anni cinque parla mirabilmente il francese* (Milan, 1723); Giovanni Maria Mazzucchelli, "Maria Gaetana Agnesi," in *Gli scrittori d'Italia* (Brescia, 1753–63), vol. 1, part 1, 198.

tant events in 1722–23. The first source of inspiration was a book: Giuseppa Eleonora Barbapiccola's 1722 translation of René Descartes's *Principles of Philosophy* (1644). As has already been discussed elsewhere in this volume, the preface of Barbapiccola's Italian edition contained a lengthy justification of women's right to learn.[3] This book found its way into the Agnesi family library.[4] It may have inspired the somewhat opaque discussion of Cartesian philosophy that figures prominently in Agnesi's oration of 1727, where she discusses the role of sex in understanding the relationship between the mind and the body. At the very least, the fact that Pietro Agnesi owned a copy of this book suggests that the arguments made by Barbapiccola in defense of a woman's right to learn and philosophize interested a father in search of models to which his educated daughter might aspire.

The following year, the Accademia de' Ricovrati sponsored its important debate on whether women should be educated in the arts and sciences. As Rebecca Messbarger has discussed in the introduction to this volume, the Paduan naturalist Antonio Vallisneri (1661–1730) sponsored and moderated this debate in 1723 in his capacity as president of the academy. He did so in a context that closely connected the activities in Padua with those in Milan. By the early 1720s, Vallisneri enjoyed strong ties with the Milanese scholarly community through the offices of his patron, Clelia del Grillo Borromeo (1684–1777). The aristocratic Clelia was a flesh-and-blood model for Pietro Agnesi's image of a learned daughter; she was conversant in numerous languages, including English and some Arabic, and interested in all aspects of natural philosophy, mathematics, and natural history. The Milanese countess first met Vallisneri in 1718, after reading his publications. Subsequently, she invited him to spend part of his summers with her in Palazzo Borromeo, experimenting and participating in her salon—against the explicit wishes of her father-in-law. In 1722 Clelia del Grillo Borromeo asked Vallisneri to become president of a new scientific academy, the Accademia Clelia de' Vigilanti, that she hoped would rival all of the other leading academies in Europe for the brilliance of its members and the modernity of its aspirations.[5] In

3. See the translation of Barbapiccola's introduction in this volume; and Paula Findlen, "Translating the New Science: Women and the Circulation of Knowledge in Enlightenment Italy," *Configurations* 2 (1995): esp. 174–85.

4. Adele Bellù, Giulio Giacometti, Anna Serralunga Bardazza, and Piero Sessa, *Maria Gaetana Agnesi ricercatrice di Gesù Cristo* (Milan: NED, 1999), 1:131. This information comes from the inventory of Don Pietro Agnesi's library at the time of his death in 1752, listing "I Principii della filosofia di Renato des Cartes—in 8°, in Torino," Archivio di Stato, Milano, *Notarile* 43911, n. 345 (April 24, 1752), c. 43.

5. Clelia del Grillo Borromeo's role as a scientific patron and emblem of learning in early eighteenth-century Italy deserves further study. A good starting point is Giuliana Parabiago, "Clelia Borromeo del Grillo," *Correnti* 1 (1998): 36–60.

other words, Vallisneri's decision to sponsor a debate on women's education occurred at the same time that he was in the midst of an intense relationship with a learned woman in Milan and traveling frequently between Padua and Milan.

It is unknown whether Grillo Borromeo played any direct role in sponsoring the 1723 Ricovrati debate, or to what extent she facilitated the publication of this debate with additional responses to it by learned women in 1729.[6] But Grillo Borromeo was the most likely means by which Pietro Agnesi and Antonio Vallisneri would have met and known of each other's interest in learned women. The Ricovrati debate occurred in the very year that a Milanese poet celebrated the linguistic ability of Agnesi's eldest daughter. Pietro Agnesi wasted no time in developing Maria Gaetana's talents in many different directions. For the next three years, abbot Niccolò Gemelli instructed Maria Gaetana in Latin. In 1725 Father Giuseppe Maria Reina, the Theatine abbot of the Church of San Antonio, became her spiritual advisor, since the seven-year-old Maria Gaetana already displayed a decided inclination toward pious pursuits. It is not clear at what point Agnesi began the study of mathematics and philosophy, which would bring her great fame through Europe with the publication of her *Analytical Institutions for the Use of Italian Youth* (1748).[7] In all likelihood, this did not occur until the end of the 1720s, after she had mastered all of the basic subjects that younger pupils were expected to know, including a strong humanistic foundation in ancient and modern languages, rhetoric, poetry, and history—the very ingredients from which her oration was composed.[8]

By the summer of 1727, Agnesi's Latin tutor, Gemelli, considered her intellectual and linguistic abilities to be sufficiently developed to encourage his pupil to present an oration. The exact circumstances that led to the oration remain unclear, but the subject of her presentation explicitly took up the themes explored by the Accademia de' Ricovrati four years earlier. In 1727 Pietro Agnesi and the tutors he employed in the education of his eldest daughter felt that Maria Gaetana was mature and accomplished enough to

---

6. The Paduan patrician Guglielmo Camposanpietro's contribution to the original debate on June 16, 1723—"Discorso accademico . . . che debbono ammettersi le Donne allo studio delle Scienze, e delle belle Arti"—contains the only direct reference to Grillo Borromeo, when he mentions Vallisneri's dedications of several of his scientific publications to "Lady Clelia Borromea, the most singular honor of our century and immortal glory of Italy's women." *Discorsi accademici di vari autori viventi intorno agli studi delle donne* (Padua, 1729), 9.

7. Maria Gaetana Agnesi, *Instituzioni analitiche ad uso della gioventù italiana*, 2 vols. (Milan, 1748).

8. Mazzucchelli writes that she initiated the study of geometry and algebra while she was perfecting her languages and subsequently studied physics, experimental philosophy, and metaphysics; see his *Gli scrittori d'Italia*, vol. 1, part 1, 199.

make this public display of her learning an occasion for Milan to contribute to the debates about women's education. The fact that they did not have the oration stand alone but presented it as part of a conversation about women's learning—otherwise conducted in poetry by male academicians who participated in the Agnesi salon[9]—suggests that this was a carefully orchestrated event.

In all likelihood, very little, if any, of the content of Agnesi's *Academic Oration in Which It Is Demonstrated That the Studies of the Liberal Arts by the Female Sex Are by No Means Inappropriate* was hers. On August 18, when Agnesi stood before her father's friends and associates to recite this oration from memory, she was only two months beyond her ninth birthday. This was an unusually young age for anyone, male or female, to give an oration, let alone to discuss publicly such a controversial subject.[10] It has been suggested by Agnesi's leading biographer, Luisa Anzoletti, that Gemelli composed the oration in Italian and asked his pupil to translate it into Latin and present it publicly in the garden of the family palace.[11] But it is equally possible that he and others closely involved in Agnesi's intellectual development simply sketched the outline of the oration and suggested texts and themes to which she might refer, allowing her to contribute in some small measure to the final shape of the text. Later that year it appeared in print, accompanied by the poems recited in defense of women's education and praise of Agnesi's miraculous accomplishments.[12]

Two years after Agnesi's *Academic Oration* appeared in Milan, it was

9. See the poetic discussion of women's education in the second half of Maria Gaetana Agnesi, *Oratio, quâ ostenditur: atrium liberalium studia à femineo sexu neutiquam abhorrere. Habita a Maria de Agnesis rhethoricae operam dante anno aetatis suae nono nondum exacto, die 18 Augusto 1727* (Milan: Per J. R. Malatestam, 1727). This material was not included in the 1729 Ricovrati publication.

10. Following the Roman rhetorician Quintilian's guidelines in the *Institutio oratoria*, Agnesi, of course, should not have given an oration at all, because this was the one kind of learning that he reserved exclusively for boys, typically imagining them entering schools of rhetoric around age fourteen or fifteen after they had completed grammar school. See George Kennedy, *Quintilian* (New York: Twayne, 1969), 39–40. Renaissance humanists generally reinforced the idea that women should not learn rhetoric, because it was a public art, though female humanists such as Cassandra Fedele (1465–1558) were clear exceptions to this general rule. See Margaret L. King and Albert Rabil Jr., *Her Immaculate Hand: Selected Works by and about the Woman Humanists of Quattrocento Italy* (Binghamton, NY: Medieval and Renaissance Texts and Studies, 1992), 8.

11. Luisa Anzoletti, *Maria Gaetana Agnesi* (Milan: L. F. Cogliati, 1900), 86–109. Anzoletti provides no concrete evidence for her conclusion, but certainly it was in keeping with the classic practice of oratory to set a topic and suggest the content for a young rhetorician who might benefit from repeating and polishing the words of her teachers. See Quintilian, *Institutio oratoria*, 2.6.

12. Agnesi, *Oratio, quâ ostenditur.*

reprinted in the *Academic Discourses by Various Living Authors on the Education of Women, the Majority Recited in the Academy of the Ricovrati in Padua* (1729). Further research may eventually establish who decided to include this text as a supplement to the original debate, but in all likelihood Clelia del Grillo Borromeo had heard, or at least read, the original oration and brought it to Vallisneri's attention. However, since she did not mention it directly in her surviving letters to Vallisneri, it is equally possible that Vallisneri chose it on his own initiative, since he was in Milan from late August through September of 1727.[13] The fact remains, however, that in 1729 only two women in Italy were invited to represent a woman's perspective on the question of women's education, and one was an eleven-year-old girl.

Translating Agnesi's oration poses a number of problems. While the content of the oration seems unlikely to have been written by a nine-year-old, the language of the oration in some places bears traces of an uncertain hand. At times, the Latin is ungrammatical and impenetrable. In a number of places, it is unclear what exactly Agnesi wished to say—perhaps a sign that she was struggling to translate into her own words adult concepts and examples that her tutors and perhaps her father had given her. Of course, it is also possible that she did not even compose the Latin oration but simply recited it. But I am inclined to believe that she did participate in the writing of the Latin version, in part, because it is often vague on a number of points where a more polished orator would have made the meaning clearer. After all, Agnesi made her initial reputation in Milan as a precocious linguist. Her eighteenth-century biographer, Count Giovanni Maria Mazzucchelli, reported that she allegedly translated Father Lorenzo Scupoli's *Spiritual Battle* into Greek after her public success of 1727.[14] Unlike her Neapolitan counterpart Barbapiccola, Agnesi was known for her ability to translate vernacular works into ancient, scholarly languages. She did not represent the new ideal of access to knowledge but a more humanistic notion of erudition that reinforced her image as a learned Christian woman in the tradition of the seventeenth-century Dutch philologist and philosopher Anna Maria van Schurman.

13. The surviving correspondence between Vallisneri and Grillo Borromeo can be found in the Biblioteca dell'Accademia de' Concordi in Rovigo: Conc. 360/32 (17/T) and 338/50. Vallisneri discusses his 1727 trip to Milan in his correspondence with the Swiss naturalist Louis Bourguet; Bibliothèque Publique et Universitaire de Neuchâtel, *Fonds Bourguet*, MS 1282, ff. 293–94 (Antonio Vallisneri to Louis Bourguet, Milan, September 16, 1727). Since Vallisneri mentions being in Florence "for almost all of August," he probably was not present to hear Agnesi's oration but arrived in Milan when all of the city was still talking about it.

14. Mazzucchelli, *Gli scrittori d'Italia*, vol. 1, part 1, 199. Mazzucchelli commented that he had found no evidence of an actual translation of Lorenzo Scupoli's *Combattimento spirituale*; nonetheless, the story reinforced Agnesi's reputation as a translator of important works.

Agnesi underscored several issues in her presentation. Her oration repeatedly takes to task those critics of women's education who restrict learning to a small circle of elite males rather than imagining learning as a public good for all of humanity. She laments the ignorance of husbands who confine women to enforced idleness upon marriage and who allow their daughters to grow up equally unlearned. Agnesi chastised her audience for condescending to women and encouraged them to think of a learned wife as the best asset of any marriage. Such attitudes reflected the emerging consensus about women's education in the early eighteenth century.[15] In a number of respects, Agnesi's oration is bolder than that of the other female contributor to the 1729 debates, the Sienese noblewoman Aretafila Savini de' Rossi, because it emanates from a more conservative source. While Savini de' Rossi argued for women's education in Italian from the perspective of an eighteenth-century woman engaged in modern literary studies, Agnesi presented the necessity of woman's education as the logical outcome of a classical education. And yet there is a decisive strand of Enlightenment universalism evident in her oration. Agnesi and her tutors, for example, considered the education of women to be an important step in unshackling humanity from the bondage of ignorance. That such a strong message would come from the mouth of a nine-year-old girl must have been powerful indeed. While constantly tempered with proclamations of modesty and statements indicating her lack of authority, Agnesi's oration nonetheless made her an example of what girls who were educated by their fathers could do.

At the same time, however, Agnesi's oration sets clear limits on women's use of their learning. Neither she nor her tutors envisioned women entering the realms of politics or religion. Neatly refuting Giovanni Antonio Volpi's arguments that men possess both strength of body and mind, she separates the two, leaving war and contests of physical prowess to men alone. Agnesi repeatedly observes that women do not participate in public life (despite the fact that a number of her examples of learned women, such as Hypatia of Alexandria, clearly contradict this perspective). She argues for "private study," even though she is well aware that it will dissolve the walls of domesticity that separate men from women. Most importantly, she argues for a return to the values of the past, when women were instructed by men and also instructed them in the most profound aspects of philosophy.

---

15. On this subject, see Luciano Guerci, *La discussione sulla donna nell'Italia del Settecento* (Turin: Tirrenia Stampatori, 1987); and Rebecca Messbarger, *The Century of Women: Representations of Women in Eighteenth-Century Italian Public Discourse* (Toronto: University of Toronto Press, 2002).

Like many of the Renaissance women humanists who preceded her in the fifteenth and sixteenth centuries, Agnesi saw history as an important resource in crafting a successful argument in favor of women's education. History demonstrated that women had not always been unlearned and that men had often encouraged their learning.[16] The history of the ancient world, Christian and pagan, was her primary source of inspiration, but she did not neglect more recent examples as well. Agnesi ends her oration with three noteworthy modern examples to complement her evaluation of women's accomplishments in antiquity. The first, Isabella Roser, was a Spanish noblewoman who sponsored Ignatius Loyola during his initial spiritual conversion and ultimately followed him to Rome in 1543 in the hope of persuading Loyola to found a female branch of the Society of Jesus.[17] Agnesi's decision to mention Roser undoubtedly reflected the anti-Jesuit biases of her tutors, since Roser had openly defied Loyola's stated desire to have the Jesuits be an all-male order by persuading Pope Paul III to enact a papal bull forcing Loyola to accept the spiritual vow of Roser and two other women. The pope's subsequent decision to allow Loyola to release the women from their vows made the Society of Jesus a definitively male religious order, to the great bitterness of Roser. Agnesi's spiritual model, in other words, was a woman who used the authority of the papacy to insist, unsuccessfully in the long run, that women should have a place in one of the most important and powerful new religious orders to be founded in the age of Tridentine reform.[18]

The second modern woman whom Agnesi singled out for praise was the Venetian noblewoman Elena Lucrezia Cornaro Piscopia (1646–84),

---

16. On the subject of humanist writing and the birth of women's history, see Natalie Zemon Davis, "Gender and Genre: Women as Historical Writers, 1400–1820," in *Beyond Their Sex: Learned Women of the European Past*, ed. Patricia Labalme (New York: New York University Press, 1980), 153–82; and Paula Findlen, "Historical Thought in the Renaissance," in *Companion to Historical Thought*, ed. Lloyd Kramer and Sarah Maza (Oxford: Blackwell, 2002), 99–120. It is not impossible that Agnesi and her tutor had access to works such as Lucrezia Marinella's *The Nobility and Excellence of Women* (1600) and Gilles Ménages, *The History of Women Philosophers* (1690), though she does not lift her information verbatim from either text.

17. Ludwig Pastor, *The History of the Popes*, ed. and trans. Ralph Francis Kerr, 2nd ed. (London: Kegan Paul, Trench, Trubner, 1923), 12:20, 27, 52–54; and W. W. Meissner, S.J., *Ignatius of Loyola: The Psychology of a Saint* (New Haven, CT: Yale University Press, 1992), 260–70. See her correspondence with Loyola in H. Rahner, S.J., *St. Ignatius Loyola: Letters to Women* (New York: Herder & Herder, 1960).

18. Curiously, this episode is omitted in John O'Malley's excellent *The First Jesuits* (Cambridge, MA: Harvard University Press, 1993), though female patronage and Loyola's subsequent rejection of the idea of having "spiritual daughters" seem to have been rather important to the early years of the Society of Jesus.

whose university degree in philosophy from Padua in 1678 made her famous throughout Europe.[19] Piscopia was also the first woman member of the
Ricovrati, admitted on February 11, 1669, so the reference to her accomplishments reminded listeners of the importance of the Paduan academy in
celebrating women's learning. Agnesi's reference to Piscopia also raises an
important question: to what extent should cultural institutions validate the
accomplishments of learned women? Women do not possess "the dignity of
teaching," she observes early in her oration. And yet the historical section
of her presentation is filled with examples of ancient women who taught.
Beneath the surface of Agnesi's comments lay a fundamental issue regarding
the place of women in the Italian universities. Was Piscopia a precedent for
women of her generation?

The idea of women graduating from and teaching in the universities
was the subject of renewed interest in the years preceding and following
Agnesi's oration. In 1722 the sixteen-year-old daughter of a Bolognese noble, Maria Vittoria Delfini Dosi, almost succeeded in getting the College
of Jurisprudence of the University of Bologna to award her a law degree.[20]
This episode was well known enough outside of Bologna that news of it may
have reached Milan. Three years after Agnesi's oration was republished, in
1732 Laura Bassi became the first woman to graduate from any university
since Piscopia's degree in 1678 and the first woman whom we can definitively document as holding a professorship.[21] We can only wonder how this
must have incited the envy of Agnesi's ambitious father, who subsequently
made her at least the equal of Bassi in her philosophical and mathemati-

19. See Francesco Ludovico Maschietto, *Elena Lucrezia Cornaro Piscopa (1646–1684) prima donna
laureata nel mondo* (Padua: Editrice Antenore, 1978); Paul Oskar Kristeller, "Learned Women of
Early Modern Italy: Humanists and University Scholars," in *Beyond Their Sex*, ed. Labalme, 91–
116; and Paula Findlen, "Imaginary Graduates: Women and the Universities in Medieval and
Early Modern Italy," forthcoming.

20. Lucia Toschi Traversi, "Verso l'inserimento delle donne nel mondo accademico," in *Alma
Mater Studiorum. La presenza femminile dal XVIII al XX secolo* (Bologna: CLUEB, 1988), 23–30. For
a more recent account, see Marta Cavazza, "'Dottrici' e lettrici dell'Università di Bologna nel
Settecento," *Annali di storia delle università italiane* 1 (1997): 109–26.

21. The most comprehensive study of Laura Bassi's life and work is Beate Ceranski, *"Und sie
fürchtet sich vor niemandem." Die Physikierin Laura Bassi (1711–1778)* (Frankfurt: Campus Verlag, 1996).
The only studies of Bassi in English to date are Paula Findlen, "Science as a Career in Enlightenment Italy: The Strategies of Laura Bassi," *Isis* 84 (1993): 441–69; and Gabriella Berti Logan,
"The Desire to Contribute: An Eighteenth-Century Italian Woman of Science," *American Historical Review* 99 (1994): 785–812; and Findlen, "The Scientist's Body: The Nature of a Woman
Philosopher in Enlightenment Italy," in *The Faces of Nature in Enlightenment Europe*, ed. Gianna Pomata and Lorraine Daston (Berlin: Berliner Wissenschafs-Verlag, 2003), 211–36.

cal education.[22] In 1749, more than twenty years after Agnesi had become famous for her youthful oration on women's education, she was offered a chair in mathematics at the University of Bologna at the encouragement of Pope Benedict XIV, who had read and admired her *Analytic Institutions.* Agnesi refused the professorship because she had no desire for a public position or any reason to leave her native city. And yet it must have been a profound source of satisfaction to be offered the very thing—a university position—that seemed unobtainable for a woman in 1727.

If Piscopia raised the question of women's relationship to educational institutions, Agnesi's third modern example reminded her listeners of more contentious questions about the role of women in public debates about culture. Piscopia had been dead for over forty years by the time Agnesi gave her oration, but Anne Lefèvre Dacier (1651–1720) was only recently deceased and the most celebrated French woman of letters in the early decades of the eighteenth century. She was well known for her 1699 translation of Homer's *Odyssey,* her 1711 translation of the *Iliad,* and numerous other translations and critical works that emanated from her position as France's most noted and prolific Greek scholar in the late seventeenth and early eighteenth century. Agnesi, like Barbapiccola, expressed great admiration for her accomplishments.

What Agnesi did not mention, however, was Dacier's controversial role in publicly defending Homer's authorship of these works as part of her wholesale condemnation of modern French literature, in particular, the novel. Wife of the noted classicist André Dacier (1651–1722), who was both royal librarian and secretary of the French Academy, and a convert to Catholicism, Madame Dacier was a powerful and articulate figure in the battle between the Ancients and the Moderns.[23] To praise Dacier was to praise the most controversial proponent of the role of a classical education as a foundation for modern citizenship in the Republic of Letters. It is pleasing to think that Agnesi might have received her first exposure to the

22. The best account of Agnesi's transformation from a youthful prodigy into a well-known mathematician is Massimo Mazzotti, "Maria Gaetana Agnesi: The Unusual Life and Mathematical Work of an Eighteenth-Century Woman," *Isis* 92 (2001): 657–83.

23. Joan DeJean, *Ancients and Moderns: Culture Wars and the Making of a Fin de Siècle* (Chicago: University of Chicago Press, 1997), 71, 97–108, 131, 135; and Julie Candler Hayes, "Of Meaning and Modernity: Anne Dacier and the Homer Debate," *EMF: Studies in Early Modern France* 8, ed. David Lee Rubin (2002), 173–95. See especially Dacier's six-hundred-page *Des causes de la corruption du goût* (Paris, 1714), written in response to a critique of her antiquarian approach to translating Homer and presenting him as the sole author of an epic that she believed to be a scrupulously realistic account of ancient Greek history and customs.

Greek epics through Dacier's translations since she seems to have learned French before mastering Latin or Greek. The reference to Dacier at the end of Agnesi's oration further reminds us of the role enlightened Catholicism played in encouraging women to use their learning to defend traditional intellectual values.[24] Selecting these three women as her role models, Agnesi presented herself as heir to a powerful tradition of learned and pious women who shaped religion, transformed the universities, and directed contemporary debates about culture. Since Dacier was the third woman admitted the Accademia de' Ricovrati, when she was invited to join the academy in 1679—the first in a long list of French women writers offered membership in the period leading up to the 1723 debate—her presence at the end of the oration further reminded her listeners of the virtues of an academy that celebrated such women by admitting them to their institution as honorary members.[25]

Agnesi's oration is not a great piece of writing, nor does it probe deeply any of the important issues it raises about separating the cultivation of the mind from the condition of the body and about the utility and desirability of women's education. Like most orations, it is a demonstration piece, an assemblage of quotes and allusions designed to display her education and familiarity with classical oratory. Yet at the same time, it is a passionate defense of education for young girls who, with the proper encouragement, could become learned companions for their husbands (and in some instances public participants in debates about knowledge). Given the subsequent trajectory of Agnesi's life after the death of her father in 1752, when she deliberately retreated from the salons, refused to marry, and shunned the publicity that her early intellectual accomplishments had brought her, it is unlikely that these were entirely her own sentiments. In 1727 Agnesi was the mouthpiece for the circle that met in Pietro Agnesi's salon on via Pantano to debate and experiment with the idea of women's education. She had little authority, as she reminded her audience, but hoped to encourage them to use their own

24. Mazzotti makes this same observation about Agnesi's own intellectual trajectory in his "Maria Gaetana Agnesi," further reinforcing the idea that the references to Roser, Piscopia, and Dacier were designed to establish a history of learned Catholic women in the early modern period in which Agnesi herself could now participate.

25. Attilio Maggiolo, "Elena Lucrezia Cornaro Piscopia e le altre donne aggregate all'Accademia patavina dei Ricovrati," *Padova e la sua provincia* 24, no. 11–12 (1978): 33–36. Prior to 1723, twenty-six women were admitted to the Accademia de' Ricovrati. All but four were French. The other four were all local talents—Piscopia and the three daughters of the French physician Charles Patin who taught at the University of Padua from 1676 until his death in 1693. During his tenure as prince of the Ricovrati (1678–79), numerous French writers and scholars, male and female, were admitted, including his ten-year-old daughter Gabriella.

powers of persuasion to improve opportunities for women's education. Do not reject "everything I dare to offer," she exclaimed. These words sound indeed like a nine-year-old making her first public appearance.

Agnesi's subsequent activities only increased the scope of her reputation. At age fourteen—the year that Laura Bassi became a university graduate and physics professor in Bologna—she became the centerpiece of a public salon that drew distinguished visitors to Milan. In this next phase of her life, she publicly debated every aspect of ancient and modern philosophy and mathematics in Latin and conversed about other subjects in modern languages. Agnesi ultimately published her *Philosophical Propositions* (1738), a record of 191 theses that she debated in the salon, prior to undertaking the writing of the 1748 mathematics textbook that would make her famous throughout Europe.[26] In short, her participation in the Ricovrati debate was a concerted effort on the part of her family and tutors to make her into one of the most visible learned women in eighteenth-century Italy.

Later in life, however, Agnesi preferred to be remembered for her piety and charity. During the 1750s, she withdrew from public life; she ceased to correspond with other scholars and devoted herself to the care of the poor. A reluctant participant in the spectacle of learning that was celebrated in the salons, the adult Agnesi believed that her learning was simply another manifestation of her devotion to God. She shunned the salons and academies that had admitted her and increasingly wrote about mystical devotion if she wrote at all. The nine-year-old orator, however, was a participant in a far more contentious debate about the right to learn. It is little wonder that Vallisneri was so eager to include her *Academic Oration* in his collection.

Paula Findlen

---

26. Mazzucchelli, *Gli scrittori d'Italia*, vol. 1, part 1, 199; Maria Gaetana Agnesi, *Propositiones philosophicae* (Milan, 1738).

AN ORATION IN WHICH IT IS DEMONSTRATED THAT THE STUDIES OF THE LIBERAL ARTS BY THE FEMALE SEX ARE BY NO MEANS INAPPROPRIATE. A WORK IN THE RHETORIC OF DANTE SPOKEN BY MARIA DE AGNESI, NOT YET QUITE NINE YEARS OLD, ON 18 AUGUST 1727.

Dedicated to the Admirable Reverend Father Doctor Agostino Tolota, Canon Regular, a Most Learned Man and Most Noble Orator

To the Most Learned and Cultured Reverend Father, Doctor Agostino Tolota:[27]

Your affection for me, and that extraordinary humanity by which you became my encourager and supporter in the cultivation of the liberal arts, moves me to bring you a girlish little gift. This oration was delivered by me in a private school of rhetoric. In order that I may act in accordance with custom (because of my age), it seems that I am permitted, therefore, to inscribe it to you with these figures and name it after you. To increase the value of the gift, I added from others what I was unable to produce on my own.[28] Whatever boredom this progeny of a newborn mind may cause your learning—for which your name flies through the mouths of the wisest men in all Italy—it will be lessened and negated by the pleasure of reading what has been added, in which, of course, you may desire nothing but the truth. And so accept this gift in the spirit that you usually show me and all my family. It has been produced from a meager storehouse, but it is advanced with great spirit because, if I sense that it has been accepted by you, I will be wonderfully inspired to be able to bestow better things. Farewell.

Most obligingly and humbly yours,
Maria de Agnesis[29]

27. Father Agustino Tolota remains an obscure figure in Milan's ecclesiastical history, though he was obviously part of the group of clerics facilitating Agnesi's education. Anzoletti calls him "Father Tolotta," but it is more likely that his name was spelled "Tolota." Anzoletti, *Maria Gaetana Agnesi*, 103.

28. From the start, Agnesi reminds her listeners that this is primarily not an original work but an oration written with the help of others, borrowing the words of the dead as well as probably relying on those of the living. She reminds us that it was designed to demonstrate her facility with Latin.

29. The Latin version of Agnesi's name reflected her father's desire to invent a nobility for his family, signified by the *de* before her surname. See Mazzotti, "Maria Gaetana Agnesi."

ACADEMIC ORATION IN WHICH IT IS DEMONSTRATED THAT THE STUDIES OF THE LIBERAL ARTS BY THE FEMALE SEX ARE BY NO MEANS INAPPROPRIATE

It will perhaps seem strange and unusual that I, not yet at the end of my childhood and having scarcely completed my youthful training in Latin, dare to speak in the presence of very distinguished men who are most well versed in every kind of knowledge, and whose minds are not accustomed to take pleasure, save by more elevated instruction, and whose ears are used to dissertations of more mature eloquence. Clearly I should be afraid, lest they turn away from the purpose of today's oration, considering it nothing more than the frivolous opinion of a clever girl, especially since nothing might appear to be more unsuitable to an assembly of manly wisdom than womanly speech. However, I am certainly aware of my weakness, but relying greatly on your humanity, every fear having been wholly banished, I am by no means afraid to descend into this arena full of risk and danger, not only on account of the authority of the most excellent men who surround me, but also on account of the justness of the cause that I am about to take up, which gives me the greatest hope.

For truly by whose judgment ever, if not by yours, very distinguished listeners, must it finally be decreed that those men who forbid women altogether from cultivation of the best kinds of knowledge[30] deal somewhat more harmfully with them when, furthermore, it is permitted to every mortal to be wise and when the ability to distinguish intelligence is related more to learning than to sex. For shame! Must the womanly republic[31] alone grow old any longer in its domestic idleness, when the schools are ablaze with literary labor? Must it alone not be allowed to speak with a learned voice, when the academies protest noisily and learnedly? As if it were taboo to have women speak eloquently, or listen to them speak. Truly we do not maintain—far from it—that feminine eloquence should be introduced onto sacred stages,[32]

---

30. Agnesi refers to *disciplina*, so she might have specific "disciplines" in mind but since she used this word frequently to talk about knowledge in a general rather than specific way, we have preferred to translate it less literally.

31. The invocation of a *muliebris Respublica* suggests the persistence of Laura Cereta's fifteenth-century ideal of a "republic of women." However, Agnesi's use of this image allows us to see how the humanist ideal of scholarly community could also have other meanings by the eighteenth century, since she uses this term to describe the predicament of women in general who are removed from the world of learning. See Laura Cereta, *Collected Letters of a Renaissance Feminist*, trans. and ed. Diana Robin (Chicago: University of Chicago Press, 1977), 80.

32. In this passage, Agnesi makes a clear distinction between the idea of learned women publicly debating knowledge in a secular environment, and the more controversial issue of women

but we contend only that it should not be entirely banished and removed from the schools. We do not reopen the court and the forum to it, but let us not close the academies and the schools: we do not intrude in the public events of civil affairs, nor do we drive away truth by private study. For all these reasons, I consider it worthwhile today to reveal to my illustrious listeners, no matter how many surround me, how contrary to the truth is the opinion of those who suppose that the studies of the liberal arts are judged unsuitable in women.

Do not expect, listeners, that following the common practice of orators, I would lay the foundation of my oration on this point, since I think I will have done my job if, however many things my adversaries are able to force upon me, I may weaken and destroy them to such an extent that the deceit of empty gildings is removed and a plain and genuine version of the truth at last appears. Therefore, even if many objections are raised against this proposition of ours, nonetheless they attack us especially by a threefold strategy. First, by custom, which, having been introduced by our ancestors, only grows in posterity. It ought to be powerful, since it is supported by that strength and that authority which has always maintained the sanctity of laws and the sacrosanct laws of peoples since the birth of mankind and has been preserved by inviolable religion. Next, they force upon the female sex its weakness, making it absolutely no match for the laborious study of letters and the difficult attainment of knowledge, which weakens and enervates even manly strength. Finally, there is a certain disturbance that, like a battering ram, breaks down and overturns all civil and domestic affairs. To avoid this it is best, indeed necessary, that female minds—as they say—having been elevated enough on their own and filled, be kept away entirely from the liberal disciplines and be content with the management of domestic affairs, busying themselves with the needle and the spindle; these things, and others of this kind, are proper to women, unlike pen and paper, since nothing is really more irritating than a learned woman in a debate. Most equitable judges, these things are the fortifications and foundations that must be overturned and destroyed. I dare to promise that the opinion of all your adversaries will be rejected by me as a thing of no importance.

And surely what mortal does not see, even more clearly than noonday light, how much more destructive customs grow stronger. It is not the fault of our ancestors, but a defect of the times. When they are at their worst, we

---

interpreting scripture and speaking publicly in church. Such statements were in accordance with Paul in 1 Cor 14:34 as well as 1 Tm 2:9–15, often attributed to Paul, both of which emphasized the virtue of women's silence and reminded the faithful that women should not teach men.

see that the ancient custom of living honestly, religiously, and wisely is corrupted and shaken. Once we reach this point, with the state and condition of everything unchanged so far with respect to the world, almost no trace of ancient probity is evident. Where indeed is the education of the body easily and readily procured? Where is that refined use of nourishment? Where is sobriety, where is temperance? Is this the custom of our ancestors? Is this the practice of the ancients? Who, at any time, has been accustomed to seek out foreign banquets beyond the seas and almost beyond the confines of nature, at the loss of wealth and life? Who always summoned new kinds of garments from barbarous regions? Who ripped open the insides of mountains, traversed the seas, and sought marble to construct enormous buildings? This was, I repeat, this was the best way of living among our ancestors. But now, truly, for shame! Such values have become obsolete in later generations, so that it is right to exclaim rather vehemently, in chorus with the prince of Roman eloquence: "O times! O customs!"[33] It would be a happy direction indeed if, as in those ages most auspicious for learning, girls too were accustomed to being educated and formed by domestic tutelage. Their parents and teachers could devote efforts solely to this goal, instructing them, as they say, from a most tender age with the best kinds of learning.[34] However many free-born children they have begotten, it is to the greatest honor of their lineage if they have returned them to the fatherland full of wisdom.

But if, rather than repeating the ancient examples of the republics of Rome and Sparta, we review more recent histories and centuries closer to us, Origen and Jerome come to mind. The one, although of a most perspicacious mind and whose ingenuity in penetrating deeper mysteries clearly was divinely made, did not disdain educating more uncultured young girls with learning.[35] By no means did he consider his work to have been wasted, but rather to have been well-employed, allowing him to strengthen the weakness of the female sex by creating a garrison of the best arts and doctrine. The other, having been transferred from the assemblies and crowds of his fellow citizens to the most holy solitude of the cave of Bethlehem on the grounds that the one thing that was uncorrupted was spending life in the desert,

33. As a demonstration of the use of Ciceronian rhetoric in this oration, Agnesi invokes Cicero's famous phrase—*O tempora, o mores!*—in his *Orations against Catiline* regarding the conspiracy of L. Sergius Cataline in 63 BCE. See Cicero, *Orationese in Catilinam*, 1.1.2.

34. Again, Agnesi refers to *disciplina* to denote different kinds of knowledge, underscoring the idea that learning itself is a form of discipline for children.

35. Born in Alexandria, Origen (ca. 185–253/254) was a Christian theologian versed in Greek learning who taught converts to Christianity and had disciples of both sexes in his famous school, despite the fact that he generally saw women as the embodiment of lust.

persevered in instructing, by means of letters, very chaste matrons who were shaped by his teaching to understand every doctrine and probity.[36] Nor can it be doubted that women received instruction by great men in learning and sanctity, since so many women, learned in every kind of knowledge, have flourished in almost every age that there is not enough time to name them all. But to what end do I mention these things, if not so that those holy men, defenders of tradition, might understand how they reject and abuse those very women who should be allowed to shine? If any woman should happen to attain such learning, they sneer, it should be rooted out and, though pure and inviolate, shamefully discarded.[37] But perhaps they wish to brand this fame belonging to our ancestors a foul thing because, although they conveyed to us examples of honesty and temperance, they judged it right—on the basis of imprudent advice—to forbid the cultivation of virtue to some among their descendants.

→But it will be objected that the soft condition of women and the slight composition of their limbs seem enough, and more, to convince us that their intelligence is by no means made for the sciences.[38] Indeed, can enough hope be shown that that sex, which nature made for leisure, will be equal to the task of scholarly labor? Some strength of a cooperative body is needed for great diligence in the cultivation of the best disciplines. Come now! Bring forth those nimble candidates for wisdom, throw open the shrine of learning to the most pugnacious athletes. For shame! Scarcely did they take in hand the learned tomes of authors, which should be lingered over day and night, when they threw them out right away, despising all the best even before they read them. Yet if they are ordered more sternly either to commit something to memory or cultivate it in writing then, like horses that are tied to the millstone once their embellishments and trappings have been

---

36. Saint Jerome (342–420) was noteworthy among the early Church Fathers for his female disciples and for the religious letters he wrote to pious and learned women. Around 385, he left Rome with the Roman matron Paula (d. 404) and her daughter Eustochium (d. 418/419). They traveled with him to the Holy Land, eventually settling in Bethlehem, where they founded a male monastery, three female convents, and a hospice for pilgrims. During this period, Jerome lived in a cave near Bethlehem while completing his Latin Vulgate with the assistance of Paula and her daughter.

37. In this rather opaque passage, Agnesi literally imagines critics of women's learning discarding their knowledge by putting it up for sale in the marketplace rather than cherishing it in the privacy of their homes. Such comments were not without a certain irony in light of her father's decision to make his family salon a public forum for displaying the talents of his two eldest daughters, an aspect of her family life that Agnesi increasingly abhorred as she grew older.

38. This section outlines the views of opponents of women's education, to indicate the ability of the orator to make the argument from both sides.

removed, they mourn, complain loudly, linger, and hang back. Certainly because women possess the structure and disposition for soft things, they cannot bear even the briefest physical labor. Therefore, let us open the world more to these womanly things: the bookcase, mirror, the curling iron, earrings, boxes of ointment, bracelets, and yet a hundred other barbarous names of the craftsman.

To be sure, these words are plausible, and perhaps we should have some confidence in them—unless, having been recalled to the scales by the great justice of the judgment of the wisest men, they are certainly found to be nearly empty and unsuitable. Act, most eminent fathers, as is dignified and proper, investigate well and weigh carefully the entirety of this great matter. Denounce, above all, the most severe Catos of our time, censors of bodies more than minds, who situate the dignity of mankind in its outer appearance, as if the more charming beauty did not lie beneath the shell of the limbs.[39] For indeed, what man of sound mind, although he inspects the disparate composition of this shapeless mass of clay, nonetheless does not doubt that we have been divinely conceived with an equal soul? Perhaps some modern sect of philosophers may arise that separates minds according to sex, or that resolves to disagree with the source of this idea, Pythagoras.[40] Truly, you may not taint the dignity of the rational soul—indeed, I do not hesitate to declare this publicly—so long as it is the companion of this mortality, using the limbs as supports which bind it to the senses. After those bodily members have been cut down and weakened, the plainly admirable force, by which

39. Marcus Porcius Cato (234–149 BCE) was consul of the Roman Republic in 195. The invocation of Cato recalls the role of public orators in campaigning against bad morals, as Cato did by criticizing the luxury and immorality of the Roman elite and monitoring the behavior of public officials. Cato's daughter Portia was also reputed to be a good philosopher, so perhaps this passage is also designed to recall a famous Roman orator who did not disdain to educate his daughter.

40. This section of the oration implicitly engages with debates fostered by certain readings of Cartesian philosophy that underscored its utility in the debates about women's education. In the hands of Cartesian philosophers such as Poullain de la Barre (1647–1723), Descartes's separation of the mind from the body became the basis for arguing for women's intellectual equality, since a disembodied, universal mind was beyond sex (see note 19 in the Barbapiccola translation). Quite characteristically, Agnesi's oration gives this idea a more ancient pedigree by invoking the ancient Greek philosopher Pythagoras (ca. 569–475 BCE), who argued that men and women were the exact opposites of each other in every respect. Pythagoras was known for his numerous (or at least prominent) female disciples, making him a worthy predecessor to Descartes as a philosopher who educated women as well as men. The general climate for these debates is discussed in Erica Harth, *Cartesian Women: Versions and Subversions of Rational Discourse in the Ancien Regime* (Ithaca, NY: Cornell University Press, 1992); and Londa Schiebinger, *The Mind Has No Sex? Women in the Origins of Modern Science* (Cambridge, MA: Harvard University Press, 1989).

the better part of mankind demonstrates that it is an image of divinity, is destroyed. Hence, without a doubt those who obtain a more refined bodily structure that releases the body from all bounds are in a better condition to acquire the sciences.[41] It is also their lot to exhibit a most ready intelligence in everything that pertains to the studies of letters.

Now consider the opinion of natural philosophers and judge carefully the disposition of the feminine body. How great the power of the purity and clarity of her blood! What vigor! What well-shaped limbs! Her voice, too, overflows with every delight; what an enticing kind of oratory it has. Next, if you examine the face, which is a sure index of the soul, does not her noble and splendid character offer itself right away to gaze upon? And therefore, who does not see that nature has provided enough, and more, for the delicate constitution of women, since in general the acuity of mind is accustomed to the burden of too great a pile of limbs, and not otherwise. But is it not more abominable that intelligence waste away in a powerful body? For who would be more learned than Hercules, who wiser than Milo, if it were possible to measure strength of intellect from strength of body?[42] Certainly, it is useful to call forth the stronger porters from the crossroads and alleys into the gymnasia, lest future leaders worthy of triumphs groan and be weakened under the weight of the heaviest burdens like the lowliest beasts of burden. Surely, we do not seek out those men about to fight in the Circus nor those about to do battle in the Amphitheater, since those playing in the literary gym need not debase themselves with those things that suffice for brandishing a boxing glove and wrestling lions. The approach to wisdom is not impassable in such a way that it cannot be accessible to women, nor has learning been placed at such heights that the weaker sex is not strong enough to climb. For this reason, the weakness of the feminine sex should not be blamed; rather, their liveliness of temperament should be envied. Their softness should not be condemned, but the mildness of their humors ought to be commended. By these means, nature wanted womanly intelligence skillfully constructed for every doctrine and erudition.

41. Agnesi specifies the kind of knowledge she has in mind as *scientia*, underscoring the idea that certain knowledge, being closer to divinity, was more easily acquired by a less corporeal body. This section of the oration implies, without stating it explicitly, that the lesser physicality of women offers greater scope for the soul to shape the body, rather than having the body shape the soul.

42. By invoking legendary accounts from Greek mythology of men known for their extraordinary strength—Hercules, son of Zeus (who was reputed to have killed a lion with his bare hands), and Milo (who was said to have conquered and eaten a bull with his bare hands, only to be killed by a lion who ate him after he had finished off the bull)—the oration makes the point that the virtues of the male body have nothing to do with intellectual pursuits, since strength of body does not necessarily produce strength of mind.

Finally, listeners, it remains only that we defend women's studies against the worst accusations of their adversaries as not only harmless but very useful in both private and public affairs. I judge that I am about to fulfill this task easily if, in order to examine the matter—to understand what it is, just as public happiness is derived from its source—it is possible to track it down. Of course, we need not investigate any further in order to comprehend it at last, since the testimony of all ages reveals that the richest vein of common goods has always emanated from the study of letters. This is why we pronounce "golden" the centuries that were dedicated more to letters, since we either envy past ages for their happiness or deplore our own calamities. And, therefore, we may rightly judge those republics to be happy insofar as they may be called learned; and as many authors from some other commonwealth will occupy the mansions of the wise as from one's own. To be sure, however, the abundant utility of the most beautiful arts cannot be contained within domestic walls; it flows in many different directions, more broadly and copiously, and it extends itself in the interest of the people. Who, therefore, does not envy the most fortunate condition of certain families, where the learning of the parents fosters their children's studies, and in which the girls and boys are consumed by a certain most noble rivalry in their studious eagerness? What can be more pleasing, what can be sweeter for parents than to see their hopes so well positioned, which will not only be useful for them but also will benefit others at some future point?

By this same principle, Pythagoras instructed Damo and Themistoclea, his daughter and his sister, in the arts of philosophy to such an extent that the one's supreme intellect brilliantly explicated the style of her father's statements, while the other applied hers to his judgments and conclusions, that is to say, to the progeny of his mind.[43] Nor truly less praiseworthy, perhaps even more admirable, was Aristippus, who prepared his daughter Arete uncommonly well in the Socratic disciplines; she afterward gave instruction to her son and soon thereafter inherited the paternal professorial chair in Libya, becoming the educator of all Africa.[44] Hypatia, wife of the philosopher Isidore, certainly seems to have surpassed nonetheless the exceptional

43. See note 21 in the Barbapiccola translation. Agnesi gets the story somewhat wrong, since it was Themistoclea who taught Pythagoras and not the reverse; see Diogenes Laertius, *Lives*, 327, 339 (VIII.8, 21). Her mistake may have come from reading Gilles Ménage, *The History of Women Philosophers*, trans. and ed. Beatrice H. Zedler (Lanham, MD: University Press of America, 1984), 47.

44. The Greek philosopher Aristippus (435–360 BCE) studied with Socrates in Athens and founded the Cyrenaic school of hedonism in the Greek colony of Cyrene (northeastern Libya). His daughter Arete (fl. 370–340 BCE) was among his followers and is reputed to have taught natural and moral philosophy after her father's death for some thirty years and to have written more than forty books. Upon her death, the epitaph on her tomb supposedly praised her as

nature of this accomplishment. Of course, she brought her mind into the stars in order to investigate the notion of the planets, which she conveyed to posterity through her most precious writings; at the same time, she professed many kinds of learning in Alexandria to listeners from all sides, assembling hastily in squadrons.[45] Hence, who dares to accuse of superficiality Socrates, the best of all the philosophers, who called Diotima his teacher and who, as Plato says, was accustomed to be present at the lectures of Aspasia?[46] Lastly, what might I say of Polla, most learned spouse of Lucan, who had such great erudition and learning that she undertook the best appraisal of the Pharsalia and, though they were unfinished, completed them with as much dignity as elegance?[47]

One must agree with the Philosopher [Aristotle] that man is a stupendous beast. For Nature, it seems, the most excellent parent of all things, has bestowed upon this one creature, the human being, as though a Cosmos in miniature, everything shining and precious that the whole vast universe can yield, who, although crude and churlish, strides forth from his creation to tower over all other living things by his spiritual force no less than by his inner worth. But still more incredible: just as iron sabers, dipped in that fabulous fountain, exchanged the savage mien and stiff asperity of iron for the effulgence and splendor of gold, so once imbued with letters, the minds of mortals lose all their crudity, and humankind lays aside completely its iron nature schooled in barbarian ways; for once those rough intellects begin to engage in literary study, they immediately develop refined modes of life and civil laws.

---

having the "beauty of Helen, the virtue of Therma, the pen of Aristippus, the soul of Socrates, and the tongue of Homer." See Mary Ellen Waithe, ed., *A History of Women Philosophers*, vol. 1, *Ancient Women Philosophers 600 B.C.–500 A.D.* (Dordrecht: Martinus Nijhoff, 1987), 197–201. Again, Agnesi slightly misstates the standard story, since Aristippus the Younger was called "mother taught" because he was supposedly Arete's own disciple. See Ménage, *History*, 35; and Diogenes Laertius, *Lives*, 1:201, 217 (II.72, 86).

45. See note 27 in the Barbapiccola translation for a discussion of Hypatia.

46. See note 22 in the Barbapiccola translation for a discussion of Diotima and Aspasia. There is a lively debate about whether Diotima (fifth century BCE) of Mantinea was a real or fictitious participant in a discussion of the role of beauty in divinity in the *Symposium*, but Ménage affirmed that "Diotima taught Socrates the philosophy of love" (*History*, 26), while Lucrezia Marinella observed that Socrates "confessed to having learned many things from Diotima, a woman of wisdom and prudence" (*The Nobility and Excellence of Women and the Defects and Vices of Men*, ed. and trans. Anne Dunhill [Chicago: University of Chicago Press, 1999], 117).

47. See note 12 of the Barbapiccola translation for a discussion of Polla Argentaria. Since Lucrezia Marinella describes her as "completing the verses begun by her husband with great elegance," it is possible that Agnesi's comments are simply an elaboration of Marinella's observations.

Evidently the faithful study of the noble liberal arts
softens customs and permits them not to be wild.[48]

And anyone is only as human as he is wise. Hence, we are ordered by the
most judicious counsel to rush forth from the embrace of our parents into
the bosom of our teachers so that our still-nascent age may learn from their
experience in the childhood of humankind to accept a more civilized pattern of life, and in school abandon all our wildness where, as Quintilian
says, those who go as beasts return as men.[49] Indeed, it happens by this skill
that the innate character of children grows into the gentlest maturity and,
by a wonderful transformation, stubborn intellects yield to the ability to
reason. For:

No one is so wild, that he cannot be tamed
if only he lends a patient ear to cultivation.[50]

Now those unjust critics, enemies of letters as much as of the human
species, who boldly denounce women, as they are accustomed to do, scrupulously take care lest they bathe the tender minds of girls in the dew of knowledge, but rather condemn them to the eternal drought of ignorance, and lead
to that barrenness and sterility which is the cause of all their trouble; indeed,
those who are without learning are rightly judged to be savages. Certainly,
when they are collected within the domestic walls to waste slowly away, fas-
tened to their seats like lowly spiders bringing forth thread from their breast,
either unrolling unspun wool in a wicker basket or devoting themselves to
other, far worse labors in their leisure, why may they not, being weary, ward
off everything with their vice-ridden thoughts and wrinkled noses? They

48. Ovid, *Epistulae ex Ponto Liber*, 2.9.47–48. The original reads: "adde quod didicisse fideliter
artes / emollit mores, nec sinit esse feros." Agnesi slightly modifies this to read "Scilicet ingénues
didicisse fideliter artes / Emollit mores, nec sinit esse feros." This translation modifies slightly the
one in Ovid, *Tristia, Ex Ponto*, trans. Arthur Leslie Wheeler, rev. G. P. Goold, 2nd ed. (Cambridge,
MA: Harvard University Press, 1988), 363.

49. The Roman orator Quintilian (ca. 35–ca.95) advocated rhetoric as the kind of learning
best suited to the perfection of humanity in his *Institutio oratoria*. The use of Quintilian as well
as Cicero further underscores the role of this oration as a demonstration of the speaker's skill
in invoking both the precepts and the language of the best Roman orators.

50. Horace, *Epistula*, 1.1.39–40. The original is: "nemo adeo ferus est, ut non mitescere possit,
si modo culturae patientem commodet aurem." Agnesi's text varies this well-known saying by
changing the final verb to *accomodet*. This translation slightly modifies the one found in Horace,
Satires, Epistles and Ars Poetica, trans. H. Rushton Fairclough (New York: G. T. Putnam's Sons,
1926), 255.

finish nothing with a calm and peaceful mind, and at last they may turn away to those things which to you, listeners, are apparent and familiar.

Truly, how easy the remedy for this ailment is, if they are bound to a stricter method of living and handed over to the holy nuns to be educated. Indeed, under no circumstances are innate qualities struck down with difficulty; some traces of inborn wildness always remain. Therefore, at last women's intellects may fly away from these narrow straits to the contemplation of things; they are sent away to the most pleasing studies of the noblest arts. Now no troublesome cry will disturb domestic tranquility, no inept effort will disturb the harmony of private life. For just as nothing is more troublesome than to struggle with the stubbornness of an unlearned wife at every moment, so nothing is more blessed than to hear repeatedly the most cultivated conversations of a learned wife, which now are considered neither pedantic nor offensive—chattering in such a way that a husband finds nauseating—nor are they insipid or annoying, destroying the ears with their babbling. Instead, she either recalls cleverly and pleasantly the famous deeds of antiquity, or she flatteringly detains her listener in most pleasing discussions. Why may she not condemn more severely the most foolish opinion of those men who believe that refined women, once married, should be shut away from the sciences as if they were infected with some plague by having married, and who rashly proclaim celebrated marriages in which Lady Wisdom might bear the torch to be under an unlucky sign?[51] As if a learned woman made a man miserable when, in fact, her learning is the best part of conjugal happiness.

PERORATION

In this place, I might have asked those very hostile enemies of female wisdom, what, in the end, they think of those women of letters, flourishing greatly with all praise, who consecrate their name to the eternal memory of posterity, either through the fame of their excellent writing or through the very noble and fruitful memorials of their intellect? Let us bring forth a few examples among many. What of Isabella de Rosales of the First Company, who more than manfully defended theological propositions in the presence of Paul III and the Sacred College of Cardinals in the past century?[52] What

51. This passage recalls the famous laws of quarantine in Italian cities during plague epidemics, when the infected were shut up in their homes.

52. Agnesi follows a typical misspelling of Isabella Roser's name and reminds her readers that she was among the original members (*Ordoniis Principibus*) of the Society of Jesus upon taking the

of Cornelia Piscopia, who is reasonably called, by that magnificent term, the oracle of seven languages, and who was bestowed with the public honor of the philosophical laurels of Padua?[53] It is certainly just that we may admire the effigies, not only of this last one but also of that first one, that are prominently displayed in painting in the Milanese Library among other images of the most celebrated men?[54] What of that Daceria, who certainly shed great light on the more obscure works of Homer, and also gave us a metric version of them?[55] Lastly, what about all those who gave the name to Arcadia and who have dispersed their celebrated nocturnal poetic compositions in praise of all wise men among the common people?[56] But now every rule of a good style demands that we release your ears from this great and, even worse, prolonged annoyance of listening. Thus, I ask this one last thing, very wise listeners, that you, who yourselves are defenders of letters and patrons in

---

vows that Ignatius Loyola wrote for her and two other women at Paul III's request. Roser took these vows on Christmas Day 1545 in Santa Maria della Strada in Rome, even though Loyola later received the pope's permission to rescind the vows of poverty, chastity, and obedience in April 1546. See Loyola's letter of October 1, 1546, in which he tells Roser that "it has seemed to me for God's greater glory that I should withdraw and separate myself from this care of having you as a spiritual daughter under obedience, having you rather as a good and pious mother, as you have been to me for several years now for the greater glory of God our Lord." Rahner, *St. Ignatius Loyola*, 288–89. In 1550 she entered a Franciscan convent in her native city of Barcelona. See Meissner, *Ignatius*, 266–69.

53. This is an explicit reference to the Venetian noblewoman Elena Lucrezia Cornaro Piscopia's degree in philosophy on June 24, 1678, which she received after defending two propositions from Aristotle's *Posterior Analytics* and *Physics* in a room filled with members of the College of Philosophers and Physicians who subsequently proclaimed her a doctor in philosophy. The decision to award Piscopia a degree in philosophy occurred after a contentious debate about her request to be examined in theology. This request, interestingly, provoked a discussion among theologians of the time, who did not all agree about how to interpret Biblical passages, most notably in the writings of Saint Paul, regarding women's ability to display learning and interpretive knowledge of scripture.

54. Cornaro Piscopia's portrait was indeed on display in the Biblioteca Ambrosiana as part of its portrait gallery of famous and saintly scholars. Visitors to the library in Milan commented upon its presence, though they had considerably less to say about Roser's portrait. Certainly, Agnesi's tutors and perhaps her father were well aware of the portrait gallery in this famous library.

55. See note 43 in the Barbapiccola translation for a discussion of Anne Lefèvre Dacier. Clearly, Agnesi's tutor was aware of Dacier's faithful adherence to Greek meter and her fierce opposition to attempts by other translators to modernize Homer to make his poetry more pleasing to eighteenth-century ears. Possibly, one of the reasons that Agnesi's oration ends with Dacier is the fact that Gilles Ménage had dedicated his *History of Women Philosophers* (1690) to her because he admired her knowledge of the history of philosophy and considered her "the most learned woman whether of the present or the past" (Ménage, *History*, 3, 63). He claimed that Diogenes Laertius had dedicated his *Lives of Eminent Philosophers* to a woman, suggesting that there was ancient precedent for his praise of a woman.

56. See note 18 in the Barbapiccola translation for a discussion of Arcadia.

your judgment of our studies, and who always promote the advancement of the best abilities with your authority, might urge more effectively than I might assert with my voice, how adverse to the truth is the opinion of those who very stubbornly insist that the studies of the liberal arts are altogether unsuitable in women.

Translated by Paula Findlen and Rachel Trotter Chaney

V

DIAMANTE MEDAGLIA FAINI

TRANSLATOR'S INTRODUCTION

On August 28, 1724, the poet and intellectual Diamante Medaglia was born in the village of Savallo in the northern Italian province of Brescia. Her father, a doctor, entrusted her moral and academic instruction to his uncle, Father Antonio Medaglia, the pastor of Santa Maria di Savallo, with whom Medaglia studied Latin, Italian literature, theology, and religious history. But it was her encounter with the poetry of the sixteenth- and seventeenth-century Petrarchan poets, so popular in her youth, that was to prove most decisive for her early intellectual formation and her later fame in the region.

As a young woman, Medaglia began to compose impassioned love sonnets and canzoni modeled stylistically on the Tuscan poets she prized, which quickly brought her to the attention of the members of the Brescian literary republic and such regional lights as the historian and literary scholar Lucio Doglioni (1730–1803) and the poet and playwright Mattia Giovanni Butturini (1752–1817).[1] Her verses, including her Sonnet VIII (which follows), also prompted her election to several literary academies, including the Agiati of Rovereto, the Arditi of Brescia, the Orditi of Padua, the Unanimi of Salò, and the national Academy of the Arcadia.

This introduction summarizes historical and literary analysis elaborated in chapter 3 of my book *The Century of Women: Representations of Women in Eighteenth-Century Italian Public Discourse* (Toronto: University of Toronto Press, 2002), 69–86.

1. For biographical information on Lucio Doglioni, see the *Dizionario Biografico degli Italiani*, vol. 40 (Rome: Società Grafica Italiana, 1991), 370–73. On Mattia Giovanni Butturini, see the *Dizionario Biografico degli Italiani*, vol. 15 (Rome: Società Grafica Italiana, 1972), 626–28.

Sonnet VIII

Rose, that at the dawn of your first years,
Lithely sprout from the maternal stem,
Why do you keep a pointed dart beneath your leaves
To plot unremittingly my ruin?

Ah, do not be so cruel, and so many afflictions
Do not wreak upon me by your thorns; the heavens
Make you lovely and true, but the god of Delos
Will quickly trim the wings of your beauty.

Forsake, forsake your pride, and on she who lays herself down
Humble at your feet do not make war, and let reign
Pity in you equal to your ebullient beauty.

Let the now nearby olive tree
(A symbol of victory and sacred peace)
Teach you not to wield arms against the vanquished, nor disdain.[2]

But Medaglia's father disapproved of her poetic vocation and the increasing publicity it brought. According to Giuseppe Pontara, one of her contemporary biographers, Doctor Medaglia arranged his daughter's marriage to fellow physician Pietro Faini when she was twenty-four, at least in part to check her literary ambitions.[3] After she married, Medaglia Faini did not entirely abandon her poetic ambitions, but she did forswear love poetry and confined herself instead to the occasional verses that contemporary opinion deemed appropriate to her new civil status. She became lyricist of the lives of sundry protagonists, including young men and women taking religious vows, brides, illustrious ladies, distinguished scholars, and other cultural and political personalities. Antonio Brognoli, another of Medaglia Faini's contemporary biographers, underlines with pointed irony the sacrifice she made on the altar of poetic integrity to satisfy the social conventions governing the public conduct of women: "Of these [occasional] Sonnets by Mrs. Faini, we have a sizable number, many of which certainly merit our praise, the most estimable being those subjects especially daunting to

---

2. Diamante Medaglia Faini, *Versi e prose di Diamante Medaglia Faini con altri componimenti di diversi autori e colla vita dell'autrice*, ed. Giuseppe Pontara (Salò: Bartolomeo Righetti, 1774), 8.

3. Giuseppe Pontara, "Vita di Diamante Medaglia Faini," in *Versi e prose di Diamante Medaglia Faini*, by Faini, xiv.

portray because of their triviality and simplicity. She has happily composed so many of these that I advise every poet who in the future is similarly put upon to turn to this rich arsenal and to reprint one of these without troubling himself in so vain an endeavor."[4]

Medaglia Faini herself bluntly expressed her disillusionment at this misuse of her talent in the last poem of her poetic career, an uncharacteristically discordant sonnet that repudiates the social constraints that obliged her to commemorate people and events of no relevance to her:

I, who until now, at others' behest, have written
Sonnets, stanzas, and madrigals
For doctors, betrothed, lawyers,
For those who take the veil and holy vestments,
No more will wrack my brain
Without gain, and for such things, waste my time.[5]

True to her word expressed in this sonnet, Medaglia Faini relinquished her muse and never wrote another poem. Yet she discovered a more gratifying font of inspiration in the "new science and philosophy." Determined to master astronomy, philosophy, mathematics, and physics, she placed herself under the tutelage of noted regional scholars. She studied philosophy and history with the Reverend Domenico Bonetti of Volciano; and she lived and studied for three months with the Brescian mathematician Giovanni Battista Suardi, the author of two influential mathematical studies, *New Instruments for the Description of Diverse and Modern Curves* (Brescia, 1752) and *Mathematical Diversions* (Brescia, 1764).[6] Indeed, her extensive correspondence indicates that for the last ten years of her life, until her death in 1770, science and philosophy were the focus of her intellectual life.[7]

In 1763, near the time of her renunciation of poetry, Medaglia Faini

---

4. Antonio Brognoli, *Elogi di Bresciani per dottrina eccellenti del secolo XVIII* (Bologna: Forni Editore, 1972), 269.

5. Medaglia Faini, *Versi e prose di Diamante Medaglia Faini*, 163.

6. On Suardi, see Pietro Riccardi, *Biblioteca matematica italiana dalla origine della stampa ai primi anni del secolo XIX* (Modena: Tipografia Dell'Erede Soliani, 1870), 479.

7. Biographical information on Faini has come from the following sources: Medaglia Faini, *Versi e prose di Diamante Medaglia Faini*; Brognoli, *Elogi di Bresciani*, 254–74; Guido Bustico, "Diamante Medaglia Faini," in *Pagine Benacensi* (Salò: Pietro Veludari, 1909), 46–50; Guido Bustico, "Diamante Medaglia Faini," in *Rassegna Nazionale* (Rome, 1941), 3–5; *Per il Centocinquantesimo Anniversario 1900 dalla Fondazione della I. R. Accademia di Scienze, Lettere ed Arti degli Agiati in Rovereto* (Roverato: Tipografia Grigoletti, 1899), 15.

came to stand before a Brescian academy, to which she not only belonged but was the elected Princess, to champion the education of women.[8] Implicitly rejecting the example of her own intellectual trajectory in her oration before the Unanimi of Salò, Medaglia Faini advocated a remarkable curriculum for women virtually devoid of the conventional literary instruction with its emphasis on poetry reading and composition. Instead, she argued for a "feminine" education steeped in philosophy and the sciences, specifically, classical and moral philosophy, religious history, logic, and, most importantly, mathematics and physics. This unorthodox proposal challenged even the most progressive Enlightenment arguments for women's education to appear during the century. Broad-minded *illuministi* like Pietro Verri, Giovanni Bandiera, and Pier Domenico Soresi, who advocated the formal instruction of women for their own sake and for the sake of society as a whole, were uniformly wary of the influence of the "sublime sciences" on the female intellect and character as tending to undermine women's primary domestic responsibilities.[9] Medaglia Faini, moreover, went on to further defy conventional wisdom by repudiating upper-class women's now-conventional literary education, especially the poetic training considered *de rigeur* during this "Arcadian age."

Yet, despite the subversive quality of her proposed curriculum, Medaglia Faini also betrayed the influence of the politics and poetics of the masculine discursive tradition, even as she exploited the Enlightenment terms available to her to suggest fundamental changes in women's condition. For example, addressing as she did a male academic elite, she adhered to the classic conventions of oratory, employed the *tono medio* of academic disputation, and built her argument upon the tried infrastructure of master narratives, ancient and contemporary. She cited Cicero, Aristotle, Plato, Socrates, and Horace to defend the primacy of philosophy and science in her curriculum. Anticipating the likely attacks on the propriety of teaching women classical philosophy, she quoted extensively from such noted theologians as Jean Mabillon, Saint Basil the Great, the French Jansenist Charles Rollin, and the Church Father Clement of Alexandria, all of whom defend the importance of the pagan philosophers to the education of Christian students. But at the

---

8. Biblioteca dell'Ateneo, Salò, MS 101 (c. 23), n. 4 (*Registri de' Ragionamenti recitati nell'Accademia detta de' Discordi di Salò, ed ora de' Pescatori Benacensi*). See entries for May 7, 1761; March 11, 1762; April 18, 1763; and May 5, 1763. I wish to acknowledge Paula Findlen for this information, which she cites in her article "Becoming a Scientist: Gender and Knowledge in Eighteenth-Century Italy," *Science in Context* 16 (2003): 59–87.

9. See Pietro Verri, *Ricordi a mia figlia*, in *Opere Varie*, ed. Nino Valeri (Florence: Felice Le Monnier, 1947), 295–351; and Pier Domenico Soresi, *Saggio sopra la necessità e la facilità di ammaestrare le fanciulle* (Milan: Federico Angelli, 1774).

same time, she rested her defense of the importance of women's education in mathematics, science, and philosophy on women's inherent intellectual frailty and vanity, her own feminine defects, and the deficiencies of her very oration; only these disciplines, she averred, could counter the primitive irrationality, impiety, and "torpid indolence" to which women naturally incline.

Medaglia Faini's oration thus epitomizes the ideological tensions and subterfuge that characterized many prowoman arguments by women during the Italian Enlightenment. Forty-four years later, amidst the boisterous atmosphere of resistance and emancipation that followed the French Revolution, Carolina Lattanzi could unequivocally condemn *The Slavery of Women*.[10] But in 1763 Medaglia Faini felt compelled to challenge women's oppression more covertly. Co-opting traditional analytic and discursive methods and flattering the misogynist prejudices of her scholarly male audience, Medaglia Faini defended women's instruction in the "new science and philosophy" not for its own sake but as the best way to enhance women's domestic skills and Christian modesty.

She begins by quoting Antonio Vallisneri's conservative judgment on the famous debate on women's education held forty years earlier by the Academy of the Ricovrati: only intellectually superior women should be allowed formal instruction. In this way, Medaglia Faini not only seeks to assuage the anxieties of the male audience before her, but by replicating the Prince of the Ricovrati's position at the academic cathedra, this Princess of the Unanimi cloaks herself in his exalted mantle of authority. This is a strategic maneuver, however. Indeed, Medaglia Faini's rhetorical and political tactics immediately reveal themselves in her truncated and selective citation of the Ricovrati Prince. She elides Vallisneri's decree to restrict women's education to the socially exceptional, "in whose veins flows clear and illustrious blood," and she eliminates as well his sycophantic praise of the noblewomen in his audience. Like Aretafila Savini de' Rossi, she opposes the traditional misogynist grouping of women into two classes: the socially privileged, slimly educated elite and the untutored masses. Throughout her address, Medaglia Faini refers repeatedly to the benefits of education for the whole of her sex and contemns the plight especially of those "rough and uncouth" women unable to express themselves cogently and clearly. By this means she underlines her support of universal education for women and directly contradicts Vallisneri's limitation of it to the exceptional few.

At the same time, she passes over in silence the arguments of other

10. Carolina Lattanzi, *Schiavitù delle donne* [1792], ed. Gilberto Zacché (Mantua: Edizioni Lombarde, 1976).

women on the same question. For example, nowhere does she mention Aretafila Savini de' Rossi's vigorous defense of women's education published in the 1729 edition of the Ricovrati debate. In fact, she cites no female authorities at all. This deliberate repression of the arguments of her precursors unmistakably aims to promote her own legitimacy among male academicians. In her insistence on women's intellectual inferiority, including her own, and her suppression of the prowoman arguments of other women, Medaglia Faini paradoxically rests her defense of women's education on a negation, both explicit and implicit, of women's intellectual integrity and authority.

Nonetheless, Medaglia Faini constructs a singular and potent argument for women's education, which incorporates the even more radical proposition that they should be taught the elite disciplines that had traditionally been closed to them. Her "devised resolution" may pragmatically have solicited the approval of men in power, but her placement of mathematics and physics at the center of her "feminine" curriculum demonstrates her commitment to women's intellectual emancipation. She claims for all women, elite and common alike, the right to read the secrets of Galileo's book of the universe. Indeed, despite her antifeminist assertions, her call to extend women's intellectual authority across the limitless expanse of the cosmos, from the deepest recesses of the sea to the farthest heavens, and from the metaphysics of the Greeks to the "new science and philosophy," tacitly unlocks women's domestic confines and confers on them new authority in both the substantive world and the realm of ideas.

Nor should the setting and occasion of Medaglia Faini's oration be overlooked. Speaking her defense from the podium of the Academy of the Unanimi to her fellow academicians, Medaglia Faini embodies in herself the new authority of women, and not only of the aristocratic class but also of the bourgeoisie, in the sphere of intellectual exchange. Unlike Aretafila Savini de' Rossi and the other eminent defenders of women, including Lucrezia Marinella, Moderata Fonte, and Arcangela Tarabotti, who were forced to defend women's intellectual integrity from the periphery of the Republic of Letters, Medaglia Faini stands within, at the symbolic apex of authority—at the same time that she occupies a liminal place within the intellectual establishment of the Italian Settecento, as the conflicted politics and poetics of her discourse poignantly reveal.

Rebecca Messbarger

AN ORATION ON WHICH STUDIES ARE FITTING FOR WOMEN

Strange will it seem to each of you, worthy and honorable Academicians, that I who am in braids and a skirt dare to appear today before your select and noble assembly.[11] I, moreover, who had never given any thought to those famous debates among the most celebrated of men, taken up at various times by the Republic of Letters, concerning that remarkable problem often discussed, and most recently broached in Padua on the sixteenth day of June 1723 by the renowned Academy of the Ricovrati, that is, "Should women be admitted to the study of the sciences and the liberal arts," yet I undertake to discuss precisely those studies that are appropriate for women. And if my own devised resolution is closely examined,[12] and if I may hope that a rebuttal is not imminent, then perhaps that much sooner might I be, if not entirely approved by you, at least benevolently excused and tolerated. Given the enduring wisdom of the judgment on this celebrated question brought by the very erudite Signor Vallisneri, Prince at the time of the aforementioned Academy, I quote:

> Let there be admitted to the study of the sciences and the liberal arts those women who are passionate about the same, whose hidden noble genius leads them to virtue, and in whom burns and sparkles a spirit beyond the norm, surpassing that which is common to the masses. Without the arrogance of tyranny, let the range of womanly duties be divided. Divide the tasks such that the superior intellect is left free. Let some women attend to household tasks and to their honest and necessary works. Let others follow the Muses most chaste where inclination transports them and, by means most necessary, let them be animated, guided, and filled with delight, so that unyielding to indolence, ignorance, and envy, they might enhance the sciences.[13]

11. Annotations by the author appear as notes with symbols below. In the first sentence of the translation, I have adhered to the author's syntax to maintain her emphasis on the word *strange* (*strano*) with which she begins her discourse.

12. Medaglia Faini's use of the term *"devised* resolution" (*divisata* risoluzione) to describe the objective of her defense for women's education is highly ambiguous, as it may signify a solution that is "devised," "planned," "systematic," and "ordered" or, instead, one that is "different," "distinct," and "disguised." These various denotations might also be said to describe the ambiguous methodology of her defense, through which she capitulates to male authority and affirms misogynist views while at the same time vigorously contesting men's intellectual subjugation of women and promoting women's education in the sciences.

13. As was noted in the translator's introduction, Medaglia Faini sharply truncated Vallisneri's final judgment, leaving out his references to social class and his direct address to the noble-

With this prudent decision in mind, my current undertaking should not be viewed as contemptible—that is, to investigate scrupulously which studies are most appropriate for the exceptional woman, and to which she might apply herself with success, and so adorn her soul. For it is incontrovertible that the female sex should not take up all disciplines without distinction, abandoning itself to its own caprice. [Rather, women should limit themselves to those select studies that are useful to them and from which they might derive the most benefit] And if what no sound mind can doubt be true, that ideas without practical use for him who possesses them do not merit to be called studies, a concept amply demonstrated by the enlightened Father Jean Mabillon in his most important work, *De Studiis Monasticis*,[*] then, if I do not err, this truth only more firmly justifies my position on the selection of the current argument.[14]

Now then, first descending from this sound principle to the lowest humanistic arts in order to ascend to the most sublime sciences, no one, in my view, can deny that these arts would be particularly fitting and convenient for women. Aside from the fact that these arts are the chief foundation of letters and that all the other disciplines turn to these as to a cardinal point, one derives great benefit from these studies for the elevation of the soul, the fortification of the intellect, and the defense of one's claims, which are rendered more admirable perhaps because they are more intelligible, as the previously celebrated Father Mabillon keenly noted.[15] For this very reason, Basil, Holy Doctor of the Greek Church, not only did not prohibit anyone from reading the profane authors, but in fact counseled all to do so without

---

women in attendance at the 1723 debate. This is a significant revision that underscores the ideological differences between the Prince and the Princess of their respective academies.

[*]Mabillon, 1: 180—*Diamante Medaglia Faini.*

14. Jean Mabillon (1632–1707), a French monastic historian and scholar of Greek and Roman antiquity, was a Benedictine monk, whose *Traité des études monastiques* (Paris, 1691–92) defended ecclesiastical studies for monks in opposition to Armand Jean Bouthillier de Rancé, Abbé de la Trappe. Refuting Rancé's argument that monks should consign themselves to a life of penitence, Mabillon argued the necessity of scriptural study to monastic life. Mabillon further maintained that knowledge of profane writings—Greek and Roman history, philosophy, and literature—was crucial for comprehending the sacred. As indicated in her footnote, Medaglia Faini here cites the Latin translation of Jean Mabillon, *Tractatus de' studiis monasticis*, 3 vols., trans. Joseph Porta (Venice: A. Poleti, 1729), 1:180, in which Mabillon explicitly defends the utility of studying the pagan philosophers, especially the Stoics and Plato, and quotes at length from Saint Basil the Great.

15. Faini's reference is unclear here. She does not indicate the text or edition of Mabillon she cites in her footnote. She is probably referring to part 1 of *Traité des Études Monastiques*, but the citation she indicates on page 180 remains obscure.

exception because, as he himself attested,[*] in this way and through these readings, the soul becomes more beautiful and illuminated.[16] Most important, I aver, is that without humanistic studies—if we wish to believe the authorities—one will never be able to express the most profound concepts with ease and coherence.

Now tell me—and heaven help you, Gentlemen—shouldn't a woman be able to communicate her own ideas? Is she not endowed with a mind and a capacity for reason as is a man? Is she utterly excluded from human discourse? Certainly not! How then, without the aid of these most agreeable studies, can she rightly fulfill her roles, those roles, or we might say, those duties virtually intrinsic to her nature? It is true, as some might perhaps argue, that even rough and uncouth women, and indeed those who know nothing of the arts, to borrow an expression of Enante Vignajolo, know how to give vent to the sentiments of their hearts.[17] These do not let the tongues with which nature armed them lie mute. Yet, if this is true, it is also true that many people will be placed on the rack and tortured by the insignificant chatter by which women very often express the opposite of what they mean to say, or else express themselves in such a vulgar manner that one distinguishes them with difficulty from children—women who believe that by shrieking they can express what they think, feel, and desire.

And if someone is gifted with natural eloquence (a situation not uncommon), it is certain and beyond doubt that if this natural gift is not guided and corrected by art, it will always remain imperfect and lacking. Thus, as it has

---

[*] S. Basilius, vol. 1, sermon 24: "Auctores idèo profani perlegi identidem poterunt, ut inde exornetur animus"—D. F.

16. Saint Basil of Caesarea (ca. 329–379), a monk, ascetic, and later the Archbishop of Caesarea, wrote a treatise entitled "Address to Young Men on Reading Greek Literature." In this treatise, Basil encourages young men to accept what is useful in Greek literature, in other words, that which stimulates virtue and aids in the understanding of scripture, and to overlook that which is not.

17. Enante Vignaiolo was the academic name taken by the Ferrarese scholar, cleric, and noted antiquarian Girolamo Baruffaldi (1675–1755) as founding member of the Vigna Academy in Ferrara. Later, it served as a pseudonym for the publication of polemical writings. A controversial figure, Baruffaldi was exiled in 1711 from Ferrara and his archive seized and sent for inspection to Rome after he was accused of supplying the powerful Este family with documents that proved their right to lands claimed by the Church. Baruffaldi was a member of the Arcadia Academy and composed numerous satirical and humorous poems. His most famous poem is a narrative poetic satire of contemporary customs entitled "La Tabaccheide" (1712) in which he celebrates tobacco, "drug of poets, elixir of scholars." In another poetic satire entitled "Il Grillo" (1738), Baruffaldi ridicules rural culture and the medical arts. Baruffaldi's play *The Poet* burlesques the eighteenth-century pedant. *Dizionario Biografico degli Italiani*, 7: 6–9.

been argued, it is clear that women must be admitted to these studies. I will not say that they must apply themselves to the humanities for many years or that these studies are designed solely for their literary formation. Women's education should be selective and in accord with those precepts and rules on which I reserve the right to expound later, in order that the tutor's care for the humanistic education of tender young girls be carried out in the best way and to the greatest profit.

Turning specifically to poetry, inasmuch as it is part of the humanities and represents a noble discipline of these same arts, it is nonetheless inappropriate to judge it as analogous to the study of classical languages, which must be learned under the tutelage of an expert instructor and in accord with the mode of life led by the individual. It will suffice to reiterate what Signor Becelli wisely wrote about poetry in his noted tract on the divisions of intellects and scholarly disciplines. "Poetry," he states, "is truly congenial to very few, because it is an extremely difficult art and by its very nature sublime. And upon reflection it is clear that few nations have had excellent poets, and these were infrequent in each century. Therefore, the useless toil must be criticized of primary and later tutors, who teach children and the young to write poetry. Poetry is the least necessary of all the disciplines and thus, as Horace says, 'the mediocre poet is not tolerated, by men, by the gods, by the walls, nor by the columns themselves.'"[18]

If we then wish to consider the poetic faculties separately, disconnected from weightier disciplines, and unsustained by any other intellectual foundation than the barest acquaintance with a few fables, it seems clear and most certain that poetry serves the majority of women only as an ornament. Moreover, writing substandard poetry will lessen women's regard among those who have the intellectual competence to judge the merits of authors, either because women's compositions are tedious, or because they lack the necessary erudition, as the poet avers: "Versus inopes rerum, nugæque canoræ" [verses deficient in substance and tuneful trivialities][19] or because the writing of poetry will tend to foment that excessive self-love that is almost second nature to our sex. Because it is imperative that we avoid the slightest hue of

---

18. Guido Cesare Becelli (1686–1750) was a poet, critic, playwright, and translator. He translated Locke's *Aphorisms*, reinserting Locke's discourse on women's education, which Locke later excluded. His *Trattato della divisione degli ingegni* privileges science over poetry. Becelli, in the current citation, refers to Horace's *Ars Poetica* (19–17 BCE), line 372: "mediocribus esse poetis non homines, non di, non concessere columnae." James Hynd's translation of this passage in *The Art of Poetry* (Albany: State University of New York, 1974) reads: "That poets should be 'of middling quality' neither gods nor men nor the bookshops have ever granted." *Dizionario Biografico degli Italiana*, 7: 502–5.

19. From Horace's *Ars Poetica*, 322. The translation is that of James Hynd. (See previous note).

vanity in our studies, as has been affirmed by many authors besides Mabillon, and because it is more important to promote the substance and the profundity of thought than surface appearances, I hope not to err when I assert with all sincerity that it is better to be condemned than to write inferior poetry. But this would be less true if writing poetry were accompanied by the rigorous study of philosophical truths and of those rules that are central to the discipline. On the contrary, such a poet would be held in the highest regard, as has been said by that most esteemed of intellectuals, Ludovico Antonio Muratori, in his tract on perfect Italian poetry: "the philosophical geniuses (these are his precise words) with the particular powers of the intellect to penetrate to the depths of things, discover the most hidden beauty of their objects, and they fill with meaning all of their parts. Their thoughts are founded on the truth, and these are often beyond the comprehension of people's ordinary understanding."[20] It is true that, because I wish to interrogate the issues raised by Muratori and to reason about the philosophical disciplines, I can justly reiterate what Cicero attributed to Antonius, who had unwillingly assumed the task of speaking about rhetoric:* "Listen," (he said), "listen to a man who will teach you that which he himself never learned."[21]

---

*Audite ver, audite, inquit, hominem docebo vos, discipuli, id quod ipse non didici, quid de omni genere discendi sentiam. Lib, 2. *De Orat.* N.28.29—D. F.

20. Ludovico Antonio Muratori (1672–1750), cleric, librarian, historian, and antiquarian, was a scholar of philosophy and law. The citation is from vol. 1, book 2, of his noted work *Della perfetta poesia italiana spiegata e dimostrata con varie osservazioni* (1703), in which the author elevates the imagination above judgment and the intellect in the creation of verse. The passage appears in chap. 9, "Tre spezie d'Ingegni, Musico, Amatorio, e Filosofico. Antichi Poeti Italiani bisognosi de' due primi. Necessità, ed ufizio del Filosofico. Difetto del Marino. Filosofia Morale, e Logica neccesarie a' Poeti. Sentimenti d'alcuni Autori Franzesi, e del Tasso, pasati. Oscurità di Dante. Lege de i tre Ingegni." In the edition published in Venice in 1724 by Sebastiano Coleti, the excerpt appears on p. 358.

21. "Audite ver, audite, inquit, hominem docebo vos, discipuli, id quod ipse non didici, quid de omni genere discendi sentiam." This truncated citation is from Cicero, *De Oratore*, book 2, chap. 7, 28–29. The full passage reads: "Audite vero, audite, inquit. Hominem enim audietis de schola, atque a magistro et Graecis litteris eruditum; et eo quidem loquar confidentius, quod Catulus auditor accessit, cui non solum nos Latini sermonis, sed etiam Graeci ipsi solent suae linguae subtilitatem elegantiamque concedere. Sed quia tamen hoc totum, quidquid est, sive artificium, sive studium dicendi, nisi accessit os, nullum potest esse, docebo vos, discipuli, quod ipse non didici, quid de omni genere dicendi sentiam." The English translation by Edward William Sutton of this passage from *De Oratore* (Cambridge, MA: Harvard University Press, 1942) follows: "Attention, pray! Attention! For you will be listening to a man from the schools, polished by professorial instruction and the study of Greek literature; and I shall speak with all the full assurance, in that Catullus has joined my audience, he whose possession of accuracy and taste in the Greek language is ever acknowledged, not only by us men of Latin speech, but by the Greeks themselves as well. Seeing however that all this art or vocation of speaking, whichever it may be, can avail nothing without the addition of 'cheek,' I will teach you, my disciples, something that I have not learned myself, to wit, my theory of oratory in all its branches."

However, in my case it is not my ignorance of the utility of and the great advantages gained from philosophical studies that leads me to exhort young women to devote themselves to the extent that they are able to such an important science. Among the greatest advantages obtained by the study of philosophy, the principal ones are, according to the best philosophers, the liberation of our minds from those many prejudices that render us incapable of reasoning and of judging things in a perfect and just way. Other advantages are the animation of the mind by universal ideas and understanding, the enabling of the mind to proceed in accordance with right moral conduct and to conceive great respect for religion, and the protection of the mind by firm principles from the false and specious reasoning that underlies disbelief. With respect to the civil government of one's small domestic province, this science will naturally instill in women those principles that are necessary to that end. Thus, among the many faculties embraced and encompassed by philosophy, it is right to choose only those that guide us in an opportune way to domestic governance, and these faculties will indeed be, if I am not wrong, logic, experimental physics, and what should certainly not be neglected, a superior ethics and a sound politics.

With respect to logic, it is important to note that this is no longer the discipline of pure pretense, nor one founded, as it once was, on the desire for victory in disputes and vain arguments, as Saint Clement of Alexandria has written with respect to the sophists: "cujus principium fuisse id quod visum fuerit disputanti, officium vero contentionem, finem victoriam" [their principle was whatever the disputant wished, his duty was contention, and his aim was victory].[22] Rather, logic is the art of thinking rationally, of distinguishing without error the true from the false, and, in a word, of correcting those intellects who, Signor Rollin claims, "interpret all things in a partial and erroneous manner, who embrace those arguments most contrary to the truth, and who, in their desire to be right in their disputes with others, allow themselves to be swayed by the most insignificant appearances, who are always inclined to excess, to a lack of equilibrium, who take sides without hesitation regarding problems they don't know or understand; and who defend their ideas with such obstinacy that they will not listen to any argument that might disabuse them of their error."[23]

---

22. Saint Clement of Alexandria (ca. 150–211/215) was a Christian apologist, theologian, and leader of the catechetical school of Alexandria. His best-known work is his trilogy: *Protrepikos* (Exhortation), *Paidagogos* (The Instructor), and *Stromateis* (Miscellanies).

23. Charles Rollin (1661–1741), French scholar and Jansenist, was author of the noted *Traité des études* (1726–28). In 1734 he included as a supplement to this text a chapter on the instruction

[As you well know, O gentlemen, we women are, more than men, strangely subject to these false judgments, I know not whether because of the condition of our sex or for some other reason. Given this situation, whoever is acquainted with this feminine predisposition which often renders women's intellect and capacity for sound judgment deficient and, conversely, whoever knows that the force of sound reasoning can erase these errors, must recognize that the study of philosophy should be viewed not only as useful but as necessary and irreplaceable for the youth of our sex.]

Having acquired, in this way, an intellectual force, a rightness, and a mental penetration that allows them, little by little, to comprehend on their own and to develop the most bewildering arguments, clearly it is through awareness of that infinity of curious information and useful ideas intrinsic to that other branch of philosophy known as physics that their intellects may enrich and gratify themselves. Everyone already knows that the principal aim of this science is to contemplate assiduously, one by one, each of the elements and to investigate the nature of the principles by which these are composed. Physics directs us to note "with what order and symmetry everything is arranged in the universe and with what uniformity the general and particular order is observed and maintained, and through this we are able to grasp the intelligence and the invisible hands that support all things."[24] This discipline penetrates the recesses of the earth and scrutinizes the marvelous processes that take place therein. It ascends to the heavens and seeks to know the movements of the stars and to observe the order and the regularity that reign there. It contemplates the waters and the creatures that wriggle within them. And it explains marvelously the prodigious phenomena that occur there. With respect to fire, it discovers its weight, activity, and nature. Regarding air, it determines the weight, mass, and elasticity of the bodies that occupy it. By this means, many phenomena, at one time inexplicable, now appear clear. Ultimately, physics allows us to comprehend how many objects below, above, and in every direction encompass man.

How many useful and pleasing ideas can expand the intellect of one

---

of girls: *Traité des études des enfans et des jeunes demoiselles.* Heavily influenced by the writings of Saint Jerome and Fénelon, Rollin argued that the general neglect of girls' education led not only to ignorance but also to frivolity and moral corruption. Rollin held that girls had the same intellectual capacity as boys. He did not, however, advocate equal instruction for the sexes. He held that a curriculum for girls should include religious and secular history (for their moral instruction) as well as every art relevant to the management of the home. Rollin cautioned against letting girls read comedies and tragedies. He also objected to the exposure of girls to music and dance because of the passions they would incite.

24. This brief section is in italics, indicating that it is a quote; however, Medaglia Faini does not identify her source.

who applies herself seriously to this discipline, and how much excitement will perhaps be kindled gradually in the soul of any woman who studies something so important? Indeed, that fervor should enhance women's day-to-day analytical abilities since these discussions about physics are derived from and guided by mathematics, a study deserving of praise, a study truly divine. And who, in truth, does not see that these praises are just? Geometry alone (when confronting the various branches of mathematics, it is necessary to depart from the simplest concepts in order to attain the most complex) rapidly conducts us from the most common assertions to the most difficult and, in almost an instant, it elevates us from the simplest principles to those most noble and sublime. By beginning with very simple and obvious truths from which anyone possessed of reason cannot withhold full approval, it follows that one will not affirm or accept any truths except those deduced by means of infallible ratiocination. At the end of this process, difficult theorems consequently appear clear that are in fact far beyond the capacity of the untutored to know and to understand. All of the operations of this art or science, whichever you prefer to call it, proceed thus from evident and infallible proofs. As such, they cannot but lead the intellects of those who dedicate themselves to their study to the most refined judgment and the most acute discernment. Have women (render justice unto what I say, most honored Academicians) perhaps never erred in their deductions? And from premises based on pure fantasy have they never derived results that they firmly believed to be more reliable than any calculated by Archimedes himself? By your marked silence, I know that you understand only too well and consider what I have said to be true. Then without further delay, I repeat: to mathematics, to mathematics direct women's thoughts and no more will you see them subject to gross paralogisms or the other errors to which even learned men fall victim who lack mathematical training.

→However, even with her mind free of every error, the most crucial component of this curriculum would still be missing for the woman who does not obey the laws of moral judgment to guide her soul to moderate the passions that boil in her with supreme force, and to oppose sound principles to those defects and vices to which she is naturally subject, as has been described in that sage stanza:[25]

25. Niccolò Forteguerri, canzone (canto) 27, stanza 6. This stanza was written by Tuscan author and cleric Forteguerri (1674–1735), a favorite of Pope Clement XI and a member of various academies, including the Arcadia, the Crusca and the Intronati. The stanza included here is from Forteguerri's *Ricciardetto* (1716–26), a mock epic in thirty cantos that satirized the Holy See, which had denied him promotion to Cardinal in 1715. *Dizionario Biografico degli Italiani*, 49: 159–62.

Woman, my brother, is an animal
Without a brain and full of malice;
She serves no purpose either for good or for evil,
In other words, for love or for hate.
So suspicious, proud and beastly
That she is overcome by envy and avarice,
And so false that whosoever trusts her
Deserves a sledgehammer to the head.

The desired moderation will fail to result without the aid of moral philosophy. To prove the validity of this assertion, it is enough to reflect on the fact that Socrates, Plato, and Aristotle, along with many other sage philosophers who flourished in ancient times, dedicated their lives wholly to the teachings of this discipline and to the demonstration of the need for this doctrine: "By means of this, woman will therefore admirably conjoin the most rigorous honesty, the gentleness, and the most welcome and pleasing benevolence. She will be esteemed and loved in her home, in the streets, and in public and private gatherings; not only on her native soil, but also abroad; and not only during her lifetime, but also after her death. She will serve as a perfect model for other women; and she will often be the object of pleasing, respectful, and gracious judgments."[26]

Through her education in moral philosophy, a great respect for religion will take root in a woman's heart. In order for you to be firmly convinced of this, it is useful for me to make fleeting reference to what Signor Rollin said about those essential moral principles found among pagan philosophers that are germane to the cause: "Inasmuch as it instructs her, moral philosophy will lead her to accept divine revelation with docility and respect. And with great ease will she understand that God leads all things to reason, including the senses, because nothing is more reasonable than listening to Him when He speaks."[27]

And if we imagine woman pictured inside the domestic walls, attentive to her household duties, and to the right government of her family, how many enlightened truths will she draw from this discipline that will help her carry out precisely these responsibilities? From moral philosophy she will

26. Medaglia Faini adds emphasis here to indicate that this is a direct citation. However, she does not identify her source.

27. See previous note in this section regarding Rollin. It should be noted here that Medaglia Faini defends women's instruction in pagan philosophy on the basis of arguments similar to those put forth by Giuseppa Eleonora Barbapiccola, whose work she likely knew.

learn fully what a precious treasure peace is, and this she will strive in every way to perpetuate and to preserve. She will discern the proper natural social hierarchy, and by her own example and her gentle ways she will subtly accustom the subaltern not to refuse the yoke of necessary dependence. She will recognize as in a pristine mirror the vile nature of idleness and the sorrowful consequences that bud forth at every instant from this corrupt root. This she will grow to abhor with the greatest revulsion.

Perhaps these maxims may at first appear too severe and incompatible with our delicate temperament as women. Such maxims might seem to suggest that a person cannot have a single hour free from unpleasant cares to enjoy a complete repose and prompt us to ask: what barbarous law is this? What harsh precepts? But no! Moral philosophy does not place on the neck any yoke that it cannot bear. It certainly does not prohibit our minds from restoring themselves for a reasonable amount of time from their usual and frequent occupations. But these hours should be viewed as times of repose, not of torpid indolence. Moral philosophy condemns a torpid indolence fully and forcefully, as it does our engaging in futile chatter with this or that company in the time that should be employed either for our own betterment or for the welfare of our families. Torpid indolence means wandering too often about in the streets for the sole purpose of securing public favor. Torpid indolence means giving too much importance to ornate attire. A woman imbued in moral doctrine will treasure the appearance of a modest gentility; she will likewise detest those embellishments that manifestly degenerate into abominable vanity. If these things are true, and they are indeed most true, not only should we women have the courage to enrich our minds, procuring noble ideas even at the cost of toil and privation, but also and more importantly those among us who are appointed to govern families should fervently dedicate themselves to the study of moral philosophy.

For brevity's sake, I will forbear to discuss the great utility to be derived from a diligent reading of sacred history, as no person can dispute the fact that these stories are made to enhance our spirits and to rightly form our hearts and principles. If we wish to reason about sacred history, since this is the foundation of religion, it will be of great use to us throughout our lives in understanding religious doctrine as it is taught in public and in reading fruitfully, particularly books of piety. With respect to the one as to the other, it is presumed that the disciple who hears and the one who reads is versed in the facts of sacred history. In the same way, the many events that occur in secular history that reveal virtue or vice can happily serve to stimulate us toward acts of virtue or to avert us from evil.

Here, provided I have not erred, I have succinctly and to the best of my abilities outlined for you those studies by which, if a woman applies herself, she will not only ennoble herself among women, but also raise herself above the many, many men who, lazy and idle, miserably waste their time with meaningless things and never cultivate the sciences.[18] Would that it pleased God that such a rich treasure not be neglected by so many and that we would again see bloom those valorous ancient Greek and Roman women who filled those possessed of only a mediocre culture with awe and fear, and who inspired the laudable envy of even the most learned. The counsel of such a sage woman would be viewed without a doubt as most sound, rather than dangerous, or at least suspect. How good it would be to engage with such a woman in delectable discourse, flavored as it would be by the finest salt. How good it would be to look into her home and see her give gentle comfort to her husband and children, if married, and, if unwed, to see her lead others by her own example to redirect their lives and to fulfill their requisite duties with devotion. How good it would be to hear her discuss events that took place in times past, and thereby energetically incite each of her interlocutors not to trust fortune completely when it is favorable, and to confront it with courage when it is adverse. Finally, how good it would be and how greatly to the benefit of all for a woman to be able to devote herself to and perfect herself by means of the aforementioned studies.

Translated by Rebecca Messbarger

28. Here, Medaglia Faini's argument unmistakably echoes Aretafila Savini de' Rossi's 1729 "Apology for Women's Education," which Medaglia Faini knew well but strategically neglected to cite.

SERIES EDITORS'
BIBLIOGRAPHY

PRIMARY SOURCES

Alberti, Leon Battista (1404–72). *The Family in Renaissance Florence.* Translated by Renée Neu Watkins. Columbia: University of South Carolina Press, 1969.

Arenal, Electa and Stacey Schlau, eds. *Untold Sisters: Hispanic Nuns in Their Own Works.* Translated by Amanda Powell. Albuquerque: University of New Mexico Press, 1989.

Astell, Mary (1666–1731). *The First English Feminist: Reflections on Marriage and Other Writings.* Edited and introduction by Bridget Hill. New York: St. Martin's Press, 1986.

Atherton, Margaret, ed. *Women Philosophers of the Early Modern Period.* Indianapolis, IN: Hackett, 1994.

Aughterson, Kate, ed. *Renaissance Woman: Constructions of Femininity in England: A Source Book.* London: Routledge, 1995.

Barbaro, Francesco (1390–1454). *On Wifely Duties* (preface and book 2). Translated by Benjamin Kohl in Kohl and R. G. Witt, eds., *The Earthly Republic.* Philadelphia: University of Pennsylvania Press, 1978, 179–228.

Behn, Aphra. *The Works of Aphra Behn.* 7 vols. Edited by Janet Todd. Columbus: Ohio State University Press, 1992–96.

Boccaccio, Giovanni (1313–75). *Famous Women.* Edited and translated by Virginia Brown. The I Tatti Renaissance Library. Cambridge, MA: Harvard University Press, 2001.

———. *Corbaccio or the Labyrinth of Love.* Translated by Anthony K. Cassell. 2nd rev. ed. Binghamton, NY: Medieval and Renaissance Texts and Studies, 1993.

Brown, Sylvia. *Women's Writing in Stuart England: The Mother's Legacies of Dorothy Leigh, Elizabeth Joscelin and Elizabeth Richardson.* Thrupp, Stroud, Gloucestershire: Sutton, 1999.

Bruni, Leonardo (1370–1444). "On the Study of Literature (1405) to Lady Battista Malatesta of Moltefeltro." In *The Humanism of Leonardo Bruni: Selected Texts.* Translated and introduction by Gordon Griffiths, James Hankins, and David Thompson. Binghamton, NY: Medieval and Renaissance Studies and Texts, 1987, 240–51.

Castiglione, Baldassare (1478–1529). *The Book of the Courtier.* Translated by George Bull. New York: Penguin, 1967. *The Book of the Courtier.* Edited by Daniel Javitch. New York: W. W. Norton, 2002.

Christine de Pizan (1365–1431). *The Book of the City of Ladies.* Translated by Earl Jeffrey Richards. Foreword by Marina Warner. New York: Persea, 1982.

————. *The Treasure of the City of Ladies.* Translated by Sarah Lawson. New York: Viking Penguin, 1985. Also translated and introduction by Charity Cannon Willard. Edited and introduction by Madeleine P. Cosman. New York: Persea, 1989.

Clarke, Danielle, ed. *Isabella Whitney, Mary Sidney and Aemilia Lanyer: Renaissance Women Poets.* New York: Penguin, 2000.

Crawford, Patricia, and Laura Gowing, eds. *Women's Worlds in Seventeenth-Century England: A Source Book.* London: Routledge, 2000.

Daybell, James, ed. *Early Modern Women's Letter Writing, 1450–1700.* Houndmills, England:: Palgrave, 2001.

Elizabeth I: Collected Works. Edited by Leah S. Marcus, Janel Mueller, and Mary Beth Rose. Chicago: University of Chicago Press, 2000.

Elyot, Thomas (1490–1546). *Defence of Good Women: The Feminist Controversy of the Renaissance.* Facsimile Reproductions. Edited by Diane Bornstein. New York: Delmar, 1980.

Erasmus, Desiderius (1467–1536). *Erasmus on Women.* Edited by Erika Rummel. Toronto: University of Toronto Press, 1996.

Female and Male Voices in Early Modern England: An Anthology of Renaissance Writing. Edited by Betty S. Travitsky and Anne Lake Prescott. New York: Columbia University Press, 2000.

Ferguson, Moira, ed. *First Feminists: British Women Writers 1578–1799.* Bloomington: Indiana University Press, 1985.

Galilei, Maria Celeste. *Sister Maria Celeste's Letters to Her Father, Galileo.* Edited by and Translated by Rinaldina Russell. Lincoln, NE: Writers Club Press of Universe .com, 2000. Also published as *To Father: The Letters of Sister Maria Celeste to Galileo, 1623–1633.* Translated by Dava Sobel. London: Fourth Estate, 2001.

Gethner, Perry, ed. *The Lunatic Lover and Other Plays by French Women of the 17th and 18th Centuries.* Portsmouth, NH: Heinemann, 1994.

Glückel of Hameln (1646–1724). *The Memoirs of Glückel of Hameln.* Translated by Marvin Lowenthal. New introduction by Robert Rosen. New York: Schocken Books, 1977.

Henderson, Katherine Usher, and Barbara F. McManus, eds. *Half Humankind: Contexts and Texts of the Controversy about Women in England, 1540–1640.* Urbana: Illinois University Press, 1985.

Hoby, Margaret. *The Private Life of an Elizabethan Lady: The Diary of Lady Margaret Hoby 1599–1605.* Thrupp, Stroud, Gloucestershire: Sutton, 1998.

Humanist Educational Treatises. Edited and translated by Craig W. Kallendorf. The I Tatti Renaissance Library. Cambridge, MA: Harvard University Press, 2002.

Joscelin, Elizabeth. *The Mothers Legacy to Her Unborn Childe.* Edited by Jean leDrew Metcalfe. Toronto: University of Toronto Press, 2000.

Kaminsky, Amy Katz, ed. *Water Lilies, Flores del agua: An Anthology of Spanish Women Writers from the Fifteenth Through the Nineteenth Century.* Minneapolis: University of Minnesota Press, 1996.

Kempe, Margery (1373–1439). *The Book of Margery Kempe.* Translated by and edited by Lynn Staley. A Norton Critical Edition. New York: W. W. Norton, 2001.

King, Margaret L., and Albert Rabil, Jr., eds. *Her Immaculate Hand: Selected Works by and about the Women Humanists of Quattrocento Italy.* Binghamton, NY: Medieval and Renaissance Texts and Studies, 1983; second revised paperback edition, 1991.

Klein, Joan Larsen, ed. *Daughters, Wives, and Widows: Writings by Men about Women and Marriage in England, 1500–1640.* Urbana: University of Illinois Press, 1992.

Knox, John (1505–72). *The Political Writings of John Knox: The First Blast of the Trumpet against the Monstrous Regiment of Women and Other Selected Works.* Edited by Marvin A. Breslow. Washington, DC: Folger Shakespeare Library, 1985.

Kors, Alan C., and Edward Peters, eds. *Witchcraft in Europe, 400–1700: A Documentary History.* Philadelphia: University of Pennsylvania Press, 2000.

Krämer, Heinrich, and Jacob Sprenger. *Malleus Maleficarum* (ca. 1487). Translated by Montague Summers. London: Pushkin Press, 1928. Reprint, New York: Dover, 1971.

Larsen, Anne R., and Colette H. Winn, eds. *Writings by Pre-Revolutionary French Women: From Marie de France to Elizabeth Vigée-Le Brun.* New York: Garland, 2000.

de Lorris, William, and Jean de Meun. *The Romance of the Rose.* Translated by Charles Dahlbert. Princeton, NJ: Princeton University Press, 1971. Reprint, University Press of New England, 1983.

Marguerite d'Angoulême, Queen of Navarre (1492–1549). *The Heptameron.* Translated by P. A. Chilton. New York: Viking Penguin, 1984.

Mary of Agreda. *The Divine Life of the Most Holy Virgin.* Abridgment of *The Mystical City of God.* Abridged by Fr. Bonaventure Amedeo de Caesarea, M.C. Translated from the French by Abbé Joseph A. Boullan. Rockford, IL: Tan Books, 1997.

Myers, Kathleen A., and Amanda Powell, eds. *A Wild Country Out in the Garden: The Spiritual Journals of a Colonial Mexican Nun.* Bloomington: Indiana University Press, 1999.

Russell, Rinaldina, ed. *Sister Maria Celeste's Letters to Her Father, Galileo.* San Jose: Writers Club Press, 2000.

Teresa of Avila, Saint (1515–82). *The Life of Saint Teresa of Avila by Herself.* Translated by J. M. Cohen. New York: Viking Penguin, 1957.

Weyer, Johann (1515–88). *Witches, Devils, and Doctors in the Renaissance: Johann Weyer, De praestigiis daemonum.* Edited by George Mora with Benjamin G. Kohl, Erik Midelfort, and Helen Bacon. Translated by John Shea. Binghamton, NY: Medieval and Renaissance Texts and Studies, 1991.

Wilson, Katharina M., ed. *Medieval Women Writers.* Athens: University of Georgia Press, 1984.

———, ed. *Women Writers of the Renaissance and Reformation.* Athens: University of Georgia Press, 1987.

Wilson, Katharina M., and Frank J. Warnke, eds. *Women Writers of the Seventeenth Century.* Athens: University of Georgia Press, 1989.

Wollstonecraft, Mary. *A Vindication of the Rights of Men and a Vindication of the Rights of Women.* Edited by Sylvana Tomaselli. Cambridge: Cambridge University Press, 1995. Also *The Vindications of the Rights of Men, The Rights of Women.* Edited by D. L. Macdonald and Kathleen Scherf. Peterborough, Ontario, Canada: Broadview Press, 1997.

Women Critics 1660–1820: An Anthology. Edited by the Folger Collective on Early Women Critics. Bloomington: Indiana University Press, 1995.

Women Writers in English, 1350–1850. 15 vols. published through 1999 (projected 30-volume series suspended). Oxford University Press.

Wroth, Lady Mary. *The Countess of Montgomery's Urania.* 2 parts. Edited by Josephine A. Roberts. Tempe, AZ: MRTS, 1995, 1999.

————. *Lady Mary Wroth's "Love's Victory": The Penshurst Manuscript.* Edited by Michael G. Brennan. London: The Roxburghe Club, 1988.

————. *The Poems of Lady Mary Wroth.* Edited by Josephine A. Roberts. Baton Rouge: Louisiana State University Press, 1983.

de Zayas, Maria. *The Disenchantments of Love.* Translated by H. Patsy Boyer. Albany: State University of New York Press, 1997.

————. *The Enchantments of Love: Amorous and Exemplary Novels.* Translated by H. Patsy Boyer. Berkeley and Los Angeles: University of California Press, 1990.

SECONDARY SOURCES

Ahlgren, Gillian. *Teresa of Avila and the Politics of Sanctity.* Ithaca, NY: Cornell University Press, 1996.

Akkerman, Tjitske, and Siep Sturman, eds. *Feminist Thought in European History, 1400–2000.* London: Routledge, 1997.

Allen, Sister Prudence, R.S.M. *The Concept of Woman: The Aristotelian Revolution, 750 B.C.–A.D. 1250.* Grand Rapids, MI: William B. Eerdmans, 1997.

————. *The Concept of Woman.* Vol. 2, *The Early Humanist Reformation, 1250–1500.* Grand Rapids, MI: William B. Eerdmans, 2002.

Andreadis, Harriette. *Sappho in Early Modern England: Female Same-Sex Literary Erotics 1550–1714.* Chicago: University of Chicago Press, 2001.

Armon, Shifra. *Picking Wedlock: Women and the Courtship Novel in Spain.* New York: Rowman & Littlefield Publishers, Inc., 2002.

Backer, Anne Liot Backer. *Precious Women.* New York: Basic Books, 1974.

Ballaster, Ros. *Seductive Forms.* New York: Oxford University Press, 1992.

Barash, Carol. *English Women's Poetry, 1649–1714: Politics, Community, and Linguistic Authority.* New York: Oxford University Press, 1996.

Battigelli, Anna. *Margaret Cavendish and the Exiles of the Mind.* Lexington, KY: University of Kentucky Press, 1998.

Beasley, Faith. *Revising Memory: Women's Fiction and Memoirs in Seventeenth-Century France.* New Brunswick: Rutgers University Press, 1990.

Beilin, Elaine V. *Redeeming Eve: Women Writers of the English Renaissance.* Princeton, NJ: Princeton University Press, 1987.

Benson, Pamela Joseph. *The Invention of Renaissance Woman: The Challenge of Female Independence in the Literature and Thought of Italy and England.* University Park, PA: Pennsylvania State University Press, 1992.

Benson, Pamela Joseph, and Victoria Kirkham, eds. *Strong Voices, Weak History? Medieval and Renaissance Women in their Literary Canons: England, France, Italy.* Ann Arbor: University of Michigan Press, 2003.

Bilinkoff, Jodi. *The Avila of Saint Teresa: Religious Reform in a Sixteenth-Century City.* Ithaca: Cornell University Press, 1989.

Bissell, R. Ward. *Artemisia Gentileschi and the Authority of Art.* University Park: Pennsylvania State University Press, 2000.

Blain, Virginia, Isobel Grundy, and Patricia Clements, eds. *The Feminist Companion to Literature in English: Women Writers from the Middle Ages to the Present*. New Haven, CT: Yale University Press, 1990.

Bloch, R. Howard. *Medieval Misogyny and the Invention of Western Romantic Love*. Chicago: University of Chicago Press, 1991.

Bornstein, Daniel and Roberto Rusconi, eds. *Women and Religion in Medieval and Renaissance Italy*. Translated by Margery J. Schneider. Chicago: University of Chicago Press, 1996.

Brant, Clare, and Diane Purkiss, eds. *Women, Texts and Histories, 1575–1760*. London: Routledge, 1992.

Briggs, Robin. *Witches and Neighbours: The Social and Cultural Context of European Witchcraft*. New York: HarperCollins, 1995; Viking Penguin, 1996.

Brink, Jean R., ed. *Female Scholars: A Tradition of Learned Women before 1800*. Montréal: Eden Press Women's Publications, 1980.

Broude, Norma, and Mary D. Garrard, eds. *The Expanding Discourse: Feminism and Art History*. New York: HarperCollins, 1992.

Brown, Judith C. *Immodest Acts: The Life of a Lesbian Nun in Renaissance Italy*. New York: Oxford University Press, 1986.

Brown, Judith C. , and Robert C. Davis, eds. *Gender and Society in Renaissance Italy*. London: Addison Wesley Longman, 1998.

Bynum, Carolyn Walker. *Fragmentation and Redemption: Essays on Gender and the Human Body in Medieval Religion*. New York: Zone Books, 1992.

————. *Holy Feast and Holy Fast: The Religious Significance of Food to Medieval Women*. Berkeley: University of California Press, 1987.

Cambridge Guide to Women's Writing in English. Edited by Lorna Sage. Cambridge: University Press, 1999.

Cavanagh, Sheila T. *Cherished Torment: The Emotional Geography of Lady Mary Wroth's Urania*. Pittsburgh: Duquesne University Press, 2001.

Cerasano, S. P. and Marion Wynne-Davies, eds. *Readings in Renaissance Women's Drama: Criticism, History, and Performance 1594–1998*. London: Routledge, 1998.

Cervigni, Dino S., ed. *Women Mystic Writers*. Annali d'Italianistica 13 (1995) (entire issue).

Cervigni, Dino S., and Rebecca West, eds. *Women's Voices in Italian Literature*. Annali d'Italianistica 7 (1989) (entire issue).

Charlton, Kenneth. *Women, Religion and Education in Early Modern England*. London: Routledge, 1999.

Chojnacka, Monica. *Working Women in Early Modern Venice*. Baltimore: Johns Hopkins University Press, 2001.

Chojnacki, Stanley. *Women and Men in Renaissance Venice: Twelve Essays on Patrician Society*. Baltimore: Johns Hopkins University Press, 2000.

Cholakian, Patricia Francis. *Rape and Writing in the "Heptameron" of Marguerite de Navarre*. Carbondale: Southern Illinois University Press, 1991.

————. *Women and the Politics of Self-Representation in Seventeenth-Century France*. Newark: University of Delaware Press, 2000.

Christine de Pizan: A Casebook. Edited by Barbara K. Altmann and Deborah L. McGrady. New York: Routledge, 2003.

Clogan, Paul Maruice, ed. *Medievali et Humanistica: Literacy and the Lay Reader*. Lanham, MD: Rowman & Littlefield, 2000.

Clubb, Louise George (1989). *Italian Drama in Shakespeare's Time*. New Haven, CT: Yale University Press.

Conley, John J., S.J. *The Suspicion of Virtue: Women Philosophers in Neoclassical France*. Ithaca, NY: Cornell University Press, 2002.

Crabb, Ann. *The Strozzi of Florence: Widowhood and Family Solidarity in the Renaissance*. Ann Arbor: University of Michigan Press, 2000.

Cruz, Anne J., and Mary Elizabeth Perry, eds. *Culture and Control in Counter-Reformation Spain*. Minneapolis: University of Minnesota Press, 1992.

Davis, Natalie Zemon. *Society and Culture in Early Modern France*. Stanford: Stanford University Press, 1975. Especially chapters 3 and 5.

———. *Women on the Margins: Three Seventeenth-Century Lives*. Cambridge, MA: Harvard University Press, 1995.

DeJean, Joan. *Ancients Against Moderns: Culture Wars and the Making of a Fin de Siècle*. Chicago: University of Chicago Press, 1997.

———. *Fictions of Sappho, 1546–1937*. Chicago: University of Chicago Press, 1989.

———. *The Reinvention of Obscenity: Sex, Lies, and Tabloids in Early Modern France*. Chicago: University of Chicago Press, 2002.

———. *Tender Geographies: Women and the Origins of the Novel in France*. New York: Columbia University Press, 1991.

Dictionary of Russian Women Writers. Edited by Marina Ledkovsky, Charlotte Rosenthal, and Mary Zirin. Westport, CT: Greenwood Press, 1994.

Dixon, Laurinda S. *Perilous Chastity: Women and Illness in Pre-Enlightenment Art and Medicine*. Ithaca: Cornell Universitiy Press, 1995.

Dolan, Frances, E. *Whores of Babylon: Catholicism, Gender and Seventeenth-Century Print Culture*. Ithaca: Cornell University Press, 1999.

Donovan, Josephine. *Women and the Rise of the Novel, 1405–1726*. New York: St. Martin's Press, 1999.

De Erauso, Catalina. *Lieutenant Nun: Memoir of a Basque Transvestite in the New World*. Translated by Michele Ttepto and Gabriel Stepto; foreword by Marjorie Garber. Boston: Beacon Press, 1995.

Encyclopedia of Continental Women Writers. 2 vols. Edited by Katharina Wilson. New York: Garland, 1991.

Erdmann, Axel. *My Gracious Silence: Women in the Mirror of Sixteenth-Century Printing in Western Europe*. Luzern: Gilhofer and Rauschberg, 1999.

Erickson, Amy Louise. *Women and Property in Early Modern England*. London: Routledge, 1993.

Ezell, Margaret J. M. *The Patriarch's Wife: Literary Evidence and the History of the Family*. Chapel Hill: University of North Carolina Press, 1987.

———. *Social Authorship and the Advent of Print*. Baltimore: Johns Hopkins University Press, 1999.

———. *Writing Women's Literary History*. Baltimore: Johns Hopkins University Press, 1993.

Farrell, Michèle Longino. *Performing Motherhood: The Sévigné Correspondence*. Hanover, NH: University Press of New England, 1991.

The Feminist Companion to Literature in English: Women Writers from the Middle Ages to the Present. Edited by Virginia Blain, Isobel Grundy, and Patricia Clements. New Haven, CT: Yale University Press, 1990.

The Feminist Encyclopedia of German Literature. Edited by Friederike Eigler and Susanne Kord. Westport, CT: Greenwood Press, 1997.

Feminist Encyclopedia of Italian Literature. Edited by Rinaldina Russell. Westport, CT: Greenwood Press, 1997.

Ferguson, Margaret W. *Dido's Daughters: Literacy, Gender, and Empire in Early Modern England and France.* Chicago: University of Chicago Press, 2003.

Ferguson, Margaret W., Maureen Quilligan, and Nancy J. Vickers, eds. *Rewriting the Renaissance: The Discourses of Sexual Difference in Early Modern Europe.* Chicago: University of Chicago Press, 1987.

Ferraro, Joanne M. *Marriage Wars in Late Renaissance Venice.* Oxford: Oxford University Press, 2001.

Fletcher, Anthony. *Gender, Sex and Subordination in England 1500–1800.* New Haven, CT: Yale University Press, 1995.

French Women Writers: A Bio-Bibliographical Source Book. Edited by Eva Martin Sartori and Dorothy Wynne Zimmerman. Westport, CT: Greenwood Press, 1991.

Frye, Susan and Karen Robertson, eds. *Maids and Mistresses, Cousins and Queens: Women's Alliances in Early Modern England.* Oxford: Oxford University Press, 1999.

Gallagher, Catherine. *Nobody's Story: The Vanishing Acts of Women Writers in the Market-place, 1670–1820.* Berkeley: University of California Press, 1994.

Garrard, Mary D. *Artemisia Gentileschi: The Image of the Female Hero in Italian Baroque Art.* Princeton, NJ: Princeton University Press, 1989.

Gelbart, Nina Rattner. *The King's Midwife: A History and Mystery of Madame du Coudray.* Berkeley: University of California Press, 1998.

Glenn, Cheryl. *Rhetoric Retold: Regendering the Tradition from Antiquity through the Renaissance.* Carbondale: Southern Illinois University Press, 1997.

Goffen, Rona. *Titian's Women.* New Haven, CT: Yale University Press, 1997.

Goldberg, Jonathan. *Desiring Women Writing: English Renaissance Examples.* Stanford: Stanford University Press, 1997.

Goldsmith, Elizabeth C. *Exclusive Conversations: The Art of Interaction in Seventeenth-Century France.* Philadelphia: University of Pennsylvania Press, 1988.

———, ed. *Writing the Female Voice.* Boston: Northeastern University Press, 1989.

Goldsmith, Elizabeth C., and Dena Goodman, eds. *Going Public: Women and Publishing in Early Modern France.* Ithaca: Cornell University Press, 1995.

Grafton, Anthony, and Lisa Jardine. *From Humanism to the Humanities: Education and the Liberal Arts in Fifteenth-and Sixteenth-Century Europe.* London: Duckworth, 1986.

Greer, Margaret Rich. *Maria de Zayas Tells Baroque Tales of Love and the Cruelty of Men.* University Park: Pennsylvania State University Press, 2000.

Hackett, Helen. *Women and Romance Fiction in the English Renaissance.* Cambridge: Cambridge University Press, 2000.

Hall, Kim F. *Things of Darkness: Economies of Race and Gender in Early Modern England.* Ithaca, NY: Cornell University Press, 1995.

Hampton, Timothy. *Literature and the Nation in the Sixteenth Century: Inventing Renaissance France.* Ithaca, NY: Cornell University Press, 2001.

Hannay, Margaret, ed. *Silent But for the Word.* Kent, OH: Kent State University Press, 1985.

Hardwick, Julie. *The Practice of Patriarchy: Gender and the Politics of Household Authority in Early Modern France.* University Park: Pennsylvania State University Press, 1998.

Harris, Barbara J. *English Aristocratic Women, 1450–1550: Marriage and Family, Property and Careers*. New York: Oxford University Press, 2002.

Harth, Erica. *Ideology and Culture in Seventeenth-Century France*. Ithaca: Cornell University Press, 1983.

———. *Cartesian Women: Versions and Subversions of Rational Discourse in the Old Regime*. Ithaca: Cornell University Press, 1992.

Harvey, Elizabeth D. *Ventriloquized Voices: Feminist Theory and English Renaissance Texts*. London: Routledge, 1992.

Haselkorn, Anne M., and Betty Travitsky, eds. *The Renaissance Englishwoman in Print: Counterbalancing the Canon*. Amherst: University of Massachusetts Press, 1990.

Herlihy, David. "Did Women Have a Renaissance? A Reconsideration." *Medievalia et Humanistica*, NS 13 (1985): 1–22.

Hill, Bridget. *The Republican Virago: The Life and Times of Catharine Macaulay, Historian*. New York: Oxford University Press, 1992.

A History of Central European Women's Writing. Edited by Celia Hawkesworth. New York: Palgrave Press, 2001.

A History of Women in the West.
  Volume 1: *From Ancient Goddesses to Christian Saints*. Edited by Pauline Schmitt Pantel. Cambridge, MA: Harvard University Press, 1992.
  Volume 2: *Silences of the Middle Ages*. Edited by Christiane Klapisch-Zuber. Cambridge, MA: Harvard University Press, 1992.
  Volume 3: *Renaissance and Enlightenment Paradoxes*. Edited by Natalie Zemon Davis and Arlette Farge. Cambridge, MA: Harvard University Press, 1993.

A History of Women Philosophers. Edited by Mary Ellen Waithe. 3 vols. Dordrecht: Martinus Nijhoff, 1987.

A History of Women's Writing in France. Edited by Sonya Stephens. Cambridge: Cambridge University Press, 2000.

A History of Women's Writing in Germany, Austria and Switzerland. Edited by Jo Catling. Cambridge: Cambridge University Press, 2000.

A History of Women's Writing in Italy. Edited by Letizia Panizza and Sharon Wood. Cambridge: University Press, 2000.

A History of Women's Writing in Russia. Edited by Alele Marie Barker and Jehanne M. Gheith. Cambridge: Cambridge University Press, 2002.

Hobby, Elaine. *Virtue of Necessity: English Women's Writing 1646–1688*. London: Virago Press, 1988.

Horowitz, Maryanne Cline. "Aristotle and Women." *Journal of the History of Biology* 9 (1976): 183–213.

Howell, Martha. *The Marriage Exchange: Property, Social Place, and Gender in Cities of the Low Countries, 1300–1550*. Chicago: University of Chicago Press, 1998.

Hufton, Olwen H. *The Prospect Before Her: A History of Women in Western Europe, 1: 1500–1800*. New York: HarperCollins, 1996.

Hull, Suzanne W. *Chaste, Silent, and Obedient: English Books for Women, 1475–1640*. San Marino, CA: The Huntington Library, 1982.

Hunt, Lynn, ed. *The Invention of Pornography: Obscenity and the Origins of Modernity, 1500–1800*. New York: Zone Books, 1996.

Hutner, Heidi, ed. *Rereading Aphra Behn: History, Theory, and Criticism*. Charlottesville: University Press of Virginia, 1993.

Hutson, Lorna, ed. *Feminism and Renaissance Studies*. New York: Oxford University Press, 1999.

Italian Women Writers: A Bio-Bibliographical Sourcebook. Edited by Rinaldina Russell. Westport, CT: Greenwood Press, 1994.

Jaffe, Irma B., with Gernando Colombardo. *Shining Eyes, Cruel Fortune: The Lives and Loves of Italian Renaissance Women Poets*. New York: Fordham University Press, 2002.

James, Susan E. *Kateryn Parr: The Making of a Queen*. Aldershot: Ashgate, 1999.

Jankowski, Theodora A. *Women in Power in the Early Modern Drama*. Urbana: University of Illinois Press, 1992.

Jansen, Katherine Ludwig. *The Making of the Magdalen: Preaching and Popular Devotion in the Later Middle Ages*. Princeton, NJ: Princeton University Press, 2000.

Jed, Stephanie H. *Chaste Thinking: The Rape of Lucretia and the Birth of Humanism*. Bloomington: Indiana University Press, 1989.

Jordan, Constance. *Renaissance Feminism: Literary Texts and Political Models*. Ithaca: Cornell University Press, 1990.

Kagan, Richard L. *Lucrecia's Dreams: Politics and Prophecy in Sixteenth-Century Spain*. Berkeley: University of California Press, 1990.

Kehler, Dorothea and Laurel Amtower, eds. *The Single Woman in Medieval and Early Modern England: Her Life and Representation*. Tempe, AZ: MRTS, 2002.

Kelly, Joan. "Did Women Have a Renaissance?" In her *Women, History, and Theory*. Chicago: University of Chicago Press, 1984. Also in Renate Bridenthal, Claudia Koonz, and Susan M. Stuard, eds., *Becoming Visible: Women in European History*. 3rd ed. Boston: Houghton Mifflin, 1998.

————. "Early Feminist Theory and the *Querelle des Femmes*." In *Women, History, and Theory*.

Kelso, Ruth. *Doctrine for the Lady of the Renaissance*. Foreword by Katharine M. Rogers. Urbana: University of Illinois Press, 1956, 1978.

King, Catherine E. *Renaissance Women Patrons: Wives and Widows in Italy, c. 1300–1550*. Manchester: Manchester University Press (distributed in the U.S. by St. Martin's Press), 1998.

King, Margaret L. *Women of the Renaissance*. Foreword by Catharine R. Stimpson. Chicago: University of Chicago Press, 1991.

Krontiris, Tina. *Oppositional Voices: Women as Writers and Translators of Literature in the English Renaissance*. London: Routledge, 1992.

Kuehn, Thomas. *Law, Family, and Women: Toward a Legal Anthropology of Renaissance Italy*. Chicago: University of Chicago Press, 1991.

Kunze, Bonnelyn Young. *Margaret Fell and the Rise of Quakerism*. Stanford: Stanford University Press, 1994.

Labalme, Patricia A., ed. *Beyond Their Sex: Learned Women of the European Past*. New York: New York University Press, 1980.

Laqueur, Thomas. *Making Sex: Body and Gender from the Greeks to Freud*. Cambridge, MA: Harvard University Press, 1990.

Larsen, Anne R. and Colette H. Winn, eds. *Renaissance Women Writers: French Texts/ American Contexts*. Detroit, MI: Wayne State University Press, 1994.

Lerner, Gerda. *The Creation of Patriarchy* and *Creation of Feminist Consciousness, 1000–1870*. 2 vols. New York: Oxford University Press, 1986, 1994.

Levin, Carole, and Jeanie Watson, eds. *Ambiguous Realities: Women in the Middle Ages and Renaissance.* Detroit: Wayne State University Press, 1987.

Levin, Carole, et al. *Extraordinary Women of the Medieval and Renaissance World: A Biographical Dictionary.* Westport, CT: Greenwood Press, 2000.

Lewalsky, Barbara Kiefer. *Writing Women in Jacobean England.* Cambridge, MA: Harvard University Press, 1993.

Lewis, Jayne Elizabeth. *Mary Queen of Scots: Romance and Nation.* London: Routledge, 1998.

Lindsey, Karen. *Divorced Beheaded Survived: A Feminist Reinterpretation of the Wives of Henry VIII.* Reading, MA: Addison-Wesley, 1995.

Lochrie, Karma. *Margery Kempe and Translations of the Flesh.* Philadelphia: University of Pennsylvania Press, 1992.

Lougee, Carolyn C. *Le Paradis des Femmes: Women, Salons, and Social Stratification in Seventeenth-Century France.* Princeton, NJ: Princeton University Press, 1976.

Love, Harold. *The Culture and Commerce of Texts: Scribal Publication in Seventeenth-Century England.* Amherst: University of Massachusetts Press, 1993.

MacCarthy, Bridget G. *The Female Pen: Women Writers and Novelists, 1621–1818.* Preface by Janet Todd. New York: New York University Press, 1994. Originally published 1946–47 by Cork University Press.

Maclean, Ian. *Woman Triumphant: Feminism in French Literature, 1610–1652.* Oxford: Clarendon Press, 1977.

———. *The Renaissance Notion of Woman: A Study of the Fortunes of Scholasticism and Medical Science in European Intellectual Life.* Cambridge: Cambridge University Press, 1980.

MacNeil, Anne. *Music and Women of the Commedia dell'Arte in the Late Sixteenth Century.* New York: Oxford University Press, 2003.

Maggi, Armando. *Uttering the Word: The Mystical Performances of Maria Maddalena de' Pazzi, a Renaissance Visionary.* Albany: State University of New York Press, 1998.

Marshall, Sherrin. *Women in Reformation and Counter-Reformation Europe: Public and Private Worlds.* Bloomington: Indiana University Press, 1989.

Masten, Jeffrey. *Textual Intercourse: Collaboration, Authorship, and Sexualities in Renaissance Drama.* Cambridge: Cambridge University Press, 1997.

Matter, E. Ann, and John Coakley, eds. *Creative Women in Medieval and Early Modern Italy.* Philadelphia: University of Pennsylvania Press, 1994. (Sequel to the Monson collection, below.)

McLeod, Glenda. *Virtue and Venom: Catalogs of Women from Antiquity to the Renaissance.* Ann Arbor: University of Michigan Press, 1991.

Medwick, Cathleen. *Teresa of Avila: The Progress of a Soul.* New York: Knopf, 2000.

Meek, Christine, ed. *Women in Renaissance and Early Modern Europe.* Dublin-Portland: Four Courts Press, 2000.

Mendelson, Sara and Patricia Crawford. *Women in Early Modern England, 1550–1720.* Oxford: Clarendon Press, 1998.

Merchant, Carolyn. *The Death of Nature: Women, Ecology, and the Scientific Revolution.* New York: HarperCollins, 1980.

Merrim, Stephanie. *Early Modern Women's Writing and Sor Juana Inés de la Cruz.* Nashville, TN: Vanderbilt University Press, 1999.

Messbarger, Rebecca. *The Century of Women: The Representations of Women in Eighteenth-Century Italian Public Discourse.* Toronto: University of Toronto Press, 2002.

Miller, Nancy K. *The Heroine's Text: Readings in the French and English Novel, 1722–1782.* New York: Columbia University Press, 1980.

Miller, Naomi J. *Changing the Subject: Mary Wroth and Figurations of Gender in Early Modern England.* Lexington: University Press of Kentucky, 1996.

Miller, Naomi J., and Gary Waller, eds. *Reading Mary Wroth: Representing Alternatives in Early Modern England.* Knoxville: University of Tennessee Press, 1991.

Monson, Craig A., ed. *The Crannied Wall: Women, Religion, and the Arts in Early Modern Europe.* Ann Arbor: University of Michigan Press, 1992.

Musacchio, Jacqueline Marie. *The Art and Ritual of Childbirth in Renaissance Italy.* New Haven, CT: Yale University Press, 1999.

Newman, Barbara. *God and the Goddesses: Vision, Poetry, and Belief in the Middle Ages.* Philadelphia: University of Pennsylvania Press, 2003.

Newman, Karen. *Fashioning Femininity and English Renaissance Drama.* Chicago: University of Chicago Press, 1991.

Okin, Susan Moller. *Women in Western Political Thought.* Princeton, NJ: Princeton University Press, 1979.

Ozment, Steven. *The Bürgermeister's Daughter: Scandal in a Sixteenth-Century German Town.* New York: St. Martin's Press, 1995.

Pacheco, Anita, ed. *Early [English] Women Writers: 1600–1720.* New York: Longman, 1998.

Pagels, Elaine. *Adam, Eve, and the Serpent.* New York: HarperCollins, 1988.

Panizza, Letizia, ed. *Women in Italian Renaissance Culture and Society.* Oxford: European Humanities Research Centre, 2000.

Parker, Patricia. *Literary Fat Ladies: Rhetoric, Gender, and Property.* London: Methuen, 1987.

Pernoud, Regine, and Marie-Veronique Clin. *Joan of Arc: Her Story.* Revised and translated by Jeremy DuQuesnay Adams. New York: St. Martin's Press, 1998 (French original, 1986).

Perry, Mary Elizabeth. *Crime and Society in Early Modern Seville.* Hanover, NH: University Press of New England, 1980.

———. *Gender and Disorder in Early Modern Seville.* Princeton, NJ: Princeton University Press, 1990.

Perry, Ruth. *The Celebrated Mary Astell: An Early English Feminist.* Chicago: University of Chicago Press, 1986.

Petroff, Elizabeth Alvilda, ed. *Medieval Women's Visionary Literature.* New York: Oxford University Press, 1986.

Rabil, Albert. *Laura Cereta: Quattrocento Humanist.* Binghamton, NY: MRTS, 1981.

Ranft, Patricia. *Women in Western Intellectual Culture, 600–1500.* New York: Palgrave, 2002.

Rapley, Elizabeth. *A Social History of the Cloister: Daily Life in the Teaching Monasteries of the Old Regime.* Montreal: McGill-Queen's University Press, 2001.

Raven, James, Helen Small, and Naomi Tadmor, eds. *The Practice and Representation of Reading in England.* Cambridge: University Press, 1996.

Reardon, Colleen. *Holy Concord within Sacred Walls: Nuns and Music in Siena, 1575–1700.* Oxford: Oxford University Press, 2001.

Reiss, Sheryl E., and David G. Wilkins, ed. *Beyond Isabella: Secular Women Patrons of Art in Renaissance Italy.* Kirksville, MO: Truman State University Press, 2001.

Rheubottom, David. *Age, Marriage, and Politics in Fifteenth-Century Ragusa.* Oxford: Oxford University Press, 2000.

Richardson, Brian. *Printing, Writers and Readers in Renaissance Italy.* Cambridge: University Press, 1999.

Riddle, John M. *Contraception and Abortion from the Ancient World to the Renaissance.* Cambridge, MA: Harvard University Press, 1992.

———. *Eve's Herbs: A History of Contraception and Abortion in the West.* Cambridge, MA: Harvard University Press, 1997.

Rose, Mary Beth. *The Expense of Spirit: Love and Sexuality in English Renaissance Drama.* Ithaca, NY: Cornell University Press, 1988.

———. *Gender and Heroism in Early Modern English Literature.* Chicago: University of Chicago Press, 2002.

———, ed. *Women in the Middle Ages and the Renaissance: Literary and Historical Perspectives.* Syracuse: Syracuse University Press, 1986.

Rosenthal, Margaret F. *The Honest Courtesan: Veronica Franco, Citizen and Writer in Sixteenth-Century Venice.* Foreword by Catharine R. Stimpson. Chicago: University of Chicago Press, 1992.

Sackville-West, Vita. *Daughter of France: The Life of La Grande Mademoiselle.* Garden City, NY: Doubleday, 1959.

Sánchez, Magdalena S. *The Empress, the Queen, and the Nun: Women and Power at the Court of Philip III of Spain.* Baltimore: Johns Hopkins University Press, 1998.

Schiebinger, Londa. *The Mind Has No Sex? Women in the Origins of Modern Science.* Cambridge, MA: Harvard University Press, 1991.

———. *Nature's Body: Gender in the Making of Modern Science.* Boston: Beacon Press, 1993.

Schutte, Anne Jacobson, Thomas Kuehn, and Silvana Seidel Menchi, eds. *Time, Space, and Women's Lives in Early Modern Europe.* Kirksville, MO: Truman State University Press, 2001.

Schofield, Mary Anne, and Cecilia Macheski, eds. *Fetter'd or Free? British Women Novelists, 1670–1815.* Athens: Ohio University Press, 1986.

Shannon, Laurie. *Sovereign Amity: Figures of Friendship in Shakespearean Contexts.* Chicago: University of Chicago Press, 2002.

Shemek, Deanna. *Ladies Errant: Wayward Women and Social Order in Early Modern Italy.* Durham, NC: Duke University Press, 1998.

Smith, Hilda L. *Reason's Disciples: Seventeenth-Century English Feminists.* Urbana: University of Illinois Press, 1982.

———. *Women Writers and the Early Modern British Political Tradition.* Cambridge: Cambridge University Press, 1998.

Sobel, Dava. *Galileo's Daughter: A Historical Memoir of Science, Faith, and Love.* New York: Penguin, 2000.

Sommerville, Margaret R. *Sex and Subjection: Attitudes to Women in Early-Modern Society.* London: Arnold, 1995.

Soufas, Teresa Scott. *Dramas of Distinction: A Study of Plays by Golden Age Women.* Lexington: The University Press of Kentucky, 1997.

Spencer, Jane. *The Rise of the Woman Novelist: From Aphra Behn to Jane Austen.* Oxford: Basil Blackwell, 1986.

Spender, Dale. *Mothers of the Novel: 100 Good Women Writers Before Jane Austen.* London: Routledge, 1986.

Sperling, Jutta Gisela. *Convents and the Body Politic in Late Renaissance Venice*. Foreword by Catharine R. Stimpson. Chicago: University of Chicago Press, 1999.

Steinbrügge, Lieselotte. *The Moral Sex: Woman's Nature in the French Enlightenment*. Translated by Pamela E. Selwyn. New York: Oxford University Press, 1995.

Stocker, Margarita. *Judith, Sexual Warrior: Women and Power in Western Culture*. New Haven, CT: Yale University Press, 1998.

Stretton, Timothy. *Women Waging Law in Elizabethan England*. Cambridge: Cambridge University Press, 1998.

Stuard, Susan M. "The Dominion of Gender: Women's Fortunes in the High Middle Ages." In *Becoming Visible: Women in European History*, edited by Renate Bridenthal, Claudia Koonz, and Susan M. Stuard. 3rd ed. Boston: Houghton Mifflin, 1998.

Summit, Jennifer. *Lost Property: The Woman Writer and English Literary History, 1380–1589*. Chicago: University of Chicago Press, 2000.

Surtz, Ronald E. *The Guitar of God: Gender, Power, and Authority in the Visionary World of Mother Juana de la Cruz (1481–1534)*. Philadelphia: University of Pennsylvania Press, 1991.

———. *Writing Women in Late Medieval and Early Modern Spain: The Mothers of Saint Teresa of Avila*. Philadelphia: University of Pennsylvania Press, 1995.

Teague, Frances. *Bathsua Makin, Woman of Learning*. Lewisburg, PA: Bucknell University Press, 1999.

Tinagli, Paola. *Women in Italian Renaissance Art: Gender, Representation, Identity*. Manchester: Manchester University Press, 1997.

Todd, Janet. *The Secret Life of Aphra Behn*. London: Pandora, 2000.

———. *The Sign of Angelica: Women, Writing and Fiction, 1660–1800*. New York: Columbia University Press, 1989.

Valenze, Deborah. *The First Industrial Woman*. New York: Oxford University Press, 1995.

Van Dijk, Susan, Lia van Gemert, and Sheila Ottway, eds. *Writing the History of Women's Writing: Toward an International Approach*. Proceedings of the Colloquium, Amsterdam, 9–11 September. Amsterdam: Royal Netherlands Academy of Arts and Sciences, 2001.

Vickery, Amanda. *The Gentleman's Daughter: Women's Lives in Georgian England*. New Haven, CT: Yale University Press, 1998.

Vollendorf, Lisa, ed. *Recovering Spain's Feminist Tradition*. New York: MLA, 2001.

Walker, Claire. *Gender and Politics in Early Modern Europe: English Convents in France and the Low Countries*. New York: Palgrave, 2003.

Wall, Wendy. *The Imprint of Gender: Authorship and Publication in the English Renaissance*. Ithaca, NY: Cornell University Press, 1993.

Walsh, William T. *St. Teresa of Avila: A Biography*. Rockford, IL: TAN, 1987.

Warner, Marina. *Alone of All Her Sex: The Myth and Cult of the Virgin Mary*. New York: Knopf, 1976.

Warnicke, Retha M. *The Marrying of Anne of Cleves: Royal Protocol in Tudor England*. Cambridge: Cambridge University Press, 2000.

Watt, Diane. *Secretaries of God: Women Prophets in Late Medieval and Early Modern England*. Cambridge: D. S. Brewer, 1997.

Weber, Alison. *Teresa of Avila and the Rhetoric of Femininity*. Princeton, NJ: Princeton University Press, 1990.

Welles, Marcia L. *Persephone's Girdle: Narratives of Rape in Seventeenth-Century Spanish Literature*. Nashville: Vanderbilt University Press, 2000.

Whitehead, Barbara J., ed. *Women's Education in Early Modern Europe: A History, 1500–1800*. New York: Garland, 1999.

Wiesner, Merry E. *Women and Gender in Early Modern Europe*. Cambridge: Cambridge University Press, 1993.

———. *Working Women in Renaissance Germany*. New Brunswick, NJ: Rutgers University Press, 1986.

Willard, Charity Cannon. *Christine de Pizan: Her Life and Works*. New York: Persea Books, 1984.

Winn, Colette and Donna Kuizenga, eds. *Women Writers in Pre-Revolutionary France*. New York: Garland, 1997.

Woodbridge, Linda. *Women and the English Renaissance: Literature and the Nature of Womankind, 1540–1620*. Urbana: University of Illinois Press, 1984.

Woods, Susanne. *Lanyer: A Renaissance Woman Poet*. New York: Oxford University Press, 1999.

Woods, Susanne, and Margaret P. Hannay, eds. *Teaching Tudor and Stuart Women Writers*. New York: MLA, 2000.

INDEX